WHITE WOMAN SPEAKS WITH FORKED TONGUE

Criticism as Autobiography

Nicole Ward Jouve

ROUTLEDGE

London and New York

For my daughter
if she'll have it
With all my love
which she has

First published 1991
by Routledge
11 New Fetter Lane, London EC4P 4EE

Simultaneously published in the USA and Canada
by Routledge
a division of Routledge, Chapman and Hall, Inc.
29 West 35th Street, New York, NY 10001

© 1991 Nicole Ward Jouve

Typeset in 10/12pt Palatino by
Input Typesetting Ltd
Printed and bound in Great Britain by
Clays Ltd., St Ives plc

British Library Cataloguing in Publication Data
Ward Jouve, Nicole
White woman speaks with forked tongue : criticism as
autobiography
1. English literature. Women writers – Critical studies
I. Title
820.99287

Library of Congress Cataloging in Publication Data
Applied for
ISBN 0–415–04952–0
ISBN 0–415–04953–9 pbk

Contents

Preface: White Woman Speaks with Forked Tongue   vii

Acknowledgements   x

Introduction: criticism as autobiography   1

Part I Bilingualism and Translation

1 'Her legs bestrid the Channel': writing in two
  languages   17

2 *Ananas*/pineapple   37

3 To fly/to steal: no more? Translating French feminisms
  into English   46

Part II French Feminisms

4 How to make a Bertha out of an Antoinette and
  why every Jane needs a Bertha: Psych et Po and
  French feminisms   61

5 'Bliss was it in that dawn . . .': contemporary French
  women's writing and the Editions des femmes   75

6 Hélène Cixous: from inner theatre to world theatre   91

7 How *The Second Sex* stopped my aunt from watering
  the horse-chestnuts: Simone de Beauvoir and
  contemporary feminism   101

Part III Forging a Feminist Aesthetics

8 Doris Lessing: of mud and other matter – *The Children of Violence* 119

9 Too short for a book? *The Thousand and One Nights*: the short story and the book 182

10 A rook called Joseph: Virginia Woolf 193

   Index 202

Preface: White Woman Speaks with Forked Tongue

No one who writes today can or should forget their race and their gender. The 'I' who has written this book is white: privileged, yes, middle class, yes; and everything it has to say is limited and coloured by unconscious western European assumptions.

Since I chose the title for this book I have come to New England. The place and its history have reawakened an awareness that had been born many years ago, when I was living in western Canada in the midst of a 'Red Power' movement. White man speaks with forked tongue. The colonists my ancestors, who, for the past four centuries, wave upon wave, landed on the shores of the non-European parts of the earth, brought violence and despoliation wherever they went. I belong to the race that has taken a few centuries only to destroy or threaten what it had taken God or nature millions of years to make.[1] Critical writing has grown in the same period. Who knows but that it is tainted with the same greed, the same tendency to exploit and to destroy. Today, in our infinite appetite for exoticism, for the new, we go on gleefully sacking all other cultures to find something exciting to write about.

The white settlers that spread into New England or Canada had two ways of speaking with forked tongue: one was deliberate: they promised one thing and delivered another. Sadly, when they meant well, were not necessarily trying to plunder and steal, they often did worse than when they were just being greedy. The notions of property that their treaties embodied had nothing to do with the Indians' concepts of ownership. The laws of the two peoples were different. The colonists were granted the use of a place; they thought it meant the right to settle and exploit and enclose the land. The illnesses they brought with their religion wiped out the populations that their settlements hadn't starved out of existence.

Perhaps every white person should affix an authorial health warning to their texts. Something indeed like 'white woman speaks with forked tongue'. It's not because you are aware of a danger, nor because you mean well, that your words or actions do no harm. Hell is paved, etc. Writing is never innocent. White writing is less innocent than any other. As Gayatri Spivak has said, every First World woman's book is typed out on a word processor made cheap by the low-paid labour of a Third World woman. Nathalie Sarraute used to say that the novel was in an 'era of suspicion'. Today, the politics of white interpretation is in an era of far worse suspicion.

There is an appropriate honesty, however, in working on, writing out of, the here and the now. In all its ordinariness and modesty. I am glad on reflection that the essays that follow have such a homely pitch. If we cannot make something out of what we are, out of what we know, how shall we ever cease to colonize others? What else today but whatever wisdom we discover in our own lives do we have to give them?

White. But also woman.

As such, insecure in relation to most of the value systems that regulate culture. Wanting to be both whore and madonna. Both good and bad. Traditional and a rebel. To be a wife-and-mother, and to shake up the establishment. Drawn to the feminist image, still attached to the feminine mystique. Wanting to be loved for both. And in permanent trouble on account of both.

To make matters even more divisive, both French and English.

White woman speaks with forked tongue: this writer writes in two languages, and about literature in two languages.

White woman speaks with forked tongue: this writer wants to find out, through writing, why she writes. She writes fiction as well as criticism. The two seep into each other. She writes as academic, straining towards theory, and as woman. Sometimes she allows everything she is to filter through into

viii

writing, and then she becomes frightened of what she's done, and she pushes it under. And the voice that grapples with reality oozes into the texts that try to be at one remove, the structures that the critical voice has erected.

The essays that follow have emerged from these manifold divisions. Over a period of time, eight years or so, it has become increasingly clear that only by allowing my voice to fork, by letting the autobiographical or the fictional surface into my thinking about something else, somebody else, by diversifying and personalizing the discourse, letting the French interfere with the English, do I ever manage to be at all adequate to the occasion, or true to myself. It seemed a pity that what had developed into a genuine practice, one that had its own logic, and purpose, and could be useful to others also in search of a different voice, a more inclusive and exploratory way of writing about literature or women's issues, should be scattered all over the place. This book is an attempt to put it together.

Forked tongues are, after all, rooted in one throat. And the serpent has ever been the friend of woman . . .

NOTE

1 As the man says in Toni Morrison's *Tar-Baby*.

Acknowledgements

' "Her legs bestrid the Channel": writing in two languages' was first published in Moira Monteith (ed.), *Women Writing: The Challenge to Theory*, Brighton: The Harvester Press and New York: St Martin's Press, 1986. ' "Bliss was it in that dawn . . .": contemporary French women's writing and the Editions des femmes' was published by Manchester University Press in Margaret Atack and Philip Powrie (eds), *Contemporary Women's Writing in France: Feminist Perspectives*, 1990. 'How *The Second Sex* stopped my aunt from watering the horse-chestnuts: Simone de Beauvoir and contemporary feminism' appeared in Elinor Shaffer (ed.), *Comparative Criticism*, vol. 9, Cambridge: Cambridge University Press, 1987. 'Doris Lessing: of mud and other matter – *The Children of Violence* appeared in Jenny Taylor (ed.), *Notebooks, Memoirs, Archives: Reading and Re-Reading Doris Lessing*, London: Routledge, 1982. 'Too short for a book?' was published in Clare Hanson (ed.), *Re-Reading the Short Story*, London: Macmillan, 1989. 'A rook called Joseph: Virginia Woolf' appeared in a French version as 'Une Corneille nommée Joseph' in the review *Europe*, special issue: *Virginia Woolf/Gertrude Stein*, Paris, 1985.

Grateful thanks are given to the various publishing houses for their kind permission to reprint the articles.

I also wish to tender thanks to the many people who have helped me, read me, listened to me, advised me in what amounts to eight years of critical writing. They cannot all be listed, but they are all in my mind and heart. Special thanks are due to Jenny Taylor for encouraging me to develop my own voice whilst writing on Lessing, and to the whole American group of Lessing fans who edit the *Doris Lessing Newsletter*

ACKNOWLEDGEMENTS

for being so wonderfully involved and inspirational – Ellen Cronan Rose, Carey Kaplan and Claire Sprague in particular. To Michèle Roberts for her exquisite grace and generosity, Rosie Jackson for being so true and uncompromising, Clare Hanson for her enthusiasm and creative thoughtfulness, Susan Sellers for her generous and joyful supportiveness. To all the people who've asked me to give the papers out of which these essays have grown, and who have responded creatively to them – to Gérard de Cortanze for inviting me to think about Woolf, David Bellos and Gillian Beer and Miriam Diaz-Diocaretz and Alice Parker and Elizabeth Meese about writing and bilingualism, Jane Aron and Helen Carr and Nicci Gerrard and Moira Dooley about French feminisms and to Françoise Van Rossum-Guyon and Helen Wilcox and Ann Thompson about Cixous. And . . . and . . . And to Jules Chametzky and the Institute for the Advanced Study in the Humanities at the University of Massachusetts, Amherst, for giving me the final institutional *coup de pouce*.

Introduction: criticism as autobiography

It is odd. There is now a massive and sophisticated body of criticism on autobiography. Autobiography as practice as well as theory. How pervasive it is. How through writing the self is invented, constructed, projected. Or remains poised on the threshold. Yet it never seems to occur to the critics who say such wise things that they themselves, through writing, may be in the process of inventing or projecting their own selves. The critical genre, it seems, makes its adepts feel that they are being miraculously transported on a magic carpet from which they can survey, or peer into, the operations of the rest of humankind, the common herd of writers as it were. They themselves are removed from the obligation of having to bother with the self that writes. They inhabit a secure, object-ified, third-person mode that protects them from having to be self-aware.

In the sixties and seventies, the so-called New Continental Criticism launched an attack on the notion that a literary or poetic consciousness is in any way a privileged consciousness. We now know, Paul de Man explained, that literary language is shot through with the same duplicities as everyday language, and that social language, in its turn, sets elaborate rhetorical devices into play so as to avoid naming the 'Unname-able': 'unmediated expression is a philosophical impossibility'. The contemporary contribution to this age-old problem, de Man went on to argue, is that the observing subject of a distant society, for instance, now knows that prior to making any valid statement, he must be as clear as possible about his attitude towards his own. 'He' (de Man goes on, presumably using he as a universal),

1

will soon discover . . . that the only way he can accomplish this self-demystification is by a (comparative) study of his own social self as it engages in the observation of others . . . The observation and interpretation of others is always also a means of leading to the observation of the self; true anthropological knowledge (in the ethnological as well as in the philosophical, Kantian sense of the term) can only become worthy of being called knowledge when this alternating process of mutual interpretation between the two subjects has run its course.[1]

Physician de Man cures himself of the need to swallow his own medicine by arguing that the complexities of the pull between observing and observed subject are such when you enter the areas of politics or psychoanalysis or indeed literature, that the critic has to adopt a combination of rational methodology and critical self-vigilance to save himself from the dizziness that threatens. Why, unlike Barthes, he could not write a *de Man par lui-même*, or, as Philippe Lejeune was to do, alternate between reflection and practice, de Man does not really explain.[2] I think it needs explaining. I agree when he says that the road to knowledge goes through self-knowledge. And that anyone today trying to reflect on others without awareness of the reflecting subject is a new kind of Candide. But then why do contemporary critics, whether they lean towards science or towards philosophy, think that their discipline is the only one in which the subject of the observer, the pull of desire or the relativity principle do not have to be taken into consideration? Are there ways of writing that are not autobiographical in the most complex sense?

I am in the University library in Cambridge. In the Reading Room, waiting for a book on the Lady with Camellias. Someone has put a reservation slip, now four days old, inside a book called *Reading Nozick*. It is a volume of essays, edited by a Jeffrey Paul.[3] I open at the first page. It describes the favourable reception of Nozick's book, *Anarchy, State and Utopia*. I read: 'That a treatise extolling the virtues of eighteenth-century individualism and nineteenth-century laissez-faire capitalism should not have elicited either hostility or silence, is both a puzzling and gratifying phenomenon; puzzling because its

themes run counter to the *Zeitgeist* and gratifying because it is a work of considerable acuity.'
  I know nothing about Nozick. Nothing about the editor, the author of this sentence. A picture of him however rises in my mind. A bit pompous: 'extolling'. Confident. Feels he's got the wind in his sails. 1981, mind you: Thatcher's star on the rise, Reagan in the US, monetarism, individualism, liberalism. Socialism is getting routed. But oh, let's not show our hand too clearly, let's pretend it's all happening through the power of good minds, Nozick for one, piercing through the clouds of the welfare state and all the mumbo-jumbo that goes with it. Is Jeffrey one of the old young men, the new philosophers? Pushing their smartly socked feet into the shoes of the old dons. Negatives: 'that Nozick's treatise should not have elicited either hostility or silence' where he could have said 'should have been so well-received'. Binary balances, and in the process of wielding them, he delights in his own capacity for classical elegance, ironic understatement: 'eighteenth-century individualism . . . nineteenth-century laissez-faire capitalism . . . hostility or silence . . . puzzling and gratifying' Let's pretend we don't know what we are doing. A kick in the teeth for all that metaphysical foreign stuff, that German neo-Marxist Frankfurt School rubbish: 'counter to the *Zeitgeist*'. An endearing appearance of modesty: we do not gloat over the success of our ideas, we are puzzled. We did not think that the signs of the times were so visible. There's hope yet for the regeneration of the old west. Competition and all that. Dog eat dog. Tough on the misfits. But there you are: society cannot thrive unless its elite, the people with 'acuity', carry the day. The elite are gratified. We are gratified.
  The author here is conveying some information about Nozick's ideas and a waxing ideology. Above all, with his elaborate third person, his disguised glee about the rise of the ideas he is 'extolling', and his disappearance into the consensus of the elite, he says a lot about himself. How much more likeable he would be if he were able to say: 'I want to defend property. And privilege. I'm sick of state control, heavy taxation, egalitarianism. It's about time the likes of me went on to the offensive. Let's pick up the discourses that argue for what I want. Look at Nozick. There's the man. Going down well too.' With a bit more self-awareness he would have said:

3

'Why do I want to defend property, extol privilege? Because I want them both. I don't want the *vulgum pecus* to have a share of the cake they did nothing to make. I want my energies and appetites to be uninhibited.' And with yet a bit more self-questioning: 'Why do I want all this? Is it that the mood is about? That I am successful, but don't reap enough rewards? That I am not successful enough? That my father, my mother, did not give me what I wanted? That I resent being preached at?' And so it would go.

But, you will say, we don't want to know about this man. This impossibly boring confessional stuff. We want to know about Nozick.

Why do you want to know?

Fair enough. Read Nozick. Agree with him. Or with Stuart Hall.

But don't forget to ask yourself why you do agree with whoever it is you find yourself in agreement with.

(Was it that I was in a great library? I suddenly thought of Virginia Woolf in *A Room of One's Own*, reading piles of books written by men about women and perceiving one thing only in what she read: anger.)

There is, of course, another way to do what the sentence about Nozick did:

'I'm talking about you-know-who', Valance
explained . . . 'Torture. Maggie the Bitch.' Oh. 'She's
radical all right. What she wants – what she actually
thinks she can fucking *achieve* – is literally to invent a
whole goddamn middle-class in this country. Get rid of
the old woolly incompetent buggers from fucking
Surrey and Hampshire, and bring in the new. People
without background, without history. Hungry people.
People who really *want*, and who know that with her,
they can bloody well *get* . . . And it's not just the
businessmen . . . The intellectuals too. Out with the
whole faggotty crew. In with the hungry guys with
the wrong education. New professors, new painters, the
lot. It's a bloody revolution. Newness coming into this
country that's stuffed full of old corpses.'[4]

I'm sure readers have recognized Salman Rushdie's *The Satanic*

Verses. This says the reverse of the Nozick. Hostility to the new ethos is voiced through dramatic irony, almost pastiche. The fiction here functions as criticism. It is also autobiographical, in that through the burlesque enthusiasm of Valance, and the punch-drunk wonder of his interlocutor, Chamcha, one senses the author's distaste for the new greed and the narrator's glee as he smothers the Thatcherite cat with cream. As a text shot through with autobiography, as I would claim that all texts are, the Rushdie fiction is infinitely more cunning and diverse than the overly objective critical piece. It produces a lot of things beside the inevitable account of self. What I want to claim is that to even approximate, or get to look towards the horizon of such richness, criticism must take autobiography into account. Only by daring to make the observing subject part and parcel of what critical observation is about, can criticism sail towards a three-dimensional land.

Thinking is not the management of thought, as alas it is too often taken to mean these days. Thinking means putting everything on the line, taking risks, writerly risks, finding out what the actual odds are, not sheltering behind a pretend and in any case fallacious and transparent objectivity. Only when it actually thinks is criticism ever a form of writing. Only then is it a total commitment to language, the way a good joiner who makes a table will choose the best wood he or she can get, attempt to serve the wood well, use his or her skill to best effect, invest everything, body and knowledge, into what the old *Compagnons* used to call a masterpiece (which could also be a mistresspiece). What Gertrude Stein deplored there was so little of. One may individually succeed or fail. The quality of the attempt is what creates a climate in which thought can thrive. In which the ethos which Rushdie satirizes can properly be challenged.

Not that each writer should splash his or her ego all over the page, like so many liquidized Gremlins. If all criticism became autobiography, it would not only become boring, it would defeat its purpose. Criticism is about the other. Its drive for an objective voice is a search for a consensual voice and an attempt at openness. Let the ego be quiet so that the other can be seen. The drive is also for an absolute. However relativistic, however studded with 'seems' or aware of rival positions the critical discourse may be, it aims at truth – in

5

the Thomist sense, as the adequation of mind to the thing. Criticism that would be primarily preoccupied with self would be narcissistic, forget about the thing over there.

Then, you will say (and George May has said), why this idolatry for autobiography? Isn't it, as Philippe Lejeune owns it is for him, a disguised desire to write?[5] Why should everyone else do it? There is plenty of the stuff about as it is. Literary criticism in any case is better deployed when it is self-forgetful. Its business is indeed to read between the lines, to detect the personal where it lurks among the other elements at play in the text. Any critic or semiotician worth his or her salt will do it. Take, for instance, Jonathan Raban's recent interpretation of the speech given by the Prime Minister to the General Assembly of the Church of Scotland in Edinburgh (Saturday 21 May 1988) in his excellent pamphlet *God, Man and Mrs Thatcher*.[6] He pounces on her praise of 'the independence of mind and rigour of thought' of the Scottish people, commenting that 'her account of the foundation of the church of Scotland has a curious doubleness to it, as if, in describing the institution, she was also sketching a thumbnail self-portrait' (pp. 21–2). And he proceeds to read the speech as a piece of hidden, proselytizing autobiography.

And so (you might go on to say), since good criticism detects the autobiographical anyway, why land us in a *Las Meninas* world in which the critic paints himself or herself into a picture full of mirrors reflecting backwards and forwards, the real sitters as chance intruders, the children or ladies-in-waiting or animals or onlookers as the pretend subjects of the painting? If Jonathan Raban were to tell us in his turn why he writes in the way he does about Mrs Thatcher, he would weaken his case, water down his polemic. I would want to suggest that had he been a woman critic he might have chosen to run that risk, and that the result might not necessarily have been weakness. I would also want to add that it is one of the great strengths of some feminist criticism in recent years that it has precisely been prepared to take that risk. But more of this anon. I would also concede that there is truth in the stricture, and that pamphlet or satire may not be the place for soul-searching. (Although I would add that the more powerful satire will come from the writer with the greater self-knowledge, one who has struggled to arrive at strongly held opinions.) But it is true that when you're on the attack, you're not going to turn confessional.

Indeed, this piece I am writing now, though I do say 'I', is not overly autobiographical, since I want to challenge and persuade. I do know, however, where it comes from: from years in which I failed to reconcile the ability I had developed to say apparently astute things about texts, in imitation or application of various discourses I had picked up, and what (as Woody Allen might say) I was really about, what I thought life was for, what I knew about other people or about myself. If you cannot ever add up, if you cannot say, 'This is what I think and this is why I think it', you are not being a critic. Though I use him for a purpose he would not have liked, I agree with de Man when he claims that criticism is linked with crisis: 'In periods that are not periods of crisis, or in individuals bent upon avoiding crisis at all cost, there can be all sorts of approaches to literature: historical, philological, psychological, etc., but there can be no criticism.'[7]

De Man is arguing for awareness of the universal crisis in language, saying that to avoid becoming aware of it is 'as if historians refused to acknowledge the existence of wars because they threaten to interfere with the serenity that is indispensable to an orderly pursuit of their discipline'. What he said in the late sixties has become true again in the late eighties. I am however arguing almost for the reverse, if on the basis of the same analysis. Not for an awareness of the endlessly mediated condition of language, the impossibility of arriving at subjecthood, but for the need to speak as a subject, and as a subject bent on self-knowledge. We have lost ourselves in the endlessly diffracted light of Deconstruction. I say 'we' meaning all of us, but especially women. For we have been asked to go along with Deconstruction whilst we had not even got to the Construction stage. You must have a self before you can afford to deconstruct it, and it strikes me that in the world of today it is very much more difficult to find or create a voice, add up mind and discourse, than to enter the proliferating ways, be they culs-de-sac or roads of excess, that open up from the infinitely evasive subject. So let me be unashamedly unmodish and old-fashioned and quote from the early Lukács, as translated by Ian Fairley:

we are talking here about the schemata of experience,
whose true generality lies concealed at the very heart
of experience; any writing that seeks to communicate
these schemata must not deny them this experiential
depth . . . truly profound subjectivity (which by no
means implies surrender to frivolity) demonstrates
laws that are genuinely positive and practical in nature.[8]

Or take Gramsci: 'The starting-point of critical elaboration is
the consciousness of what one really is, and is 'knowing
thyself' as a product of the historical process to date.'[9] Isn't it
nice to have some of the Marxists with you (even though they
are the eccentric ones, or these are eccentric passages) when
you want to argue for the importance of self-knowledge, or
rather the quest for self-knowledge, in the writing of criticism?
Not only because Marxism has, through some of its prac-
titioners, often been used to excise the self as some culpable
excrescence, but because it's good to be reminded that there
are good material (physical, economical, historical) reasons for
counting it in. These reasons endure. Unless criticism springs
out of genuine analyses of the real world, and in its turn
affects it (and in the word 'real' I include the self that lives
out of and in history as well as writes), then it inhabits the
realm of fantasy. It perpetuates a sterile state of fantasy, like
cogs that no longer clutch into the dents of a wheel, and turn
in the void, mad with their own unimpeded speed.

The mess arising out of *The Satanic Verses* recently has shown
how divorced the critical intelligence had become from reality.
There has been a vast distance between the violence triggered
by the book (evidencing however paradoxically, the power of
the Word) and the inability of the countless commentators
(with some notable exceptions) to say anything truly apposite.

The cult of the new, in the past twenty years, has been a
sign of vitality: it has also done a great deal of harm. The
pace of consumption has been too fast, generating panic, the
constant need for more, the greed to be stimulated and to
absorb and digest and move on. And so, the old and the not-
so-old have been drawn upon to fuel the machine. It has often
been a theory machine. Often fed from abroad, the Central
Europeans, the Russians, the French. The critic has tried to
imitate, refute or apply whichever model he or she found most

attractive. You could almost say, returning to de Man, that the critics of what he calls 'crisis', the genuine critics, have been turned by managers into 'approaches to literature'. Pretend that there isn't a war on. Take theory and make more in the same vein. Alternately, take theory and apply it to the text. If you do this, you will be regarded as a serious, a what is called 'professional', person. Let us not forget what 'professional' means if you are a woman. Let us not make profit out of other people's truths. Far better to say, 'a poor thing, but my own'. If you imitate and follow and apply, you emasculate what you follow. 'The mistake we make when we choose a model', Anaïs Nin said, 'is that we choose the point of arrival.'[10] The only way in which you can be genuinely stimulated and fed by discourses you admire or find congenial is if you dare conquer a voice of your own. Then you will understand why for you it is Kristeva rather than Irigaray, Spivak rather than Derrida, Bakhtin rather than Barthes.

It is not because criticism is your craft that you are removed from the obligation that is, or ought to be, upon every writer, to go to the end and the fullness of what writing can be for her or him. I had rather have Baudelaire's 'Phares', lighthouses answering each other through the darkness, as an image of the way artists dialogue through the ages, than Bloom's fathers-and-sons 'anxiety of influence' model. As a woman, not only do you not know where to enter this fathers-and-sons game,[11] you also know that you are not just a daughter, you are potentially, if not in effect, a mother too. You may be a learner, you may not be so clever or so gifted as those you admire: it does not mean that you should turn into their zombie. You may be only a little lighthouse, your small light making safe a tiny reef or corner of the coast. That is still better than stealing a flame from the big house and going round the foot of the tower proudly shining your torch on bits of rock that the big beam had given warning of anyway. And you can go to the lighthouse, become your own lighthouse, only if you recognize that, however different your craft and your skills and your object, you are still in the same business as the artists themselves. The business of making sense of life which means as a first step making sense of yourself.

But (you might say) what you propose is incredibly naive. Contemporary theory has problematized the subject in

9

manifold ways, ways that preclude the search for the self that you propose. Psychoanalysis would demonstrate to you, through Lacan in particular, that 'I' is always another, first grasped as an imago. And what about the unconscious, the divided self and all that? Self-knowledge is a mirage, a hangover oasis from the Greeks. And you speak about the autobiographical voice as if there was such a thing, as if the prodigious wealth of recent studies on autobiography, first male then female, hadn't endlessly questioned its existence as a genre. Is it form? Is it content? a mixed genre? an inferior genre? necessarily ruptured and discontinuous? Does it involve a contract with the name of the author? Is it meant to make a fallacious whole of the disparate elements of the personality? to separate, or to connect, private and public self? How can you so glibly assume that by saying 'I' you will somehow make everything add up?

I take the point. It is no easier to say 'I' than to make theory. The contruction of relations, of sense, is infinitely hard, whichever way you go at it. Yes, 'I', today, is perhaps more problematical than it has ever been. I say 'perhaps' thinking of Montaigne, who has always been a great love and a source of strength to me. Here is a man who went from a third-person voice and would-be philosophical debates and critical commentaries on the texts of others to his own script. A fall from his horse, making loss of consciousness totally painless; seeing the natural stoicism with which country people all around him were dying of the plague, changed his whole manner of thinking about death, made years of meditations on philosophy at one remove irrelevant. He no longer thought all the forces of the mind should be deployed to learn to die, be it stoically or through growing accustomed to a sceptical view of things. 'M'est avis que c'est le bout, non le but, de la vie.' Death as the end, not the aim, of life. 'Essaying' his faculties, directly relating what he was, found himself to be, what he perceived and discovered, to the great texts he had become familiar with, became his object. Or his subject.

An exercise. The creation of self through process and relationship.

In any case, as I have tried to show at the outset, any writing constructs and betrays a subject. It is not a question of choice. One might as well make something of the process. It is not

because consciousness can never be full, never more than fragments or a patchwork, that the enterprise is fallacious.
Indeed, it is because subjecthood has become so difficult,
has been so deconstructed, that there is need to work towards
it. This is particularly so for women. It has often been pointed
out in recent years that women's autobiographies carry a sense
of their being somehow 'unfinished' human beings. The awareness of being 'different', pain arising from that sense of being
somehow incomplete, unable to add up, to see your existence
as related to, let alone symbolic of, the world at large.[12] Just
as the writing of autobiography has been, for many women,
the road towards selfhood, so writing criticism as autobiography may be the way to a fuller, more relevant voice. If, as
bilingual or trilingual or transcultural being, you are never all
in one place – if you are, of necessity, as woman, split – you
have to say 'and'. You have to say 'both', or all three, or yes
and yes and yes. You cannot say 'either/or', for that would
mean banning part of yourself. Perhaps you have to learn to
say 'as'. You can only be genuinely at home in relations.
Relations are never more than relations: metaphors for
instance, like my 'white woman speaks with forked tongue',
which enables me to hold for a while, and to relate, various
aspects of myself to politics and history and interpretation, yet
remains an image and a relation. None the less true for that.
Relations never amount to identity, never are fixed. They exist
as movement, they enable. But then, life is movement. And
if you wish for balance, the contemplative life, this too has to
be reached through a relation, an equilibrium.

But isn't this desperately predictable? Don't women always
go for the autobiographical, as Colette made an imaginary
'man' blame her for in The Break of Day? Am I not just reinforc-
ing another cliché? Are women, yet again, to produce 'body',
autobiography, metaphors, for men to do the serious thing
with, that is, analyse and theorize?

'Patience', Colette replied. 'I am not making my portrait.
This is only my model.' Spell it out: I am not giving you
anything fixed, present or past, to theorize. If you think you
can theorize what I've given you, you're a simpleton. I am
creating something ahead of me, something I can work
towards, something that may help you work towards your
own model. It's a praxis, a process. Not a static thing.

11

It is white women's paradoxical advantage that in the past few hundred years and in the nineteenth century in particular they have been 'relegated' to the realm of the so-called personal, put in charge of the emotions, the ethical. It is white women's further advantage that twenty years of feminism have made them question everything radically, and primarily themselves. For white women who care to think, the idea of crisis is very much alive. The way the world is going, as well as the new awareness of the limitations of their, so bizarrely called, whiteness, ensures that it will remain alive. We have not lost touch with ourselves, or not so radically that we cannot still think in the full sense of the word.

NOTES

1 Paul de Man, *Blindness and Insight: Essays in the Rhetoric of Contemporary Criticism*, Minneapolis: University of Minnesota Press, 1983, pp. 9–10.
2 Philippe Lejeune has written a series of books that cover the whole register: from critical monographs about autobiographers to theories of autobiography (e.g. *Je est un autre: l'autobiographie de la littérature aux medias*, Paris: Le Seuil, 1980) to writing/co-editing his own family history to a mixture of the genres: *Le Moi autobiographique*, Paris: Le Seuil, 1986.
3 Jeffrey Paul (ed.), *Reading Nozick*, Oxford: Blackwell, 1981.
4 Salman Rushdie, *The Satanic Verses*, London: Viking, 1986, pp. 269–70.
5 Lejeune, *Le Moi autobiographique*, p. 31.
6 Jonathan Raban, *God, Man and Mrs Thatcher*, London: Chatto & Windus, 1989.
7 De Man, *Blindness and Insight*, p. 8.
8 Georg Lukács, 'Notes on literary theory', p. 41 of Ian Fairley's translation. It is still unpublished, and is to form part of a York Ph.D. thesis on the works of the early Lukács.
9 From *Prison Notebooks*, quoted in Edward Said's *Orientalism*, New York: Pantheon Books, 1978, p. 25. Ranjana Khanna made me think about this particular passage.
10 Anaïs Nin, 'The personal life deeply lived' in A. Stone (ed.), *The American Autobiography*, New Jersey: Prentice-Hall, 1981, p. 162.
11 I refer both to Freud's trouble with femininity – his repeated returns to the question of women's sexuality and the controversies that have arisen from it, about which feminists have copiously and brilliantly written over the past fifteen years – and to the immediate application of the various possible models in S. Gilbert and S. Gubar's recent *No Man's Land* (New Haven: Yale University Press, 1989), to the imaginary roles adopted by women writers in

the past century or so: as the father's son, or the father's rebellious daughter, or the mother's daughter . . .

12 The field of studies of autobiography in general and women's autobiography in particular is now so rich it is impossible to represent even minimally here. I refer the reader to the bibliographies in Lejeune's books, *Je est un autre* and *Le Moi autobiographique*, or to the useful summary in the introduction by Estelle Jelinek in *The Tradition of Women's Autobiography: From Antiquity to the Present*, Boston: Twayne Publishers, 1986, or to Shari Benstock (ed.), *The Private Self: Theory and Practice of Women's Autobiographical Writing*, London: Routledge, 1988.

Part I

BILINGUALISM AND TRANSLATION

1

'Her legs bestrid the Channel': writing in two languages

His legs bestrid the Oceans; his reared arm
Crested the world . . .
                    (*Anthony and Cleopatra*)

They give birth astride a grave
                    (Becket, *Waiting for Godot*)

I live and write in two languages: French and English. No great shakes to be striding such a divide: thousands do it; many women feel themselves caught between three, four, five, languages; between a local and a national language. Many have swum the Channel. My arm isn't reared and if it were, all it could crest is my own head. Sorry, Cleopatra.

Yet it's not because a predicament lacks grandeur and originality that it isn't interesting. For doing the splits geographically, linguistically, poses problems of identity. It's a more graphic form of what women who strive to speak with their own voice experience anyway. Indeed, it's precisely because the situation is so widespread, because *mobility*, in terms of place, culture, speech, imaginary projection of self, affects more and more women, that it might be useful to try and work out what my own 'bilingualism' entails.

(And while I'm clearing my throat let me cough up a bit of phlegm.

I labour at, am in labour over, two languages. Yes, there is a divide, there is a gap between the two and I'm not that keen on bridges (more on subterranean tunnels?). But whatever else, the divide isn't death, isn't negation. Let me send the Godot-trapped pair, Didi and Gogo, back to back in their womanless hell. We do not give birth 'astride a grave'. The

17

Channel, a pretty polluted and busy sea but a sea all the same, ebbs and flows between my two 'countries'. The grey-breasted robin that keeps perching over a slender bamboo stake above some yellow wallflowers, tipping its pretty head and swallowing the odd fly as it goes by, cares nothing for death. The man who gave me a book about bird-watching was buried yesterday. This morning, looking at the robin, what I want to do is mother the man quietly on into ongoing life, rejoicing at what he would have rejoiced at.

Bilingual Beckett, you cast a long shadow. I've been in it. Now I'm out.)

'MOITIÉ-DE-POULET' GOES ON SOME ERRANDS

I am French – still. I have retained my French 'nationality'. Was born and bred in Marseilles and Provence, finished my 'studies' in Paris. I married a half-Irish 'Englishman' over twenty years ago, and with the exception of one year in Paris have been living in England (and English-speaking Canada) ever since. I have three 'English' children: bilingual, complex, with a wanderer's instinct about them and a taste for the cosmopolitan: but British. Going on like this makes me feel like a concentrate of the Smith family in Ionesco's *Bald Prima Donna*, where Mrs Smith announces that they drink English beer and eat English soup. A French journalist from *Elle* obviously saw me as such, writing, 'she wears English trousers and extraordinary laced-up English shoes' (beautiful antiques, seven quid in a jumble sale, and I was so proud of my find!). Ah well. To return: I recently calculated that exactly half of my life had now been spent in France, half in England. At this stage of equilibrium, I am a perfect mongrel.

There is a (French?) fairy-tale about a creature called 'moitié-de-poulet', 'half-chicken'. The illustrations show it as cut down the middle lengthwise, from head to tail. Moitié-de-poulet hops busily on its one foot and runs critical errands for the king. That's me. My French moitié-de-poulet perches on walls and meditates at windows, flapping its one rather ineffectual wing and on occasions using it as a parachute to glide down from the branch where it has imaginatively managed to perch. My English half-chicken pecks and pokes, generally looking for grub.

'Moitié-de-poulet' is about right. Half is half. My presence in one country, one language always means my absence from the other.

I had no childhood, no youth in England. Have none of the instinctive knowledge, the intimate relation to – green and water and 'long summer days' and the Battle of Britain and Monday wash and Thursday baking and 'Grammar' versus 'Comprehensive' and miners' cottages and terraced streets and pop music and India – which growing up in England in the 1940s and 1950s and early 1960s would have given me. I can hear class and region in accents, I can't reproduce it. I can in French, though. My English voice is the most peculiar mix of a foreigner's frozen state of development, short of the right intonations and rhythms, with an eerie pliancy, a large vocabulary. A freak. But a twenty-year-old freak. Old enough to vote (which I don't).

Conversely, I have no adulthood in France (or had virtually none till I started publishing with the Editions des femmes). May '68 I experienced through the English media and the reports of French friends. I know how crucial it was in the making of the consciousness of my generation and the generation immediately following it. I know that the disillusionment that followed was lethal for some. It wasn't so for me. I take 'dips' into the French political – I was going to say 'arena', but then my 'dips' would be sand-baths – here you are, you see: I am fumbling around for an 'English' equivalent for a nascent French metaphor: 'j'y ai trempé; je n'y ai pas été immergée': look at the mud I'm churning up! Well, I have not been immersed in May '68. The same applies to everything that's been happening to France in the last twenty years or so from Pompidou to Simone Weil and the resurgence of racism and the expansion of *ordinateurs* and *vacances de neige* to the odd and multifarious ways in which streets change while remaining the same and idioms and coinages and slangs mutate from one year to another. When I go back, which is fairly frequently, I do notice bits and pieces in the papers I read, the speech of my friends and of my friends' children. What do I do about it? Learn the new idioms 'by heart'? To 'modernize' my French? How odd, to be learning one's own language as if it were a foreign language. Or do I choose to speak and write a more and more antiquated French, quaint,

like the silk of one's first ball-dress, kept in moth-balls in a
carton or some out-of-reach drawer – without even the comfort
of thinking that it'll come back into fashion (for language unlike
fashion has no recurring cycles)? Is my 'native' language,
through lack of air and moisture, becoming threadbare, its
fibres paper-thin? Will the day come when I can no longer
write in it, when it will tear, flimsily shred like ancient silk?

No wonder I am obsessed with Miss Havisham.

Alas! it is not as if I had made all that good use of English
during these my adult years. For I have in some ways only
half lived in England. Sometimes when it was cold and muddy,
or even when August was lush, its light somehow tinged with
black, I've been pining for the dryness, the cleanness of the
smells, the bare rocks of my mediterranean south. Sometimes
feeling the place, my Yorkshire place, was *unreal* (which is a
weird and worrying feeling), the people – dare I say it –
not quite 'human'. 'English' detachment brings out of me,
perversely, my most aloof and unavailable self – what my
husband rightly rails at as my 'holier-than-thou' moods – a
cataleptic stiffness of which I only become aware when something makes it break down. I was recently visited out of the
blue, by an Irish mother-of-two who was unselfconsciously
friendly, offered me her free train voucher, and went away
warmly shaking my hand, having talked about *herself*. As she
closed the door I was trembling with pleasure, and caught
myself thinking, 'How good it is for a change to talk to a
human being', which then made me blush because of all it
implied. But then, there you are. Better own up. It's not a
question of being French or English. It's a question of not being
on the same wavelength. I'm sure English women who've, for
instance, lived in Paris will have had similar experiences.

Politically too, it's very difficult to 'be' anywhere. Living so
long in England and reading the English press, etc. makes you
feel sympathetic to British positions, but at the same time you
don't stop being sympathetic to French ones. So that whenever
the two countries clash, which they frequently do, I find myself
defending whichever one I'm not in to the people of the 'other
side' – with predictable unpopularity. I make myself think of
my mother, complaining that whenever she tried to 'explain'
my brothers' 'position' to my father, he accused her of betray-
ing him; whenever she tried to make my brothers see their

father's 'point of view', they accused her of being biased. The fact is, you're not on *either* side. They're just not you. I can't, for instance, get reconciled to the anti-Europeanism of the British Left: how could *I* be anti-European? I dislike the lack of excitement about 'intellectual' matters in this country, the suspicion about theory, about ideas. I find the way in which everything remotely connected with the 'avant-garde' (e.g. a few years back, structuralism) gets classed as 'left-wing' (even when it's somebody as right-wing as Lévi-Strauss) quite bewildering. On the other hand, I've been so distanced from 'theory', through lack of intellectual support and through the sheer 'materiality' of my life, that I now find some of the 'French' intoxication with, for instance, the language of psychoanalytic concepts nearly comic. Well, not quite. I find it strange, but I'm also peeved that I'm not more familiar with it. I certainly am more startled by it than I would be if I'd stayed in a slowly evolving milieu. I can still remember my sheer delight when a friend said, about another woman she disliked, 'She's got a superego as big as the Ritz.' It said it all perfectly. But I would never have come to such a formula in a month of Sundays. (I would have had to wait for the 'semaine des quatre jeudis' for that to occur to me in French.)

Talking English, I felt for a long time very much like a parrot. I was so aware of my efforts to adapt to the world of academic learning by imitation of mannerisms and formulas. I even remember noting words down when listening to university or 'clever' talk (you then said things were 'complex' and 'ambiguous' and you were 'concerned'; the only word I can congratulate myself on having abominated from the start is the awful 'surely'). I wanted to be able to use the 'tools' myself, you see. It took the fool that I was years to realize that tools shape your hand – words shape your mouth, your mind – that they equip you for the production of bookcases when it's perhaps bird's nests you'd like to be making. But there is no knowing that until you've suffered from having your desire knocked out of you. I once wrote a book about Baudelaire: the best bit was when on a rainy day I suddenly let the pattern of raindrops on the window-pane in front of me lead me to a reflection about how I came by metaphor. The publishers said, all in a chorus, 'It's all very pretty, this "personal" touch, but really, you know, not quite serious.' So I cut it out. You have to do a lot of unlearning before you get to the position when you start growing a tongue of your own. Let official voices now fill somebody else's lungs.

I am talking about criticism. Which is what I have always written in English, my second, or second-hand language. Conversely, all my 'creative' prose has been written in French. It just happened that way. I didn't think consciously about it until a few years ago, when I was asked at a women's meeting to talk precisely on this subject of bilingualism, and I was suddenly struck by how consistent the split had been. Moitié-de-poulet indeed.

I had always 'written' in secret, ever since I had been a child. This need for secrecy, for privacy, no doubt was fostered, or enhanced, by the kindly oppressiveness of the adult world round about me. I grew up in a large family town house which had been built by my great-grandmother. It did have something of a matriarchal set-up, my grandmother, whose favourite I was (I slept in my grandparents' bedroom till I was ten), very much ruling the roost. In the end, my grandparents ended up living on the third floor; my parents, three brothers and I, on the second; my uncle, aunt and four cousins, on the first; sundry (often spinsterly) relatives on other floors, the 'maids' on the fifth floor. Several of the maids got pregnant and had babies. Yet when I expressed to my mother my decision when I was grown-up to have children but no husband, she told me this would be impossible. I spent a lot of time with the maids, a lot of time with my grandmother, learning from them both the 'feminine' arts of sewing, knitting, crochet, embroidery, etc. I went to a kindly but deeply 'processive' Catholic school; and was so penetrated by a conviction of the righteousness of the adult world, that I remember once telling my mother that it must be a great relief to be grown-up, because then you did not sin any more. She answered, much to my surprise, that adults sinned too. But I didn't believe her: I was touched by how kind she was trying to be to me.

Adults, at school and home and church, watched you like hawks. The other children did too. When I first started with periods (which the women in the family, who all knew about it, treated as a nice catastrophe), you used washable towels. Mine were soaking in the bidet when my eleven-year-old cousin peeped in, took a good look at the bloody water, asked me with a big grin on his face whether I had hurt myself – the rage and embarrassment and sense of *impotent* exposure. So guess what I did when I finally got my own bedroom, and my grandmother bought me a desk with a secret drawer? Sorry to be so archetypically banal, but yes, of course, I wrote poems and stories and kept a diary and hid my notebooks in the secret drawer with dire warnings to anyone nosy enough to pry. I've always had a soft spot for spells.

Writing, I could cease to be 'good'. Cease to produce the show I felt the much-loved grown-ups required of me. I could dare and dream and be passionate, and pretend to be taller and wiser than myself, and nobody to call my bluff. Later, when I found myself married, a teacher and a mother, in a strange place, under a lot of strain, wanting to be a good wife and a good mother and a good housewife and a good teacher and frequently making a mess of things, the writing started again. Of course, at least half of the pressure originated in me. It was my fault, I presume, if I had this oversize superego (which a little something, thank God, just stopped short of being as large as the Ritz). If I had had 'character', I would have rebelled, and fought head on, in childhood as in adulthood. Instead of which I resorted to the old way out: I started writing fiction in French.

But it wasn't just escapism; not just 'return' to a childhood habit, seeking refuge in my 'native' language as something that was free from the adult pressures English and the academic life had come to represent for me. I was also trying to deal with the present in what was beginning to look as 'my' language: nothing like exile to make you tearfully, *viscerally* patriotic. The cord has been stretched, it's tugging at you. When it was nicely coiled in a corner, you never realized it was even there. So in some ways French began to function for me as a language of 'origins'. As a 'maternal' language, in opposition to English which I must have cast in the role of a 'patriarchal', a 'symbolic', a law-giving language. I didn't at all realize what I was doing at the time. But this must be why *Shades of Grey*, which I began to write in the late 1960s, opens with a story about a young French mother. She's just had a baby daughter; she's in an English, a strongly regimented, 'hysterical' maternity ward. She feels herself being gradually estranged from her

23

own body, her own baby, by the rules and etiquette of the hospital. The English everyone talks about her becomes the expression of this estrangement. It is like the outside, the bleak air into which she is being forcibly delivered. She clings to soft, 'babble-like', 'poetic' French reminiscences as a defence against this. Revealingly, those bits proved untranslatable and were left out of the English edition. So were the pieces of exploratory, associative, dream-like prose at the end of the volume, the attempt by the narrator to 'grow a tongue' of her own. I readily agreed with the publishers that the 'English reader', that mysterious entity, just wasn't keen on that sort of writing. I must have been unwilling to have all that ground gained in French translated into the 'other' language: unwilling to come out of the 'womb' (?) where I had gone for shelter.

So, my practice would in some respect fall in with Cixous's (and Kristeva's) notions of a 'maternal' language. One that is 'of the body', pre-Oedipal, plentiful. What Cixous talks about when she describes her mother's linguistic intercourse with her as a child, as *milk*. As nourishing. Like those juices which Clarice Lispector's 'orange' produced for her. Also, in so far as French, which for months at a time I neither heard nor spoke, was being driven inwards and downwards, perhaps it assumed something archaic that had not been there before. That repressed and ideally unbroken language/self came to balance the multiplying incomplete selves that my 'social' life was creating: I was a 'different' person in the Yorkshire countryside where I was living from the academic self I was when at work from from from. I was turning into Dostoyevsky's double, selves springing up from the pavement. French then played the role of a dark 'unconscious' stabilizing force secretly taking me along the road where some day, some 'truth' might be found.

But that was also far from being the whole story. For the 'creative' French I started writing when I found myself living in England was a continuation (in a new setting) of a French I had attempted to devise whilst *growing up* as a reaction to the adult world which surrounded me, and the French 'culture' I was being introduced to. It had never been 'natural'. I had always experienced it as reactive, as constructed. For that matter, I think that not just me, but a lot of children who write start with a kind of imitative rhetoric. The models are

24

different for boys and girls, and it would be interesting to work out what the differences are: but in my experience the *imitative* pattern is similar; only very *small* children (perhaps later very rebellious children) draw or write those things we associate with impromptu surrealist genius. When children are over eight, or nine, or ten, especially of course when they are on a good-book-reading diet, they aspire to that magic self which they implicitly know is both behind and ahead of them, with 'literary' means. The books, poems, tales told by the grown-ups, have made them glimpse it. They think they've got to tread those paths to get to it. So it was at least for me. I remember thinking I was going to write *real* books for children, because the grown-ups being grown-ups had forgotten what it was like to be a child, and I knew. Well, I never did. The mirage of projection, of desire, concealed from me what some other part of me knew was essential. And so, paradoxically, English rendered me the service of making my French more 'natural' (in the sense of less and less conscious and controllable, cut off from models and a context, with 'roots' even further away from sight). French, which I might be starved of, which might be starved of social, of 'external' sustenance for months on end, which might so totally disappear that I even dreamt in English, continued its subterranean or submarine existence somehow, mutating, I realized when it surfaced, in symbiosis with what had been going on in my 'conscious' spoken English world – in fact, developing social and political dimensions which had been there more faintly earlier. God knows how all the 'translations' occurred. What was interesting was that the French became deep – that when it did me the favour of coming out, I felt it was welling up.

But – I seem to be losing sight of the point – it was also a reaction to the present. Work upon the present. Transformation of the present. It was also a resistance to, a complicated game played with, censorship, where French and English weren't necessarily in the roles the previous 'maternal/patriarchal' opposition might suggest.

The impulses are so contradictory, so mixed up with those issues of secrecy Adrienne Rich powerfully indites, I can only work them out one at a time. I do it because, whilst I feel I am guilty of many of the failures in courage she describes, being honest about it is my only way ('back'?) to 'truth'.

25

I always write in secret. Individualism: the 'bourgeois' luxury of 'inner life'. Some of it is the superstitious fear that the power to write will evaporate once writing has made contact with air, been read by others, or even talked about. In that sense, writing in a 'foreign' language is a defence, like mirror-writing when one is an adolescent: I was very good at it. The more distant my 'French' writing life is from my English life, the safer I feel. But some of this compulsive privacy also goes back to the period when I knew I could be naughty when I wrote – to the unavowed conviction that it is 'wicked' to write. The sources of the taboo are too numerous and too complicated to be gone into. But that it is *also* 'real', also 'external', was proved to me when I wasn't really expecting it, upon the French publication of *Shades of Grey*. I thought the book was quite tame, didn't think of it as likely to give offence. So much water had gone over the bridge. So I was surprised when I heard from a relation that, for instance, my uncle's family had almost come to blows over it. That they were shocked, indignant. There was one good reason why they could have been, I knew – and felt afterwards rather penitent about it. But they sermonized me about my bad taste, bad language, for talking about what 'we all know about but don't talk about'. There was a (discreet) buggery scene in one of the stories. Two months later, my uncle and aunt sent me as a consciously innocent (I'm sure of that) Christmas present (their usual gift): two popular French books. One was an historical novel about my native Provence, and it started with the violent rape of the heroine. The other was the fond memoirs of an old Provençal hunter and man of letters, and it started with his recalling how, as a child, he used to enjoy poking his finger into the anus of a deer freshly killed by his father. And I really got going over why what was being regarded as so monstrously shocking when I wrote about it from the point of view of the 'victim', and 'realistically', was so inconspicuous as to be almost nice, nicely 'literary' and polite, anyway, when men(?) wrote about it. I felt very strongly (it's one instance among many) that the lid was being slammed. It made me realize that I had gone 'north', had gone to live in England *also for freedom*: because there, I thought (till my children started being worried about what I was likely to write about), I felt there was nobody I cared about who cared about what I wrote. I didn't belong,

I was nobody, I was anonymous. Well, I think I was wrong: you can't escape. But perhaps if you moved all the time, changed countries and identity fast enough, you could keep that particular censoring dog at bay. I tried. I wrote *L'Entremise* as an attempt to operate within the suffocating field of censorship. On one level it paid: it's been the only non-critical work I have written which my family found likeable. On another level it starved me, turned into a Doppelgänger story . . . and of course, the forbidden at the end made such a return that it deeply affected my mother, so strong was one moment of 'recognition' for her.

That whole period made me both 'see' the taboos and take a despairing measure of my own inescapable tendency to give offence. Of course, in a way, everything is taboo: your family, your friends, all sexual matters, deep feelings. How come I can't write 'nice' books like so many people? Is it that I am particularly wicked, perverse? And so I have flirted with the possibility of anonymity – better than even a foreign language, the possibility to write *as far as you want*, and not to have to live with the consequences . . . I nearly did, when I published my case study of the Yorkshire Ripper case. I felt that by putting my name on it, I was stepping even more clearly into the danger zone: 'he' can see you . . . I was helped there – helped to a name, that is – by the fact of writing in French, of having French at work on the data, foreignness to give distance to the case. I also enjoyed the support of the Editions des femmes: the enterprise became plural. I wasn't alone. But the fact remains that there are things I have written, and many more I want to write, which I couldn't bear to own up to. So whether to keep them 'hidden' for ever, wait till I'm so old nothing matters anymore, or go for anonymity . . .

This is where a contradiction is at work. I also 'inherited' from long religious training a belief in 'writing as salvation', 'writing as truth'. That whole western tradition of transference of the religious to 'art' – that's got me too. So while on one level I feel writing = bad = secret, theft, treachery, I am also persuaded that writing = salvation = the truth at *any* cost, and somewhere, something in me *means any*. And there 'secret' means 'what will eventually come out', means 'sacred'. Pressure, taboos, mean the building-up of the necessary steam, something like revving up. Lies mean, not lies but creating the elaborate conditions within which 'truth' might be glimpsed. And here another twist occurs. Recently, it happened that two pieces came out 'in English', and that they seemed to be driving deeper, into areas of the mystical, areas also of my infancy and my children's infancy, areas that I had come to suppose only French could get to, or back to. Part of the reason why this was so, I suppose, was that, feeling terrified by my sense of the peculiarity of my English, I was trying to descend somewhere where English, such as something in me can feel it, could make its own 'essential' noise. Sound like itself, in so far as my own bizarre linguistic gifts and inadequacies could allow it to sound at all. I went deep-water fishing, that is, but wonderfully it turned out that, as I didn't know where I was in relation to the water (whether above or inside, nor how many waters inside waters there were), it got me to feel I might write about things I hadn't dared touch upon in French. There was something impersonal about English that made a certain type of quest possible. French phrases, like old boots and rusty tin cans, came up at the end of my book . . . Wouldn't it be lovely if that led me into that 'maternal' kingdom I thought English was denying . . . And if it did, in what language would that happen?

TRANSLATION AND SCHIZOPHRENIA

For many bilingual women, Jacqueline Risset most notably perhaps,[1] translation is an activity by means of which the 'natural' bond 'meaning-language' can be transgressed. It is a state of continued suspension – a living process, ever beginning anew, allowing, in Walter Benjamin's words, 'the post-maturation of the foreign speech, the birth throes of one's own speech'. The process, therefore, is eminently 'feminine'. When you translate, the absolute status of nouns, the 'Name-of-the-Father', is shaken. Exchanges between words are no longer 'full', that is, guaranteed by the law of the Father, the law of significance. Identities cease to be stable. You escape from definition, from the law which rules and partitions women, which prevents femininity from coming into being. Translation = no man's land = woman's land?

Whilst translating, black and white cease to be the rule: you positively move inside the spectrum of grey. But I discovered, somewhat to my cost, when I was translating *Le Spectre du gris* into *Shades of Grey* that, instead of making me inhabit a transgressive or birth throes state, translation turned the spectrum of grey into the *spectre* of grey. The punning is not so flippant as it sounds; it has a long, a real history. The activity of translating destroyed whatever bit of identity the writing of the stories had constructed for me in French. It threw me back into the horror of indifferentiation, of possible non-sense. I found that in order to translate, you have to have a non-questionable identity in one language. You simply can't afford to do it, if you're split, if you're two bizarrely osmotic 'moitiés-de-poulet'. Translating made me feel sick. What had happened was that, in some of the stories at least, I had already 'translated' mostly 'English' experiences into (a) fiction, (b) French, (c) layers of significance that had to do with those other translations. Moving into English was retrogressive, 'realistic' in the wrong sense of the word. I was unweaving what I had woven. I was destroying a painfully elaborated . . . not identity, but a way of being that enabled you/me to be free from black and white, to move inside working contraries, inside a form that stopped things from being definite. The form did function in French, partly because certain contexts, allusions, were immediately perceptible, partly because the fiction/translation was being woven at first hand. Trying to put it all into English gave the fabric the wrong sort of status (too definite) as well as making it unmatchable and bizarrely vulnerable. Above all, I realized that my own mental sanity depended upon my operating as *two* people, two writers: one French, the other English. That I did not like *moving* from the one to the other: in fact I do everything to perpetuate and feed the difference. I'm glad there *is* a Channel, that the sheer journeying from one place to the other is so burdensome. Every time I do that journey, I feel as if I'm going through mutations as strong as those that befall Alice when she eats cakes and nibbles at mushrooms. A similar thing happens when I have to translate 'for keeps' (the job of impromptu, fluid, run-of-the-mill interpreting, translating as you go poses no problems). Possibilities proliferate. The two languages become gaping chasms. The perspective of having to arrive at a finished, 'written' object that would posit a living and *perceptible* correlation between the two languages is somehow unbearable to me. The sense of being suspended in mid-air, the way the two languages start affecting each other, like spilt watercolours that run into each other, gradually makes me unable to know where either is. I become anguished about spelling; words, phrases, become odd; I no longer know whether you can 'say this', whether it is 'correct'. I realize then that I need the partition, the cut between the two. I am perhaps not so far away from schizophrenia as I'd like to think. I can live as two people. I'd go mad if the two people were forced to acknowledge each other, rather than go their separate ways, the way it pleases each.

The only solution I found to translating my own stuff (I try to avoid having to translate others') was to re-write. Make it into a different object. Let the grain of whatever language I'm moving in impose its pattern. If it's oak it's tight. I love the way English can rely upon prepositions, short words, imperative or telegraphic modes. By contrast, I have found that I often get on to something interesting, or simply get to wherever I feel that I must be, by doing, with French, what Philippe Sollers calls 'flocculation': abundant flowering, thick as the petals of a carnation, hovering like a hummingbird, whose multiple spiralling wing-beats maintain it in the air long enough for it to get at a flower. What is certain is that the decision to write in one language rather than another is going to lead to something different. I shall never end being amazed by how heterogeneous France and England are. Where would I be if I could do the same thing in both?

Drowned, of course: in the grey waters of the Channel.

POSSESSION

Yet I am also in the business of connections.

Connections with what is, or seems to be, totally different from me.

Taking a character who is as unlike me as I can possibly imagine. The beautiful model of *L'Entremise*, its narcissistic heroine – and seeing 'ce qui reste quand on a tout enlevé'. What's left when you've removed every way to identification with, love for, a character. (Interesting what it did to George Eliot when she created Rosamund Vincy.)

Trying to create 'people' whom, on account of class, colour, a whole range of experience, I could never hope to know – who would neither wish to know me themselves, nor feel I had any right to get to know about them, write about them. And yet write about them, because somehow there *is* a bond between us and it is important to see what it is. But it is just as important not to take possession, not to 'give' people a 'voice'. Not to make them signify, be recuperable, exploitable. I get very moved by the way Virginia Woolf 'did' Septimus Warren Smith in *Mrs Dalloway*. You can feel she was 'trying', you can feel the strain, and there is nothing perhaps more lovable in the writers we love than where they haven't quite pulled it off, where the ropes show: their passing weakness suddenly touches our prevailing weakness; we feel the warmth of their 'humanity'. Virginia Woolf knew she had little in common with a 'lower-class' young man suffering from shell-shock: she'd never even *seen* the war. And yet she knew with a knowledge bought at the cost of madness that there was a link between Septimus Warren Smith and Mrs Dalloway, and she set about discovering it. Her hovering round that bond (the way Mrs Ramsay tries to make her dinner-party work) that *is* translation, of the kind Jacqueline Risset talks about.

I understood something of this when trying to end my analysis of the Yorkshire Ripper case. I wrote a piece of fiction, mostly in the second person, the '*tu*' of one of the victims who came from Spain originally. I wanted to reaffirm the 'humanity' of those women whom everyone, the killer and the police and the judiciary and the media, had been almost systematically defacing. I called the piece 'An Elegy for a Dead Prostitute', and I tried to make it into a song, something 'open', as close to 'poetry' as I could get. I thought of Genet's 'transformations', of his covering his convicts with flowers. I used '*tu*' because I knew I couldn't be her, I had no right to say 'I', or 'she', to pretend that I knew either way. But saying '*tu*' is also a way of being fraternal – of making it happen to the reader as well. The 'bond' was that, however privileged I might be and underprivileged she had been, we were both 'immigrants' from the Mediterranean. No, that wasn't enough. But yes, it was enough: I wasn't trying 'realistically' to produce her voice: in any case, she would have spoken some sort of Spanish English, and I was writing in French: in fact, I could *hear* the top of her palate rubbing over some consonants. I was trying to create an area of language where a voice such as hers might be heard.

Still, about connections: what is odd is that you may work on, discover, something that seems totally private, even eccentric, in a state of total isolation – and it turns out to have an unexpectedly political, a public, face. Sometimes the discovery is pleasant. Many times I have dreamed of a book, cherished an idea, in the secret of my brain or chambers or wherever one thinks privacy is at its greatest, only to discover that I was plottting, or doing, exactly what large sections of the French 'intelligentsia' were up to. It nearly makes you believe in all sorts of suspect things: 'nationality' (somehow, something – what? – the 'formation' you've been given? the language? – makes you remain on a wavelength even though you're abroad, in another context altogether, and you don't know that you are); the famous *Zeitgeist*; or Doris Lessing's concentric circles, what she calls 'ripples from the storm': the same thoughts, 'fads', mysteriously carried by atmospheric mental waves, reach a wide range of apparently disconnected people. Whichever way it is, I have seen the phenomenon occur so often that I now take it for granted: if I have this wonderful 'original' idea, ten to one that a lot of other people are having it too. For instance, I worked on the case of the Yorkshire Ripper in total solitude and with a certain 'pioneering' feeling; I found on arriving in Paris when the book came out that the whole town was ablaze with interest in *fait-divers*: countless books were coming out, special issues of magazines, debates in the Pompidou Centre, even an exhibition in the Musée des Arts et Traditions Populaires. I nursed in secret for years plans for a picaresque erotic novel about a woman's multiple loves, only to find on my last visit that a large number of other French ladies had written exactly along those lines – not least among them Kristeva – and that Sollers had produced the male counterpart to my idea. But nothing like this is happening in England that I can see: it's all debates about 'pornography' or 'romance' . . .

Also, sometimes one has the hallucinatory feeling that what's happening on a local, or private, level is the *expression* of a larger public event. Thus my university department had its own incestuous mini-Watergate at the time of the American one. What was amazing was how the stages of its development

seemed to be mimicking the other, how it all seemed to lay
bare the same inner structures or political predicament as the
'real' one. Whether the mind is so thirsty for metaphor that it
projects all this, or whether, like a major disease, a particular
'crisis' proliferates secondary ailments all over, I don't claim
to know. One summer many years ago I became obsessed by
the Fisher–Spassky chess confrontation. As day after day I read
the papers about it, it looked as if its episodes corresponded to
the vicissitudes of a relationship I was going through at the
time. I nearly learnt to play chess on the strength of this!
Thinking that perhaps, once I understood the *actual* moves of
the game, I might get to the bottom of what was possessing
me. The mood passed, Spassky (with whom I had identified,
of course) lost, Fisher disappeared into the solitude of some
New York hotel bedroom.

What is more worrying is to discover that you've been
moved by something – again, something public – that you
didn't know at the time was moving you. More pretentiously,
let me say that the writing of fiction (which is supposedly
'private', imaginative) can turn out to be the expression of
something much larger, more impersonal. It's all very well to
say this is a pretty old 'sociology of lit.', or 'Marxist' idea: it's
a different matter studying the thing and having it happen to
you. For me, *L'Entremise* started with the tale of a woman who
overhears her own voice in the *back* of the car she's driving,
then sees her own double's *aged* face appear in the rear mirror
in the place of her own *young* face. She then gets hounded by
her double, who always creeps up on her stealthily, from
behind. I had actually heard my own voice in the back of the
car – and been frightened of what was at the back. Anyway
the book came out; and it was only two years later, when I
had finished work on the Ripper case, that it occurred to me
that perhaps I had displaced on to a fictional model what was
an *instinctive* fear felt by northern women at the time. We were
afraid of 'his' 'creeping' up on us from behind – I certainly
was – yet how did we know he came from behind, since
details of the attacks were only released after the man's arrest?
I also discovered then that Sutcliffe was 'car mad' – that he
spent his spare time playing with motors. *Shades of Grey* has
a story called 'La Roue' ('The Wheel'), in which a man becomes
fanatically fond of his car as a refuge against the 'predatoriness'

33

of his wife and mother. Another story, 'The Immaculate Conception', is about a woman whom frustration and thwarted motherhood drive to compulsive and ultimately suicidal housecleaning. This seemed to be what had happened to Sonia, Sutcliffe's wife. Reading descriptions of her behaviour, her way of dressing, what her house looked like, I recognized details I had *invented*. Is it that there are universal forms of behaviour which the 'imagination' perceives, or had I been driven to work on Sutcliffe because I somehow sensed that I had 'been there' already? If the latter, what does it mean about me. Or had I 'been there' for the same reasons that the Sutcliffes and Sonias of this world come into existence? Or again, are the types of displacements that lead to the double 'schizophrenias' of a Sutcliffe and a Sonia also present in anybody who strains under a *dual*, a *bilingual*, situation? By 'dual', I mean that instead of being 'in control', having 'one being' which is French *or* English, working-class *or* middle-class, 'male' *or* female (*and* enjoys a 'proficiency' of some sort in the 'other' mode) you are – 'moitié-de-poulet', quoi.

OF TRUTH; 'SNAKETHINKING'; AND SAFECRACKING

How to arrive at truth. The right relation to truth. The right image for truth. If you speak with bilingual tongue. But perhaps white woman always speaks with bilingual tongue. White woman speaks with forked tongue.

Create a field, perhaps. A field full of contradictions.
This first:

There are phrases which help us not to admit we are lying: 'my privacy', 'nobody's business but my own' . . .
. . . Does a life 'in the closet' – lying, perhaps of necessity, about ourselves to bosses, landlords, clients, colleagues, family, because the law and public opinion are founded on a lie – does this, can it, spread into private life, so that lying (described as *discretion*) becomes an easy way to avoid conflict or complication? can it become a strategy so ingrained that it is used even with close friends and lovers?[2]

Now for a bit of translation:

34

Above all she remembered to distrust paradoxical thoughts. Because they are true serpents, the disciples of Milton's beautiful Snake, she knew something about it: there is a curve in their slimness which has always unaccountably seduced her; what held her was not the message but the enigma of its logic; and the enigma was how at a certain point in the speech what began as truth ended up as falsehood . . .

In the end this snakethinking sickened her. She felt that the paradox was only thinking through imitations of thought . . .

Thought she'd known for a long time that the secret of its seductiveness was perhaps nothing else but its secrecy. Because everything that is hidden, is seductive. And it is the oldest secret in the world, and it would long ago have ceased to be secret, if it wasn't being lost and hidden again every time.[3]

Both bits as a possible comment on the following supposedly bilingual image:

Craftsmanship. Labour. Patience. But I don't get a crop. I don't have a birthright. More: I suddenly think as I look at myself writing sentences, forward, backward, no, not quite there, got to adjust them so the paragraph works, so that it should finally click, can't have that. Try this one. More like a burglar who's skilled at opening safes. Ear to the delicate clock. Listen to the faint whirring of the dents as you move from one to the other till the magic, the barely perceptible pause tells you you've got the right number there. Next. And next. Till at the end of the day, oh wonders of wonders, you give a little shove, a little pull, and instead of all the sirens caught in the act race away like hell, the heavy door glides gracefully open.

Yes. It has to do with theft: both in French and in English. Silence. Secrecy. Daring: the cracking of *safes* is full of risks. No violence, no thrusting or penetrating pens and what-nots (only an 'I' to add, can't do that in French, 'pens' + 'I' = One = safe identity), no rape of the virgin page, of the soft body of language pah pah pah. None of that. In any case, you know perfectly well that you're *also* the safe. You haven't got a wife to play that role for you.[4] But your ear, so attentive, the clock is like a bird to tame (plenty of time; I won't hurt you; relax). Every sound it makes you've got to interpret. And no two safes are alike. Not just because the codes and right and left are different in different countries, you don't drive on the same side of the road and driving-wheel and gears are on different sides, do you change hands when you write in French? Do you write English with your left hand? But because each is fitted in a different place, for a particular function.

Have I cracked this one? Yes. I see wads of notes, some typescript pages, perhaps a few banknotes. Yes, I have cracked it. Useful to have done so. But as soon as it clicked open, I realized that the lady of the house, canny lass that she is, had removed the valuables to some other hiding place. She only let me have a go at this one because she knew that what she truly treasures had been secreted away from it.

NOTES

1 See 'Traduire', in *Des femmes en mouvement*, mensuelle, 4 April 1978, p. 78
2 Adrienne Rich, *On Lies, Secrets and Silence*, London: Virago, 1980, p. 190.
3 Hélène Cixous, *Limonade tout était si infini*, Paris: Editions des femmes, 1982. Needless to add, 'my' translation.
4 This obscure crack is levelled at a particularly objectionable French writer, Jean-Edern Hallier, who in his book, *L'Enlèvement*, which is full of the most violently misogynist images, boasts of having burgled his own wife's safe.

2

Ananas/pineapple

A
Ananas
An
An–
Âne/Ânonner
Ananthe
Ana–
Anapeste
Anabaptiste
Anaglyphe
Anachorète
Anaphylaxie
Anabase

ANABAS

The more criticism I read, the more I think that it is a scrambled form of autobiography, which seeks to conceal the self in the writing. This article attempts to reveal what makes me tick.

Let me follow the precepts of M. Jourdain's philosophy master, in Molière's *Le Bourgeois gentilhomme*, and begin at the beginning, with a knowledge of letters. Vowels, which 'express the voice'. The first is A, which you form (in French) by opening the mouth wide: A. M. Jourdain says 'A', and is delighted to find out that he can, that he's been doing it all his life. 'A veut tout tems qu'on la bouche oevre', says a thirteenth-century French maxim, quoted by Littré. Ah, but. 'A' for 'Apple'. Twice I have stretched aside the corners of my mouth instead of opening it. Bilingualism begins with A.

There is a rather entertaining dictionary game: you open the Larousse at random, you read out the words on the page. Neither you nor anybody else knows a quarter of the words. Very gratifying, if you're the one with the dictionary, and the others have to guess. I played the game with myself once when looking for the etymology of *ananas*. I had read an article on Jamaica that spoke of the pineapple as one of the emblems of the island. Had *ananas* got anything to do with *an* (*année*, year), *anal*, *âne* or *anarchiste*? It has not. It comes from a Peruvian (Littré), more precisely a Tupigurarami word (Robert, 1544/78) meaning both the plant and the fruit. At that point *anas* began to jump at me from the page. The meanings were multiple. *An*, year, comes from *amnus*, *am*, Sanskrit for time. *An-* means without, as in *ananthe*, without flowers. But the prefix *ana-* (I spare the reader the suffix) indicates repetition and reversal. The logic that connects *anapeste* (striking twice) with *anabaptiste* (christened again) could perhaps be grasped. But what about *ana-* meaning 'often' in *analogue*, from down to up, in *anaglyphe*, 'backwards' in *anachorète*, 'the other way round' in *anaphylaxie*, and the action of going up as well as the expedition to the inside in Xenophon's *Anabase* (a title borrowed by the twentieth-century poet Saint-John Perse). Ana . . . Nananana . . . In my experience as a mother, this was the first sound a baby makes. I thought of primary drives. Babble. *Anonner*, from *âne* (donkey, *anus*, yet another word) means to read or recite in a halting way (as a donkey brays?). It is some comment on Kristeva's distinction between the semiotic, primary sounds connected with the maternal, and the symbolic, where language as law, as connected with the father, rules, that this spectrum should appear as soon as you open the sound an, ana: the most elaborate and different concepts are at work through the same sounds, and these sounds are primary. The two extremes touch. The overlapping, the slippages made me feel crazy. I was going to say, hysterical, if the word had not become so charged with meaning. Perhaps it is the right charge, since the mothers of sounds were opening like so many Pandora's boxes.

I did lapse into uncontrollable laughter when I finally landed on *anabas*, next to *anabase*. It is, the Larousse said, 'an insect-eating fish of the indo-chinese coastal bushes that breathes air. Its usual name is *souris*' (mouse). A fish called mouse that lives in the trees and breathes air. All else confusion. I remembered a sequence from the film *Mondo Cane*, where, after an atomic explosion, fish on a Pacific atoll had taken to living in trees, hopping from branch to branch. Madness.[1]

It was all the fault of *ananas*. If I forgot its sound, and just thought of it, such as I had seen it, eaten it, been told about it, I imagined a tallish plant with trailing leaves, movingly bearing its one precious fruit as the aloe does its one unrepeated flower. A fruit with a many-tiered spiked crown, a pale honey juicy fibrous flesh radiating from a solid hub, and a carapace the colour of walnut wood. Each scale of the carapace diamond-shaped, eyed with a little black ring, staggered in a honeycomb pattern. Was it the pattern of that carapace that had led the British, Englishing their colonies with true-Brit aplomb, to name 'pineapple' the Indian *nanas*? 'Nanas' can indeed be called a primary sound, since not only is there no known 'mother' to it, but I am told that the black American word 'nanny', nanna, means mother. Yet for me, pineapple meant *pomme de pin*. That was what the large pine-cones of my Provençal childhood were called. They had *pignons*, pine-kernels, between their staggered wooden petals, hard oblong nuts that you cracked between two stones to get at the exquisite kernel, hardly larger than a cooked grain of rice, and that melted in the mouth . . .

The slippage began when *ananas* refused to equate to pine-apple. It precisely expressed the relation of my French to my English. Not that my French is colonial, or foreign, imported as *ananas* is. I was born and grew up in Marseilles, a Southern French city, and had a perfectly ordinary, i.e. riveting, middle-class childhood and youth. But ever since I started writing as a 10-year-old, my French has had an imitative or secondary quality. I was producing verse, stories, in imitation of those I was reading, or as a gesture towards them. The writing was something precious, guarded by a carapace of secrecy against the heat – against the prying and powerful grown-ups. It was a gesture both towards and against the overbearing largely patriarchal milieu in which I was. Having settled in England as an adult, however, having married an Englishman and holding a university job in which, the language, the culture, the critical concepts being different from those I had come to expect, I felt astride everything – ill at ease, lost – I began to write fiction in French. Pineapple, an English, a conceptual word, made *ananas* into something more primary than it had ever been. English, being clearly secondary, for cultural and institutional reasons, did my French the service of making it archaic. French became deep, something silenced, pushed under, that when I wrote helped me discover some form of identity.

And so, not realizing what I was doing at the time, I began to write fiction in French, criticism in English. Assigning roles to my languages must have been, for me, a way of keeping to some sort of order. I was quite taken by the harmonious version of bilingualism produced by Philippe Sollers when I first came across it:

> The national, the maternal language, does not dream itself, it makes a subject dream in its dream. But the dream of one language may be the wake of another, and when it is night under one latitude, it may be daylight under another.[2]

I liked the expansive, fluid sense of the relation of self to language this gave, the rhythmic, cyclical view of bilingualism that was being offered. Whilst one language is being spoken or written, it is daylight for it. The unspoken other language has gone under, is in the dark. But as earth keeps revolving and everything on it exists, the dark language, even when unheard and invisible, continues its antipodean existence.

On reflection however, for me at least, things are just not so. Languages are not tangible solid rotating hemispheres. You as a subject are not the place where language lives and occurs, in turns illuminated and plunged into darkness. For a language to live in that way for you, you must be in the country where it is being spoken, written, where it evolves and grows. You must be in it, as a fish in the sea. If you are not, instead of a blissful, animated, recuperative night, you've got a gap: a vacancy, that nothing in that language will fill.

I had no childhood, no youth in England. Nothing will ever make me into a native daughter, give me the instinctive bodily knowledge of grass and seasons and schooling and English politics that having grown up in the place would have given me. However much I get used to landscape and people, however much I like them, they will always remain strange to me. Conversely, I have had virtually no adulthood in France. What has been happening to French sensibilities and politics from De Gaulle to Michel Rocard in the past twenty years or so somehow eludes me. When I go back, I feel I am learning new words, noticing changed attitudes and different topics of conversation as if I were in a foreign country. I belong to both places. I belong to neither. Comfort and completeness are nowhere: everything continually needs to be adjusted to.

It strikes me, not only that the bilingual person, the bilingual writer in particular, is in a much more uneasy situation than Sollers allows for, but that this situation exemplifies what Catherine Clément describes as the anomalous position of *woman* in culture. Women, she argues, along with the cham-anns and witches evoked by anthropologist Marcel Mauss, belong to two opposite orders at once: as human beings, they are on the side of the Rule, the Symbolic, what orders the natural. As biological beings, having periods, pregnancies, they are seen to be on the side of natural rules. They are *réglées* (regulated/regulating, have periods) in two different ways.[3] Which of course you can only translate in a heavy footed way, the term 'period' suggesting something quite different from *règles*. *Ananas* aren't pineapples, I keep telling you.

For years I tried to separate night and day. I wrote fiction in French, criticism in English. I did not know why I did this, nor why I chose to write those particular books. With hindsight, patterns appear. My first attempt was at Baudelaire, a poet I loved and whom an entourage of students and colleagues regarded as peculiarly French: celebrating him, I was glorifying my own strangeness. He had inverted the meanings of terms such as 'nature' and 'artifice' to deal with a changing world, a world in which nature was becoming coarsened and estranged from mankind, in which the artificial was becoming a new nature and appeared as the only source of values. I was looking to him for a dialectic (a binary, a patriarchal one, it now occurs to me, in which woman was resolutely bracketed with nature) – a dialectic that would help me cope with the contradictions that French and English, the city in which I had grown and the country where I was now living, the clashing values of childhood and adulthood, posed for me.

I was closer to my object the second time around. Interestingly, that time I wrote the book in French first, then I rewrote it and made it into something else: in English. *Un Homme nommé Zapolski* (in English *The Streetcleaner*) was concerned with a multiple murderer, Peter Sutcliffe, whom the media had called the Yorkshire Ripper because of the similarity they saw (or sought) between his murders and those of the Victorian Jack the Ripper. I wanted to understand, not only why the man had done what he had done, but also why, throughout the entire case, there had been such a tragic trail of errors: from the killer thinking he was on a God-appointed mission to 'clean the streets' to the police failing to catch him even though they had questioned him nine times. Sutcliffe thought he heard the voice of God coming from the grave of 'a man called Zapolski' in the Catholic part of the Bingley cemetery where he worked as a gravedigger. The slippage from being Sutcliffe to being Zapolski, possessed by Zapolski, the schizoid paranoid identity, were to me recognizable. All his life, Sutcliffe had suffered from being persecuted as a sissy, a mummy's boy, a man lacking in recognizable maleness. The voice from the grave appeased the anguish, gave him a distinctive male identity. Later, the voice told him, in answer to agonizing problems of identity, both social and sexual, that it was all 'the fault of prostitutes', that he had to 'clean the streets' of their litter. He chose the most violent image of the Master of the City in a bid to solve his problems. He became the exterminating angel.

Here was a man who in a sense was bilingual. Both male and female. Able to be neither. The need for him to be male turned into a will to murder, repeated murder. As if masculinity required that the world be made black and white, that the Rule be mercilessly and absolutely imposed. That people – that *women* – should be seen as good *or* bad, 'decent' or prostitutes, and that masculinity should be asserted through the extermination of the bad: 'cleaning the streets' – through the definition of women as bad through murder. Here was the beginning of the trail of errors. Women are neither good nor bad. Indeed, Sutcliffe, in his random descents upon the cities of Yorkshire killed *both* so-called good women, and prostitutes. But there was a disturbing endorsement of his deeds and this division of women into good and bad by the media, the many men who identified with the killer, the police and the judiciary. There was a will (the will of masculinity? of the Symbolic?) that women should be so divided, so regulated. Sutcliffe's parodic masculinity posed huge questions, among them the question of whether something called the feminine lay in being *neither and both*. No wonder, given the way of the world, it was difficult to be bilingual. No wonder it was difficult to be woman. The world did not like 'neither and both'. Yet 'neither and both' seemed to stand for something like life, whereas 'either/or', in that case, had been the way of murder.

After so much death, I needed life. I worked on a life-loving writer, on Colette. I found her incredibly healing. Not only does she integrate bilingualism ('J'habite à jamais un pays que j'ai perdu') but she has one, powerful voice, one, powerful identity that for instance subverts gender divisions. As in that marvellous pen-name of hers, a girl's (and her only daughter's) first name but also her father's surname. When somebody, in her books or in life, calls her 'Madame Colette', they're calling her by her mother's name. At one stroke, beyond binary oppositions, she is her father, her mother, her daughter, herself . . . In the process, she finds a way of writing about things that makes them acutely real, material: beyond the Mallarméan ideality of language, the absence/presence couple that forever seems to haunt modern literature. The thingness of Colette's writing is balm to the bilingual reader. For when the names totter, when schizophrenia threatens, when the pineapple refuses to become *ananas*, reaching out for the materiality of the pineapple in language is the only path to sanity.

Which is not to say that there aren't many sane and splendid ways of being bilingual, or multilingual. The people of Eastern Europe, for instance, whose native experience is that of a pluralistic culture, who grow up with several languages, inhabit difference with joyful fluidity. Besides, bilingualism is a much more widespread condition than is commonly recognized. Denouncing the notion of genius as *Geist*, as the crystallized inner history of one nation, the quiddity of native speech, George Steiner points out that this is a Romantic construct. Bilingualism, he reminds us, used to be the norm among the European elite until the latter part of the eighteenth century. People spoke Latin or French as well as the national language. Bilingualism or multilingualism have been becoming the norm again this century through the many writers in exile, or the writers astride languages. Steiner names Joyce, Beckett, Nabokov, Borges.[4] I would add Cixous, Lispector, half-Russian Nathalie Sarraute, Indochina-born Marguerite Duras, Africa-bred Buchi Emecheta or Doris Lessing, and many more.

There is no doubt, however, that for me bilingualism has been a difficult state to inhabit, a source of enduring confusion, of shifting sands. Until recently, writing fiction in French[5] did make me feel I was keeping alive a link with my mother country, an ancient/secret self. But now the length of time I have been in England (twenty-five years), my increasingly meagre or rusty French, no longer fed, or oiled, by a milieu of living speech, mean that the temptation to write fiction in English is growing. The sense of slippage which I tried to convey through *ananas*/pineapple, which led my youngest child to say 'pish' when he wanted to say at the same time fish and *poisson*, may have to do with the panic that the possibility of losing my language creates. Something in me is saying: if I cannot keep my bond with my nanny, I shall fall into gibberish. I shall say, 'anapple'; 'anapple, Annabel, anabas' . . .

Something else is saying: perhaps if I try to find form, to find life, in *that* language in the first place, without having to translate or rewrite, perhaps I'll turn into a full-size creature?

It has recently occurred to me that you have to earn the capacity to be bilingual. It is a question of strength of identity. Control of the mirror-image at some fundamental level, where you choose who you are, choose to be where you are when you are there, and hold fast. Bilinguals like myself are Pilates. They are always here and somewhere else at the same time. 'What is truth said jesting Pilate, and would not stay for an answer.'[6] Pilate wants to serve both Christ and Caesar. Kill Christ and keep his hands clean. I am not sure where, writing-wise, the choice will be made, the form will be found, that will enable me to live my bilingualism without being driven insane by its sudden spontaneous deconstructions. But I know that it urgently needs to be decided, and that bilingualism may ultimately be a question of character.

Deciding who to be, and writing (walking, hobbling, swimming or flying) towards it.

Anabas does live in trees.

NOTES

1 I found *anabas* recently, quite happily hopping in suspended basins in the Indochina jungle, in Marguerite Duras's evocation of her childhood in *Les Parleuses* (interviews with Xavière Gauthier, Editions des femmes, 1975, recently translated as *Woman to Woman*).

2 Philippe Sollers, 'Joyce et Cie', *Tel Quel*, 64, 1975, p. 15. My translation.

3 H. Cixous and C. Clément, *The Newly Born Woman*, tr. Betsy Wing, Manchester University Press, 1986, pp. 7–9.

4 George Steiner, *Extra-Territorial: Papers on Literature and the Language Revolution*, London: Faber & Faber, 1972, pp. 3–5.

5 I have published at the Editions des femmes both *Le Spectre du gris* (1977) and *L'Entremise* (1980).

6 The opening sentence of Francis Bacon's essay 'Of Truth'.

3

To fly/to steal: no more? Translating French feminisms into English

Jacqueline Risset, the French poet and translator of Dante, has described the translator as both midwife and mother. As midwife, the translator delivers the foreign speech from its possibilities in the other speech. As mother s/he gives birth to the text in the other language, is forever beginning, and suspended: through translations all identities reveal their frailty. All words are treated like names: each has to be dealt with individually. All names are treated like words: each can be substituted for another.[1]

Take these two sentences by Hélène Cixous:

Voler est geste de femme. Voler dans la langue, la faire voler.

To fly	is gesture of woman. To	fly	in language
To steal	epic		steal	tongue
Flight	saga			
Stealing				
(Prometheus)				

to make it fly/steal.

This is particularly tricky. Almost every word has a variety of meanings. As you read the French, the meanings unfold like a fan, spread yet remain suspended like a cloud of gnats. But as soon as you attempt to translate, each word threatens to fall apart, the sentence sways and strains and you don't know how to hold it. Once *voler* can be replaced by 'to steal' or 'to fly' or 'stealing', there is no fixing it. It's a matter of almost hopeless choices. Should you (like the translator of *The Newly*

Born Woman), have two words, linked by a stroke: 'To fly/steal', which is cumbersome, and in English seems arbitrary? The sentence enacts what Risset is talking about when she says that translation is specifically of woman, for woman has no stable identity. Through verbs and nouns, normally the most stable of words, it inscribes mobility as identity. As you try to translate, the instability is increased.

You cannot quest, Risset adds, for a female identity. Meaning, I take it, stability, essence. That may be a matter for argument. But I think that Risset is right to speak of the translator as occupying a (culturally speaking) female or feminine position. It is a position which I recognize.

The translator is a being in-between. Like words in translation, s/he endlessly drifts between meanings. S/he tries to be the go-between, to cunningly suggest what readings there could be in the foreign language other than those the chosen translation makes available. Is there a word in English that, like *langue*, designates both the bodily organ and the existence of words, the structure of speech? Should it be language, should it be tongue? You are led to reflect on how particular translations become constructed. What gets lost, what is gained, what and how altered, in the passage from one language to the next.

A French-born and French-educated woman who has been living, writing and teaching in England for most of my adult life, I still read what is written in French from a French perspective. And I never cease to be bewildered by what happens to French writing when it is translated into English.

So-called French feminisms in particular have been transformed in the process, made to fit certain Anglo-Saxon parameters which have a complex history. A history that is different in Great Britain and in the United States, and that would need to be told in detail. There isn't the space, and I shall simply produce an outline of how things seem to me to be in England, which I know better. Because of the celebrated pragmatism and empiricism of the British tradition, the strong linguistic orientation of British philosophy for a long time, and the social orientation of linguistics and psychology, because also the subject 'English', after its tussle with science in the fifties, was made into a central humanizing (=male) discipline, theory has come to be a fringe element of various departments

47

of literature, English departments in particular. It has become the custom over the years for theory to be brought in from Russia, Germany, Central Europe, France, and to be considered left-wing. That is of course because much of the theory was left-wing (Marxist theories in particular). But the fact that there has been, in the last two or three decades, mainstream opposition to theory has pushed it to the margins or to the left, whether the theory itself was left-wing or not. This has been full of paradoxes: psychoanalysis and Structuralism, with a frequent right-wing leaning, have thus been perceived as left-wing: the very fact of dabbling in them meant you were subversive.

The reception of French feminist theory has occurred in this loaded context. It certainly is a sign of the resistance to anything theoretical that it should have taken a foreigner, Toril Moi, to do so much to popularize it.

In the process of its importation so-called French theory has changed face. Though it has always been recognized that each writer was different, Kristeva from Irigaray from Cixous (not to mention Wittig in the USA) they have tended to be grouped and discussed together, when in France they are, if not at daggers drawn, at least not on speaking terms. In the Anglo-Saxon description they become, in Rachel Bowlby's expressive image, equally beautiful goddesses, and it is simply a question of (Paris-like), your choosing which one appeals to you most.[2]

The construction of (in Toril Moi's phrase) a 'Holy Trinity' of French feminist theory not only blurs or defaces what the writers effectively do but it says a great deal about the needs from which it stems. The need to dialogue with positions which, being foreign, inherit the left-wing prestige of theory and thus make it possible to challenge the more interesting, theory-minded element of the Anglo-Saxon establishment. The need to find radical discourses that could fertilize Anglo-Saxon feminisms. The very proper search for a philosophical dimension to feminism. But also, the need to perpetuate the somehow pleasing British myth that all theory is foreign, and to construct the foreign as pure theory, as the Other of Anglo-Saxon pragmatism, so that it can be critiqued at a distance. The relation between the Anglo-Saxon mind and theory often seems to me to have the character of a dialogue with, or the invocation of, an Other. In this elaborate process of translation, you might say literally, dis-placement, the actuality of the French discourse *as* discourse becomes lost.

I am particularly concerned with what has happened to Hélène Cixous: partly because she's been more than the others the target of attacks, a kind of French Aunt Sally epitomizing all that is wrong with the twin vices of 'essentialism' and 'biologism', partly because she is (like Wittig, but Wittig being more of an American than an English presence, I shall leave her aside for the time being) a writer of creative as well as theoretical prose. She is also relevant to the stance taken here, because the shifts of identity in her prose partake of what Risset describes as the drift of translation: I hope the fly/steal quotation from which I started suggested that. Cixous is the most misrepresented of the 'Trinity' in that her theoretical texts have been more translated and read than her fiction: only two or three of the fictions are available in English when there must be over twenty in existence, whereas essays like 'The Laughter of the Medusa' or books like *The Newly Born Woman* have made the rounds. And only one of the plays, the Dora one, has been translated. Thus a continuing and fast-changing, evolving practice is patchily represented, the few available fictions (like *Angst*) solidified into a false representativeness. Also, there is no clear-cut distinction between what passes for theory, what passes for fiction, or drama. The theory is creative and written as such, the fiction is critical and works on theory. Ironically, up to the last few years, the essays have been easier to read than the fiction. 'It changed my life, it so moved me', I have heard people say of 'The Laughter of the Medusa'. In the essays, the self of the author, and of the narrator, comes across more readily.

You wouldn't guess that any of this was at play when you read some Anglo-Saxon accounts of French feminisms. Here K. Ruthven makes mincemeat (or attempts to) of Cixous's refusal to have her position codified as theory:

> attempts to define feminist writings are looked upon with suspicion . . . 'It is impossible to *define* a feminist practice of writing', Hélène Cixous warns, 'and this is an impossibility that will remain, for this practice can never be theorized, enclosed, coded – which doesn't mean that it doesn't exist'. But we all have a rough

idea of what feminist writing is like, even if we cannot define it exactly. And the same is true of feminist criticism. Cixous' dismissal of definition as an impossibility in the case of women's writing masquerades as a warning to the foolhardy but is clearly protectionist towards a feminism which, fearing the foreclosure of its activities, wisely promotes openness and plurality as its distinguishing features, but grounds itself vulnerably on the theory that it cannot be theorised. A working definition of feminist literary criticism does not strike me as being either impossible or undesirable.[3]

By supposedly unmasking the real odds ('masquerades as a warning to the foolhardy'), which suggests that Cixous is trying to deceive, but only the imbeciles will be taken in, and then by further implying that here again, folks, is a woman who isn't aware of her own logical contradictions, she can't argue to save her life ('grounds itself vulnerably'), Ruthven claims that he's established that feminist criticism can be defined. His faulting of Cixous's (feminine?) logic is all the more comic as the only piece of logic he himself has to offer is a bizarre appeal to a universal, ungendered, vague common sense: 'But we all have a rough idea of what feminist writing is like, even if we cannot define it exactly.' And so one can expect that the definition of feminist criticism he is about to offer will be rough, inexact – impressionistic and intuitive per- haps? But the position he thinks he has established is one in which, having denied Cixous's claim, the claim that stood in the way of his enterprise, having answered the sphinx with roughness and inexactitude, that is, he can now proceed: con- struct feminist criticism into something that can be defined, disproved, and eventually – for this is the real goal – got rid of. You say it masquerades as the real thing, but that you don't have to be taken in, become tangled in the sphinx's skein. You say it is a fashion, that will pass, like other fashions.

Toril Moi's influential *Sexual/Textual Politics* is more sophisti- cated than the Ruthven, better informed, and generally con- ducts its arguments at a higher, more mobile and inventive level. It has been useful to many: I do not wish to play down that usefulness, but to alert the reader to the rather insidious ways in which it plays tricks not altogether dissimilar from Ruthven's. As such it must be taken, not only with a pinch, but with a jarful of salt:

> Cixous's predilection for the Old Testament is obvious, but her taste for classical antiquity is no less marked. Her capacity for identification seems endless: Medusa, Electra, Antigone, Dido, Cleopatra – in her imagination she has been them all. In fact, she declares that 'I am myself the earth, everything that happens on it, all the lives that live me there in my different forms' . . . : This constant return to biblical and mythological imagery signals her investment in the world of myth: a world that, like the distant country of fairy tales is perceived as pervasively meaningful, as closure and unity. The mythical or religious discourse presents a universe where all difference, struggle and discord can in the end be satisfactorily resolved.[4]

Moi is fully entitled to her position. It is her right to dislike or disapprove of Cixous as much as she likes, and some of this is quite witty. The irony however would be more appropriate if the piece accompanied a widely available piece of writing by Cixous: the text might then defend itself, or one could balance what Moi says against whatever reading one would want to do of the text itself. What is wrong here is that the material is being presented in such a way as to be discredited before it's been heard. The quotation occurs not only out of context, but inside a hostile context. Cixous's texts come across as utopian and megalomaniac. Is there a hint of Pater on the Mona Lisa ('She is older than the rocks among which she sits; like the vampire she has been dead many times, and learned the secrets of the grave') in the 'in her imagination she has been them all'? If so, the point would be interesting, but so complex that one little stroke barely touches it. But isn't there here an unconscious misogyny? We women keep complaining that women do not easily adopt an epic, or a mythic, or a titanic voice. Here is one that does: is it right to slam her for immodesty before one has heard her? Would Moi say what she says if she were producing a swift-running account of Shelley's poetry instead? It would apply, you would only need to change the names to Prometheus or Ozymandias. Is it the case that what a Blake or a Milton or a Shelley are allowed to do suddenly becomes improper, ridiculous and utopian when a woman does it?

There is more: Moi shows no awareness that she herself is writing, she herself is using language. She acts as if her right to use discourse frees her from the implications of discourse that she is so quick to point at in others: Writing, 'in fact she declares that "I am myself the earth . . ."', Moi confuses the 'she' of a person called Cixous with the supposed 'she' (what if s/he is bisexual?) of the author/narrator. She does not explain in the name of what position (presumably Marxist/materialist?) she is condemning the utopian solution of all 'struggle and discord'. In any case, there is no such solution. The play on Cambodia and the *Indiade* and indeed *Manne* end up in a state of anguish, with no solution found, only a ray or principle of hope, something desperately fragile the other side of despair.

At other times Moi presents the texts so much as pure theory that unless you are thoroughly versed in the vocabulary she uses you cannot understand the analyses – whose purpose remains thoroughly dismissive:

> From a psychoanalytic perspective, it would seem that her textual manoeuvres are designed to create a space in which the *differance* of the Symbolic Order can co-exist peacefully with the closure and identity of the Imaginary. . . . we have seen that even the openness of the Giving Woman or the plurality of bisexual writing are characterized by biblical, mythological or elemental imagery that returns us to a preoccupation with the Imaginary. The difference and diversity in question thus seems more akin to the polymorphous perversity of the pre-Oedipal child than to the metonymic displacements of desire in the symbolic order.[5]

Leaving aside the schoolmistressy 'we', the oversimplifying assumption that a 'preoccupation with the Imaginary' is a bad, retrograde thing, how can the reader follow unless s/he is familiar with Lacan, Derrida, Kristeva? The writing here seems tailor-made to justify Ruthven's attack:

> Like a good deal of recent French criticism, French feminism assumes in the reader an advanced

knowledge of linguistics, philosophy and
psychoanalysis; it assumes a passion for abstraction,
particularly the theorising of theory, which is in marked
contrast to the anglophone tradition that the only
theories worth bothering about are those which have
practical applications to particular texts. Because
French feminist criticism is correspondingly difficult to
read for people not educated in the French tradition,
the presentation of it to anglophone feminists has been
accompanied by exactly the same blend of mystification
and snobbery which characterized attempts to introduce
structuralism into non-feminist anglophone criticism.
Francophile feminists often adopt a patronisingly more-
Parisian-than-thou attitude to their anglophone sisters,
who are seen as muddling along in conditions of
benighted empiricism instead of getting themselves an
adequate theory of the text.[6]

And doesn't he purr as he sets the sisters at each other's
throats! You do have to wonder what the purpose in writing
such a book must be, when spite and meanness are so prevalent. There is a heart-warming attempt at sisterliness, though,
in Ann R. Jones's essay on 'Writing the Body', in the Showalter
anthology. Yet even she groups and summarizes French feminisms into a bundle of ideas and positions:

Although Kristeva does not privilege women as the only
possessors of prephallocentric discourse, Irigaray and
Cixous go further: if women are to discover and express
who they are, to bring to the surface what masculine
history has repressed in them, they must begin with
their sexuality. And their sexuality begins with their
bodies, with their genital and libidinal difference from
men.
    For various reasons, this is a powerful argument. We
have seen versions of it in the radical feminism of the
United States, too. In the French context, it offers an
island of hope . . . If men are responsible for the
reigning binary system of meaning – identity/other,
man/nature, reason/chaos, man/woman – women,
relegated to the negative and passive pole of this
hierarchy, are not implicated in the creation of its

53

myths . . . and the immediacy with which the body, the id, *jouissance*, are supposedly experienced promises a clarity of perception and a vitality that can bring down mountains of phallocentric delusion . . .

But *féminité* and *écriture féminine* are problematic as well as powerful concepts. They have been criticized as idealist and essentialist . . . ; they have been attacked as theoretically fuzzy and as fatal to constructive political action. I think all these objections are worth making. What's more, they must be made if American women are to sift out and use the positive elements in French thinking about *féminité*.[7]

There is something touching in the goodwill. Something comically pious too in the way in which the body and *jouissance* are written about: strange foreign goods that after due scrutiny, and customs approval, must be allowed on the supermarket shelves if 'American women' are to have the best of all worlds. Neo-colonialist almost. You would think that the writing, and the search for an economy of pleasure and giving, which Cixous invites her readers to quest for, made up a keep-fit programme, a magic diet that would give you vitality: like Popeye's spinach, after you partake of it you can bring down 'mountains of phallocentric delusion'.

As I read her, Cixous's texts grope for, adumbrate, a way of being, of becoming rather, that involves both the wish to go forward and the courage to lie still, to wait, to dive inside. Only by actually doing it, which is costly, riddled with frustrations and difficulties and errors, only by committing oneself – believing, hoping, trusting, giving – can one get *to* (not, get) what the writing is *for*. It is not a matter of returning it to the writer, however megalomaniac or narcissistic 'she' may appear – it's a matter of taking over, as in a relay, and trying to get to where the best and the deepest of you can take you: the scope that the 'I' of the writing has given you is epic so that *you*, reader, may know no bounds. It is visionary so that *you* may be empowered:

Je la vois 'commencer'. Ça s'écrit, ces commencements qui ne cessent de la lever ça peut et doit s'écrire. Ni noir sur blanc ni blanc sur noir, pas dans le heurt du papier et du signe qui s'y grave, pas dans cette opposition des couleurs qui se détachent l'une sur et contre-l'autre. C'est ainsi:

Il y a un sol, c'est son fond, – enfance, chair, sang brillant – ou fond. Un fond blanc, inoubliable, oublié, et ce sol, recouvert d'une quantité infinie de strates, de couches, de feuilles de papier, – c'est son soleil. Et rien ne peut l'éteindre. La lumière féminine, ne vient pas d'en-haut, ne tombe pas, ne frappe pas, ne traverse pas. Elle irradie, c'est une montée, lente, douce, difficile, absolument inarrêtable, douloureuse, et qui gagne, qui imprègne les terres, qui filtre, qui sourd, qui enfin déchire, humecte, écarte les épaisseurs, les volumes. Depuis le fond, luttant contre l'opacité. Cette lumière ne plante pas, elle fraie. Et je vois qu'à cette lumière, elle regarde de tout près, et elle aperçoit les nervures de la matière. Dont il n'a que faire.

Son lever: ce n'est pas une érection. Mais diffusion. Pas le trait. Le vaisseau. Qu'elle écrive![8]

I see her 'begin'. That can be written – these beginnings that never stop getting her up – can and must be written. Neither black on white nor white on black, not in this clash between paper and sign that en-graves itself there, not in this opposition of colours that stand out against each other. This is how it is:

There is a ground, it is her ground – childhood flesh, shining blood – or background, depth. A white depth, a core, unforgettable, forgotten, and this ground, covered by an infinite number of strata, layers, sheets of paper – is her sun (*sol . . . soleil*). And nothing can put it out. Feminine light doesn't come from above, doesn't strike, doesn't go through. It radiates, it is a slow, sweet, difficult, absolutely unstoppable, painful rising that reaches and impregnates lands, that filters, that wells up, that finally tears open, wets and spreads apart what is dull and thick, the stolid, the volumes. Fighting off opacity from deep within. This light doesn't plant, it spawns. And I see that she looks very closely with this light and she sees the veins and nerves of matter. Which he has no need of.

Her rising: is not erection. But diffusion. Not the
shaft. The vessel. Let her write![9]

The translator, Betsy Wing, has been faced with the devil
of a task. Not only is there a word order in English that makes
accumulation of epithets clumsy before a noun ('it is a slow,
sweet, difficult, absolutely unstoppable, painful rising')
whereas in the French, the epithets coming after the noun
means that their progression is like an evolution, the rising of
the light that as the epithets succeed each other and alter,
transforms itself into water. Having 'rising' at the end arrests
the movement. The pronouns in French are more fluid: where
English has 'this' and 'that', French has *ce, cette, c', ça*. They
carry a different history. *Ça* at the beginning of the second
sentence suggests the Freudian 'Id' and the *la* of the first
sentence ('Je la vois "commencer" ') can refer equally to the
writing, which is feminine, and the woman who writes. Similarly, *lumière* is feminine; so is *eau*, water, not named, but
powerfully rising throughout the second half of the second
paragraph. So that the 'Qu'elle écrive!' at the end refers to
she, writing, the light, the water . . . This is important: *elle* in
Cixous, like *je*, is always a multiplicity of beings, who are not
being imaginatively *appropriated* but are being travelled into,
are shifting into each other. The identity that is being created
by the text is a becoming, an endlessly metaphoric capacity to
shift into some other mode.

This is, as I claimed at the beginning, the realm of the
translator. But it makes the translator's task near impossible.
Thus 'ces commencements qui ne cessent de la lever' in the
second sentence mean 'these beginnings which do not cease
to make her rise', literally like dough (*levain* is yeast) as well
as 'that never stop getting her up' as Betsy Wing has it. She
is forced to choose, and she tends to go for meaning rather
than an equivalent pun. One can sympathize with her trouble
when she adds in parentheses '(*sol* . . . *soleil*)' to explain to the
reader who might think the jump from ground to sun is a bit
large that in French *sol* and *soleil* have the same basic sound.
But the effect is still to make the whole thing sound arbitrary,
or precious, whereas in French there is a long poetic history
of such punning (as in Nerval's famous 'El Desdichado'

sonnet, where *soleil* is also made to pun with *seul* (alone) and *inconsolé*; *désolé*, *consolé* (desolated, consoled))[10].

Similarly *fond* is bottom, base, the background of a painting ('Un fond blanc', a white background, mistranslated here I think as 'A white depth', though the meaning is there also): but the painting image makes the series of images imaginable: as in a Rothko you might have some basic colour, red or black, irradiate through the other strata of colours, you could imagine it as the sun Cixous is talking about. And yes, I am using comparisons with male writers or artists to explain what Cixous is doing but she herself is forever moving in and out of male writers and artists: but to alter them. What else is there to do? You cannot erase thousands of years of writing at one fell swoop. There is Joyce, of course, the book on Joyce, somewhere in the *fond*, but she is not trying for an alternative fixed female self, rather an alternative process.

In Valéry's 'La Jeune Parque', a poem about poetry-in-the-making, a male voice speaks through the body of a young female figure of Fate/Death. Cixous writes 'La Jeune née': searching for a poetic voice that would not be a form of possession, but the voice of a body forever in the process of being born, not dead: the young just-born; the newly she-born. In the passage I quoted earlier, the use of a sliding feminine mode in *elle*, *écriture*, *eau*, *lumière* enabled the writer to let nature speak without its being a colonization, an occupation. 'Nature: the roaring inside her', as in Susan Griffin's title. If you choose the way of the translator, if you accept being in a state of suspension when you read Cixous, then you become, not only aware of, but empowered by, a sense of mobility, speed, grace. Not 'black on white', or the clash of sign and paper. The text invites something deep inside you to blossom, to well up, to fly: if you'll let it. The best way of letting it might be to write yourself, with a similar degree of readiness and openness, searching for what, in the specificity of the English language, which has little gender but wonderful poetic richness, would be born of the attempt. Then, if you found it was not for you, you would have discovered something *real*.

Wouldn't translating in this way, being both mother and midwife to the text, be more fruitful than accusing it of being 'akin to the polymorphous perversity of the pre-Oedipal child' (what a clever child that must be) or 'theoretically fuzzy'? Isn't the will to theory, here, the will to reduce, and control, and dismiss? And isn't it at the cost of the text, its living appeal to us, that it erects itself?

NOTES

1 J. Risset, 'Traduction/trahison', *Des femmes en mouvement*, mensuelle, 4, April 1978.
2 In a paper given at the South Bank, 20 May 1989.
3 K. Ruthven, *Feminist Literary Studies*, Cambridge University Press, 1984, p. 20.
4 T. Moi, *Sexual/Textual Politics*, London: Methuen, 1985, p. 116.
5 ibid., p. 120.
6 Ruthven, *Feminist Literary Studies*, p. 21.
7 Ann Rosalind Jones, 'Writing the body: l'écriture féminine', in E. Showalter (ed.), *The New Feminist Criticism*, London: Virago, 1986, p. 366.
8 *La Jeune née*, Paris: Union générale d'éditions, 1975, p. 163.
9 'Sorties' in *The Newly Born Woman*, tr. Betsy Wing, Manchester University Press, 1986, p. 88.
10 Je suis le ténébreux, le veuf, *l'inconsolé* . . .
      Ma *seule* étoile est morte, et mon luth constellé
      Porte le *soleil* noir de la Mélancolie.

      Dans la nuit du tombeau, toi qui m'as *consolé*,
      Rends-moi . . .
      Le fleur qui plaisait tant à mon coeur *désolé* . . .
                          (Nerval, 'El Desdichado')

Part II

FRENCH FEMINISMS

4

How to make a Bertha out of an Antoinette and why every Jane needs a Bertha: Psych et Po and French feminisms

Gordon Burn's biography of Sutcliffe, the Yorkshire Ripper, is called *Somebody's Husband, Somebody's Son*. Amazingly, not seeming to realize anything was amiss, Burn set out to reconstitute the man, what he was, through the testimony of men only: the father, the brothers, the male friends. The mother was dead, the sisters said little. Sonia, the wife, refused to speak to Burn. So, 'somebody's son' is a father's son only. Sonia, the 'somebody' whose husband became a multiple murderer is described by hostile witnesses alone, her in-laws. She never speaks in the first person. She did publish a disclaimer in *The Guardian*. But the book accounting for her remains, and has a powerful impact. Another woman silenced, her point of view misrepresented.[1]

I have been appalled in recent years to discover that Sonia's fate was the one that was being inflicted on the French women's group 'Psychanalyse et Politique'. With some exceptions (Marks and de Courtivron, Michèle Sarde, Juliet Mitchell) it's got a bad press. This is understandable on two counts: the positions of their enemies, such as Christine Delphy,[2] are much closer to mainstream Anglo-American positions, and have received a wide audience. Also, their own aggression, paranoia, choice of being underground 'moles' as it were and their paradoxical will to censorship have meant that they have been suspicious of anyone willing to listen to their side of the story, but ever likely to go over to the enemy side: thus Claire Duchen has twice been refused permission to quote from her various translations of articles that appeared in the various journals edited by Psych et Po.[3] The result is that there has been no representation of their point of view, except indirectly,

61

or through summary interviews, whereas the objections, alternative accounts and attacks of their opponents have been much publicized. The result is bizarrely similar to what happened to Sonia Sutcliffe. You get the impression that they are being portrayed by hostile in-laws. This is worrying not only because it suggests that there is a rampant misogyny among women; but because a great deal of the writing done by women in the heyday of the women's movement in France was produced or promoted by them.

Psych et Po has always been close to the position outlined by Hélène Cixous when she said that you cannot theorize woman. Indeed, they called their publishing house and their magazines 'des femmes': multiple, and with an indefinite article. Not only has their refusal to be theorized, to become part of the mainstream (or even co-exist with others) been translated in effect in the way in which they have remained *'forclos'* (one of their favourite terms), that is both excluded and interned, in France. But in the translations that have been occurring in the past ten years or so on the Anglo-Saxon scene, translations of French feminisms into English, histories of the French women's movement, above all the growing interest in so-called French feminist theory, they have been portrayed as a wicked and disruptive lot, fortunately incapacitated so that they are prevented from doing any harm. Now 'the group presents no threat', Toril Moi said in an article in the *Women's Review*.[4] She had just been rejoicing that the 'imaginary projection of French theory as our own Other' should be breaking down, with the new interest in concepts such as the 'semiotic', 'monolithic homogeneous structure(s)' and 'proliferating network(s) of displacement and deferral of meaning'. One reason why French theory need no longer frighten Anglo-Saxon feminists, Moi suggested, was that Antoinette Fouque, the leader of Psych et Po, had emigrated to California. It was as if, the group that was sticking in the gullet of theory having been removed, England could now enjoy its benefits unimpeded.

Moi doesn't seem to have remotely taken in what was outlined as early as 1978 by Françoise Collin, the editor of the *Cahiers du Grif*. Her warning against theory is all the more powerful as her position wasn't aligned with that of Cixous, or Psych et Po. She stood as if it were midway between them and the so-called *féministes*:

The women's movement is not an ideology which, suitably formulated and defined, would set out a new norm for individual and social action, based on an old or new conception of woman, and leading to a feminist society. This need for theoretical and practical orthodoxy, which masculine thought deplores our lack of and is constantly trying to make us establish, is in fact characteristic of masculine thought itself. To give in to it would, therefore, be to give in to its Order.[5]

If there is any truth in saying that woman is what cannot be theorized, or that seeking for theoretical orthodoxy is giving in to the Order of masculine thought, wasn't the banishment/containment that was thus being imaginatively imposed on Psych et Po tantamount to the recognition that they did stand for something you'd have to call woman – or perhaps women? It seems hugely appropriate in this context that the figurehead of Psych et Po should indeed be called Antoinette. In *Wide Sargasso Sea*, Jean Rhys's rewriting of *Jane Eyre*, Mrs Rochester, Bertha Mason as she is called in *Jane Eyre*, the madwoman who will be locked up in the attic, and die setting fire to the house, is not mad. She is driven to appear insane by Rochester's and her brother's treatment of her. And she is called . . . Antoinette. Literature has funny ways of obliquely connecting, letting the repressed speak. At least, this is very much what Antoinette Fouque might have said. Her present predicament – semi-paralysed by illness, pushed to the outskirts, wilfully ignored and still formidable – continues to pose a burning, emblematic and insoluble problem.

It is doubly difficult to present Psych et Po. Nobody can speak 'for' them. Their practice has been by choice anonymous, underground. They have been 'moles', as Antoinette Fouque termed them. I first got to know the group through the Editions des femmes, the publishing house they founded together with a bookshop of the same name in 1974. It was then situated in the rue des Saints-Pères: the irony was lost on no one, since the practice of erasing the Name-of-the-Father as one way of resisting the Symbolic order was then important. Spivak's summary of Derrida's critique of phallogocentrism is an apt description of what they were resisting:

the patronymic, in spite of all empirical details of the generation gap, keeps the transcendental ego of the dynasty identical in the eye of the law. By virtue of the father's name the son refers to the father. The irreducible importance of the name and the law in his situation makes it quite clear that the question is not merely one of psycho-socio-sexual behavior but of the production and consolidation of reference and meaning.[6]

So, in 1977, when I got to know them, surnames were taboo. It could be confusing: you would ask, 'Which Brigitte?' and might be answered 'Brigitte B.' in opposition to Brigitte G. Only first names appeared at the bottom of articles written for the papers or reviews. 'Leur unique prénom', as *Les Guérillères* says, one like the eye of the Cyclops.[7] No names appeared on the books: it was 'des femmes', the product of collaboration, people often doubling up as reader, editor, press attaché . . . Sophie, a painter who designed some very good covers, never figured as the designer. It was all collective, multiple. Members of the group lived together, pooled their finances together (it was of course very convenient that one of the group, an American, turned out to be rich – but why not, after all? How were poets and artists such as Breton, or some of the Lost Generation writers, supported, and how could Joyce have published without Sylvia Beach? For once the *mécène*'s money was going to women, to a women's press, a women's bookshop.) Many members of the group lived in couples, scattered here and there, frequently meeting to decide on a particular course of action, to analyse things. None of them wrote, not books at any rate, including Antoinette, the main inspirer and doer. It was all done orally. As the years went by, there was a sense that writing steals from life, from orality. That the writer-in-the-house is a spy. I developed this notion with them, talking about Walter Scott, the way he had stolen the ballad from the old women who trustingly, because that was the way, sang to him. It evidently struck a chord. And so, how can I, now, pretend to write the history of these days, (heady days they were, in the first few years for me)? I would be stealing, I would also be misrepresenting. Only the group, now burst, could do the telling, if they decided to get back together. Which they won't.

To make the job of the putative historian worse, the group began to be riven by contradictions, to give way to mechanisms of expulsion and silencing which were sadly like what they claimed phallocracy was doing to them, and what other groups saw them as doing to the women's movement. The human dramas, tragedies even, that have occurred over the years, could only be told by a gossip of genius, and I know such a one. But she won't print. It would cause too much pleasure in the wrong quarters. Those who know won't tell. Those who tell don't know.

And – a new turn of the screw – the contradictions led to the very things that had been most avoided being adopted. Institutions were used as weapons to fight other women with. They were quite early on sued by some of their authors (a prostitute from Lyons, a worker from the Lip watch factory where there had been an occupation of the premises by the union), who claimed that they were not being paid their royalties, or being supported properly. I think there must have been simply a lot of chaos, of bad liaising. But the mood was set. The arm of the law was used against them; they started using it in return. The Name-of-the-Father came back. Antoinette Fouque, who admires writing immensely, who was the dynamo that made things happen, who had been enormously supportive of others, increasingly suffered from her self-imposed obscurity. The mole was choking on her earthern diet – understandably so: the mole-hills were being praised. Perhaps illness, the struggle with death, the dramatic decrease of feminism in France, and the stardom of other women, made her anonymity unbearable. She surfaced with, through, a name: 'Antoinette Fouque présente' began to head the spoken-word tapes of authors reading their own works. Now 'Antoinette Fouque' is on the cover of the books, above the symbol representing the women's movement. Many of the former members of the group who gave away their names and years of their lives to the cause of women, and women's writing, suffer this as the ultimate theft, the ultimate affront.

Should one with the ease of hindsight quote again from Spivak on phallogocentrism? 'Hermeneutic, legal or patrilinear, it is the prerogative of the phallus to declare itself sovereign

65

source. Its causes are also its effects: a social structure – centred on the sovereignty of the engendering self and the determinacy of meaning (phallogocentrism).'[8]

I know full well that this account of squabbling women, ending where they'd started, at least in terms of ideological effects, will delight many Anglo-Saxon women, and most men who hear me: I need think only of the undisguised glee with which my husband welcomes any tales of in-fighting at a feminist conference . . . But I wish to avoid none of the issues. The women's movement in France has gone quiescent. Our daughters think it's all been done. Our granddaughters will wake up again. There are lessons to be learnt, reflecting on what we have done, and failed to do, on what our actions have revealed to us about what we are, and what society is. There is after all a Bertha. Perhaps I have been giving you the Charlotte Brontë story: the tale of Mrs Rochester. Perhaps the tale of *Wide Sargasso Sea*, the female sea, the mobile seaweed sea where eels breed, will one day be told. Let us not forget that Rhys's Antoinette could fight like a cat.

So: this history cannot be written; it would have to be collective, multiple; it would be of contradictions. But still: how could Psych et Po be presented? I'll have a go, prefacing everything with the reminder that what I say has no authority but that of my own authorship.

Around October 1968 three women emerged from the many that were full of dissatisfaction at the way May '68 had turned out. One was Monique Wittig, another was Antoinette Fouque, the third shall remain nameless. Years later, as she was analysing the way in which matriarchal figures were becoming prominent, Antoinette said, 'Have you noticed? there are the three Simones [Simone Weil, the minister who had passed the law on abortion; Simone de Beauvoir, who was supporting *Questions féministes*; and Simone Signoret, heading a TV serial about a woman judge] but the three are always four, as with the three musketeers, or the Brontë sisters, for whom there was a fourth – Branwell, the brother, who was the discarded one, their placenta. Well, the Simones are really four. There is also Françoise Dolto [a woman psychoanalyst who was very much laying down the law about children at the time].' I wondered retrospectively who had been the fourth of that initial threesome. Whether the one I have left nameless was the placenta, and somebody more famous, possibly Christine Delphy or one of the women described in the various histories of French feminism, came to be the known third . . . At any rate, in the struggle for dominance that ensued, Antoinette won. Monique Wittig went to the USA, where she has continued to be most influential. Many other groups, many other figures came to prominence in the years that followed.[9] But a cohesive and close-knit group gathered round Antoinette. The name Psych et Po, as I understand it, came from the decision to borrow freely from psychoanalysis as the single existing discourse that had grappled with the question of sexuality, and in particular the question of hysteria, a burning question at the time, the question of woman's alienation from language. Psychoanalysis was practised among members of the group. The name also expressed the search for a link between psychoanalysis and politics. Marx as well as Freud was the source of the discourse. The personal was political, yes. But the political at large could be read as sexual, shot through with forces that were unconscious, that manifested themselves as symptoms: the group's analyses were trying to make them visible. The supposedly universal discourse of politics, they argued, was in fact laden with gender assumptions, forever putting women in the inferior hierarchical position, using female sexuality for its own ends. In effect, they were psychoanalysing the political.

Des femmes en mouvement, the monthly they were editing in 1978, wrote for instance about Chinese denunciations of Quang Jin, Mao's widow, and the 'Gang of Four', as well as about western endorsements of these denunciations:

> No one ever speaks about Quang Jin's political activity during the Cultural Revolution; or else it is, at best or at worst, wrapped up by feminist magazines in a new image, that of a woman who has conquered the greatest power, the arch-feminist . . . As for the Cultural Revolution, it is described through the very metaphors that phallo-centrism uses to describe its fear of femaleness, of the void: 'abyss', 'repression', 'chaos', 'anarchy', etc. As for China, 'she' is meant for the Western Prince, she is Sleeping Beauty there to be

raped again: 'Will China awake from her Maoist sleep?'
– or else, it is portrayed as a cannibalistic savage'.[10]

Though all the members of the group were lesbian – they
did not use the term, believing it to be too clannish, a male
term – and some bisexual, the group welcomed heterosexual
women as friends or fellow-travellers or writers. They stressed
that they were not anti-men, but anti-phallocracy. Women
could be as phallocratic as men: for example Mrs Thatcher.
Indeed, there were lots of analyses of the difficulty there was
for a daughter in being a *fille* rather than a *filse*, a son–
daughter, keen to inherit the kingdom of the phallus, to gain
recognition in terms of the Symbolic.

From what I have written so far, it will be clear that there
were recognizable presences there, though not all were named.
Derrida was, I think, important, and much could be said about
the relation of Psych et Po modes of thinking to Deconstruction. Indeed, the whole critique of contemporary discourses
the group were conducting had to do with reading the metaphor of woman into the texts that pretend it is not there. As
with Quang Jin: they organized a huge petition in *Le Monde*
to save her life. Lacan was an obvious presence: there was a
war on against him, though as Freud's interpreter he provided
much of the discourse (the 'ladies' whom he begs, in *Encore*,
to tell him what woman's *jouissance* is, are Antoinette and the
group). Another censored, but to my mind, active presence,
was Luce Irigaray. I was told she had been Antoinette's tutor
and analyst, and that the relation had come to grief. I do not
know whether this is true. What I did notice however was
that when I first read *Speculum* and *Ce sexe qui n'en est pas un*,
and remarked admiringly to some of the group how close
Irigaray's positions were to theirs, I was greeted with evasive
silence. I also witnessed how Luce Irigaray, invited by Antoinette to the 1989 6th March celebrations, prefaced her rivetting
proposals for a Declaration of Women's Rights with: 'It's
women's day today. Feast day! A day of truce'. Be there war
or truce, Irigaray's thinking about *altérité*, otherness, not difference – her work on the figure of the mother, and on the
impossibility of defining man's discourse as man's, since it
claims to be universal – all this is close to the thinking I've
heard Psych et Po do.

But what is, to me, in a sense most characteristic of the work of Psych et Po was the attempt to create spaces in which being woman could come into existence. Women-only spaces, both physical (conferences, meetings, debates, beautiful spaces in the bookshop, art or photography exhibitions) and textual. There was – and there still continues to be, it is one of the things that has survived – a fostering of creation by women, artistic, visual (painting, pottery, photography) and literary. The Editions des femmes have given many, many women writers their first chance: for example Chantal Chawaf, Annie Cohen, Catherine Weinzaepflen; much support has been given to Hélène Cixous, Jeanne Hyvrard, etc. The *livres-cassettes*, recordings by authors of their own work, have, through a deliberate policy, come to include every major woman writer today (as well as, for older texts, the voice of many a great actress). Antoinette Fouque talks of the need for women to occupy imaginary spaces, to make women come into being as a 'leap forward': what cannot be defined symbolically has to be invented in a sense. There was a mothering metaphor at work. The idea that great writers have often been their mothers' favourite sons. The attempt was to make women into favourite daughters through the group, the publishing house, the magazines, creating a space (call it placenta perhaps?) in which women could come into self-love, and perhaps into greatness. And there was a heady pressure for change, for a revolutionary consciousness, coming from Antoinette: the stress on the word 'movement' in *Mouvement de libération des femmes*. The need to change in order not to become defunct, like all previous revolutionary movements. What has caused most angst, most divisiveness, most aggro against Psych et Po has been their official inscription of the letters MLF as the name of an – their – association. Other women felt they were stealing the movement away from them. Who knows whether this was purely a bid for power, or part of a strategy of inscription, of symbolic inscription, similar to the subsequent return to surnames, as part of an overall strategy of movement and dialectical self-reinvention?

Whatever the interpretation, the deed created mayhem. Incendiary bombs were thrown into the bookshop on the rue des Saints-Pères, once almost burning down the building. The printing-shop of the rue de la Roquette was raided on women's day, the presses battered with hammers, the typewriters flooded with ink. It was women who did it all right. Some, Manson-like, daubed the walls with signatures: 'les cocottes-minutes' . . . '1980 [the year of the registration by Psych et Po of the title and logo MLF] will . . . be a year of scandal', Christine Delphy wrote: 'This is only the latest stage in a long process of embezzlement . . . Today, telling the whole truth is the only way to save the movement.'[11] Telling the truth meant exposing Psych et Po, ceasing to present a false image of unity: at the march of 8 May, radical feminist lesbians from the Jussieu group 'went to the head of the march and kicked Psych et Po out of the esplanade'.[12] The sad irony is that the rift had a knock-on effect. Through the logo, the words, 'women's liberation movement' being institutionally inscribed, something like an angst of definition seemed to grab hold of the French women. As if there were a sudden urge, not only for everyone to define their positions, what liberation or being a woman stood for, but also to be seen to be speaking for the right position, the only one, almost in the same breath as the deep divisions inside the movement were being recognized. Monique Wittig had published an article called 'La Pensée Straight', attacking heterosexuality as the 'normative and oppressive structure underlying all institutions and all thinking and concepts'.[13] In 'On ne Nait pas Femme', she went on to place lesbians outside the category man and the category woman, arguing that political lesbianism was the only way forward. Counter-articles were published. The editorial collective of *Questions féministes* split into two rival groups. A new journal, calling itself *Nouvelles questions féministes*, was born. There was a fight over that title . . . The terms 'lesbian', 'homosexual', 'heterosexual', 'feminist', 'feminine', were caught in the tornado of the term 'Women'.

A woman I met recently, who had been part of Psych et Po, told me she thought that the pervasiveness and violence of the rifts inside the French women's movement had had to do with the pervasive influence of Lacan and the Freudian School: who practised exclusions on an unbelievable scale (thus Luce Irigaray was expelled for heresy, rebelliousness and related other faults). And who practised, and went on to practise, fights almost to the death for the inheritance of the father: Freud first, then Lacan. It is worth pondering whether the contradictions inside the women's movement were due to internal causes, the fundamental impossibility to theorize 'Woman', or were engendered by the surrounding phallogocentric culture, the product of contradictions in the French psychoanalytic movement, as well as the unsolved questions of class (and to a lesser extent, race: it is worth pointing out that the Editions des femmes have always striven to give support to so-called Third World women, through publications, series, collective actions – as well as to European dissident movements such as the Basque separatist women or the Baader –Meinhof group).

What then are the odds? If we now try to think about all this, what were Psych et Po, and the other groups too, after? Representing (and therefore leading) all women, regardless of class, race, creed? What was the goal? Liberating all women, including those who did not want to be liberated? This is where you begin to have to say what woman, or women, are. And where you need terms such as 'feminist' or 'political lesbian'. But th n if their action posits itself as universal, the same questions arise.

Is the goal to make women the equals of men in all things? Once they are, how will you define woman? Through sexuality? Motherhood? The dreaded body reappears . . .

Are women definable as an oppressed class, and is the body to be dismissed as the pretext for cultural oppression? If so, when resistance which gives unity to that term 'woman' is no longer needed because women will have won, what will woman be? Shall we have a sexless, or genderless society, as Marxists once dreamt of a classless society?

It's a merry-go-round.[14]

The question, 'What is woman?' is wrong as a metaphysical question and as a social question. It could only be asked if woman's domination became equal to, and lasted as long as, man's. If the slave became the master, and the master, the slave. Then, women might ask what at present, curiously, they do not ask: 'What does man want?' Do we want that? Indeed, can you any longer today ask 'What is man?', in a world of supposedly decaying colonialism, supposedly diminishing sexism, supposedly shrinking privileges and wealth gaps?

And so, you see, I return after all to Psych et Po. I think they had the right end of the stick. They were posing the question from the two positions that are tenable. That continue to be tenable.

The one is as a critique of phallocracy: What organizes the endless banning of people of the female sex to the position of the Other? What could bring about a recognition of Otherness, not as difference (from a norm, something hierarchically better) but as a value? What would open the One? What would force the subject to perceive others as subjects too, and to perceive himself or herself as also an object? Instead of using sexual difference (which is cultural as well as biological) as what enables the dominant party to articulate oneness and subjecthood and universality? Or as Spivak argues, the question remains: What *am I, a woman*? What does it mean, saying that? how come I live in a culture that does not help me to answer that, or only very little? that only really helps if I am prepared to be either an excised woman or an honorary man? so that I have to ignore it and search for the wisdom of our mothers and grandmothers?

The other position is what Antoinette Fouque has called going 'beyond the reality principle'.[15] Making something which has never been allowed to be come into existence. Birthing, giving birth to, the splendour of woman. Obviously I want to read birth into Bertha (isn't berthing a ship putting it into a larger or better lane? In this case I would also want to read berth into Bertha. Deconstructionist games aren't inappropriate here). This birthing implies leaps forward as well as leaps backward: creating, in all possible ways, what the practice of the Editions des femmes has made possible for many women for years. Digging deep into ourselves, our subconscious, travelling back to what Freud used to think of as the pre-Minoan civilization behind the civilization of Greece. Inventing woman, thanks to the best things there are about women all over the world, as something better than what there is: our utopia, yes, but utopias are written so that things will come to pass. Things that have to do with peace, joy, *jouissance*, generosity. Not because women are better than men: they're not, and what I am saying is that it makes no sense to say 'women' as a definable referent. But because, being less implicated in what history has been so far, they can find the road to the better things more easily perhaps.

'Well,' you will ask, 'with all you've been telling us about the wars of Psych et Po, how can you say that?' I wish to distinguish yet again between the history of Bertha and the history of Antoinette. At present, certainly, *forclose* as she is, ridden with contradictions, she seems to embody that endless *de trop* which Lacan says makes out woman. That thorn in the side of truth. A certain impossibility of universalizing, the impossible unity of self and self, danger that the house might be set on fire. But in so far as the critique and the dream are there, she is, for good as well as evil, our madwoman in the attic. Her laughter rings in our ears when we meditate on what it is to be a woman. We ought to be grateful to her for embodying our deepest selves, with which we must come to terms if we are to be self-fulfilled.

NOTES

1 There is more discussion of this whole issue in my study *'The Streetcleaner': The Yorkshire Ripper Case on Trial*, London: Marion Boyars, 1986.

2 Christine Delphy's *Close to Home*, translated by Diana Leonard, has been very well received. It is now in the series Explorations in Feminisms, published by Hutchinson.

3 Claire Duchen has written a *History of French Feminism* (London: Routledge, 1986) and has also edited an anthology of texts from the French women's movement (*French Connections*, London: Hutchinson, 1987), also published in the Explorations in Feminisms series.

4 3 April 1986.

5 Françoise Collin, 'Au revoir', in 'Où en sont les féministes?' *Les Cahiers du Grif*, 23/24 December 1978, p. 14. An extract from this article is translated in Claire Duchen's *French Connections*, pp. 135–43.

6 Gayatri Spivak, 'Displacement and the discourse of woman', in Mark Kropnik (ed.), *Displacement: Derrida and After*, Bloomington: Indiana University Press, 1983, pp. 169–95, p. 169.

7 Monique Wittig, *Les Guérillères*, Paris: Editions de Minuit, 1969, p. 15.

8 Spivak, 'Displacement'.

9 For details see Duchen's *History of French Feminism*. It is to some extent partial, largely owing to Psych et Po's refusal to grant permission for the publishing of their texts, but it gives a good idea of other wings of the movement.

10 *Des Femmes en mouvement*, mensuelle, special issue on China, 11, pp. 22–3.

11 Duchen, *French Connections*, pp. 40–3.

12 ibid., p. 86.

13 ibid., p. 78.
14 Derrida: 'There is no such thing as the essence of woman, because woman averts, she is averted of herself.'
15 Duchen, *French Connections*, p. 54.

5

'Bliss was it in that dawn . . .': contemporary French women's writing and the Editions des femmes

When I first got to know the Editions des femmes I thought I had landed in women's paradise. The publishing house had been founded in 1974 and went on thriving and expanding until the late seventies. It was the golden age of the women's movement in France. In Wordsworth's phrase about the early stages of the French Revolution, 'Bliss was it in that dawn to be alive'.

The publishing-rooms above the bookshop in the rue des Saints-Pères, and the printing-house in wonderful rue de la Roquette, near the Bastille and not far from the old 'artisan' quarters of Paris, were beehives of activity. Everything was happening at once, in the same spaces: the reading of manuscripts, the pursuits of journalists on the telephone for the press campaign of a book about to be published or to protest about an article in *Le Monde* misrepresenting an action by women, the setting-up of meetings to discuss the current political situation; deciding who would see such a play or such a film, review it for the monthly, later on for the weekly, review. Manuscripts were pouring in. Kate Millet was visiting, or Nawal-el-Sarawi, or a woman novelist from the Lebanon who had written about the war. *Almanach des femmes russes*, an anthology by Russian women about life in Russia, which someone had managed to smuggle into the west, was being translated. A huge petition was being drawn up for Quang-Jin, the most implacably pursued of the Gang of Four: she had just been sentenced to death. How to drum up support for Eva Forest, a Basque militant, or for the imprisoned Baader–Meinhof militants, was on the agenda. There was chaos in some ways, but also extraordinary energy, joy, militancy. Women's achievements in all fields were being celebrated, from artists, dancers, film-maker and trapeze expert Coline Serreau to women politicians. They gave me, one of the writers they were publishing, the feeling that the world was ours for the taking. There was a breathtaking sense of curiosity, but also of sympathy, from many journalists, in the press or radio or television. Men who interviewed you were sitting up and listening.

It was the era in which women's presses were multiplying, women's collections sprouting all over, in some of the most staid of publishing houses. Women's voices were getting louder, were being heard. They were going to change the world.

THE GROWTH OF A TONGUE

A voice for women was being reclaimed from all the quarters of patriarchy that claim a woman cannot speak, cannot write. Hélène Cixous, the first to use the tale of Sleeping Beauty as a metaphor of where woman is always found throughout culture – in bed and asleep, waiting for man to wake her – was also telling the story of the hundred or so wives of the Chinese emperor. The emperor asks the famous general Sun Tse to make soldiers of his wives. Sun Tse tries to get them to march in step to the sound of a drum. The wives giggle and fall about laughing. So Sun Tse makes an example: he chops off the heads of the two favourite wives. Then the others march: in silence. 'Le Sexe ou la tête.' Women have been threatened with either decapitation or castration (have had their heads or their tongues, their sex, metaphorically chopped off), if they refused to endorse the masculine Order.

The Cahiers du Grif, which first published the Hélène Cixous piece[1], and were then on the best of terms with the Editions des femmes, in one of their most remarkable numbers, dedicated to women and language, recalled the story of Marie Grelard, a seventeenth-century girl. She had had smallpox, as a result of which her tongue had withered and dropped out. But, the medical document reports, she had such a passionate desire to communicate that with her stump of a tongue she managed first to make articulate sounds, stammer, then gradually recovered the power of speech.[2]

76

Women were fighting against all the discourses that place woman in the position of the Other. The quest was for a difference: 'Every woman who wants to hold a discourse that is her own cannot evade the extraordinary urgency upon us all: to invent woman', Annie Leclerc was writing in *Parole de femme*.[3] There were all sorts of topical and formal searches for such a voice, from books like Victoria Thérame's slangish *La Dame au bidule*, about a woman taxi-driver's experience, to Marie Cardinal's *Les Mots pour le dire*, the words to say 'it' – things such as menstruation and pregnancy and female madness. The Editions des femmes published books by escapees from psychiatry such as Emma Santos or Marie Vaubourg. Jeanne Hyvrard in the same period was writing about the terror of the mental home in her wonderful *Mère la mort*. There was every kind of refusal of the mastery of the logos, in terms of syntactical or narrative structures, from interest in translation as a typically female procedure, one that makes you enter the realm of dispossession instead of that of appropriation[4] (and there again the Editions des femmes developed the practice of publishing many translations from women writers all over the world, from Sylvia Plath to Clarice Lispector) to books based on games, the combination of chance and an arbitrary set of rules freeing the textuality from the will of the author (as in Denise Le Dantec's *Les Joueurs de go* and Geneviève Mouillaud and Anne Roche's *La Cause des oies*). Catherine Weinzaepflen was beginning her extraordinary destruction of authority/authoriality within the text, creating a texture whereby each aspect, voice-of-the-author, reader, characters, word associations, words inside the sentence, was regarded as having as much importance as every other aspect, as being equal, equidistant. The title of her first novel, *Isocelles*, published by the Editions des femmes (an *isocèle* triangle is one whose sides are equal), aptly announces a practice that was to grow and strengthen into beautiful poetics. Eugénie Luccioni's *Marches* tended towards a similar equipoise, a search for alternative rhythms. These two in a sense were in the field of Marguerite Duras or Nathalie Sarraute ('the character . . . is a neutrality that writes itself. Almost anonymous', the latter says). But these new formal searches either had a political dimension, or were acquiring it: Duras's work, and the reception of her work, were changed by those years.

These voices, and many, many more, have to be heard in the particular context of women's new-found awareness of the patriarchy. There is a degree of irony in reflecting not only that Simone de Beauvoir, in the early chapters of *The Second Sex* (1949), describing how woman differentiates herself in relation to man, and not the other way round; how she is constructed as the 'inessential as against man, the essential', how in E. Levinas's words 'Otherness becomes accomplished in the feminine' (in woman), had set the terms of the debate, a debate in which she would become part of a camp, the camp opposed to Psych et Po; but also, that though she cleverly spotted from which disciplines in particular the onslaught on woman was coming, it took twenty years, years in which those disciplines very much developed, for what she had seen to become visible to women at large. Postwar years this century have tended to send women home, to depoliticize them. But the changes in the social order of the years of Gaullism and its immediate aftermath, the massive access of women to areas of education in which, till then, they had been an elite, their increasing access to professions traditionally regarded as male professions, their access to greater judicial and political equality (and let us not forget that French women got the vote only in 1947, immediately after the Second World War), all this meant that women experienced greater potentialities and exigencies, but found themselves subjected to inferior positions in all domains. 'Women's drama is the conflict between the fundamental demand of any subject that always posits itself as the essential, and the exigencies of a situation which always constitutes her as inessential.' Read in the context of May '68, the words of *The Second Sex* ring true indeed.[5]

WOMAN AS THE OTHER

The Second Sex, inspired by period Sartre, had drawn upon the Hegelian dialectic of the master and slave to account for women having arrived at the position in which Julien Benda could write: 'Man is the Subject, the Absolute; woman is the other.' The book was dedicated to exploring how for the phrase 'woman is the other' one could substitute the phrase 'woman becomes the other': 'On ne naît pas femme; on le devient'. In after years, when she had become friends with the group of

Questions féministes, Simone de Beauvoir would borrow from Sartre's new, neo-Marxist category of 'scarcity' (as developed in the *Critique de la raison dialectique*) to explain how it was against a background of scarcity, of there not being '*assez*', not enough, that the 'same' could appear as a 'counter-man', as an Other. Woman remained defined as another being 'biologically destined' to repeat life instead of risking her life through war: it is 'not by giving life, but by risking his life, that man becomes elevated above the animal; that is why, in the history of human kind, superiority has always been granted not to the sex that gives birth, but to the sex that kills'. The master-and-slave, or the scarcity model, enabled her to describe the misogyny at work in so much Surrealist literature as well as in rationalist or indeed existential philosophy in the first half of the century. She had the nous however also to pick up two newer types of discourses that were also constructing, or had been constructing, woman as the Other: psychoanalysis and Structuralism.

Lévi-Strauss, in *The Elementary Structures of Kinship* (1947),[6] roughly argued as follows. Culture is born of communication. The ability to communicate depends upon a will to have relations, which Lévi-Strauss calls an alliance, a pact, an exchange. Women are the object of that exchange, as they represent the only natural 'stimulant' the satisfaction of which can be deferred (unlike food or drink). It is necessary that women should be exchanged for the life of groups to be possible. The incest taboo on which exogamy (the necessity of marrying outside the group) rests, far from being a natural phenomenon, is but the indispensable condition of the circulation and exchange of women between groups.

Taking up and discussing Lévi-Strauss's ideas in *L'Erotisme*,[7] the Surrealist writer Bataille stressed the use Lévi-Strauss had made of Marcel Mauss's famous essay on the gift. Mauss had shown that exchange appears, in its primitive form, less in the form of transactions than of reciprocal gifts. The father must allow the wealth constituted by his daughter, the brother that constituted by his sister, to enter the circuit of exchanges. The comparison is with champagne, which it would be mean to keep to oneself, which one must share with one's friends. 'The meaning of a woman given away in marriage is close despite everything, to that of champagne in our customs.' Marriage is thus 'placed on the side of feasts'. 'Thus women appear essentially destined to communication.' 'The sexual relationship itself is communication and movement, it partakes of the nature of feast; pp. 224–9).

In his capacity to thus defer the satisfaction of his instincts, deny himself the immediate enjoyment of his women (sister, daughter), man passes from the animal to the human stage. This is different from the Hegelian model in which it is through risking his life that man accedes to humanity, but the structure is similar, since it is also by a negation, rising above the immediate animal instinct, self-denial rather than self-preservation, that humanity comes about. A dialectic is at work in both. 'Man's essence is given in the incest taboo and in the gift of women, its consequence', Bataille writes. It only remains for him, in typical Bataille logic, to reverse the movement: man asserts his humanity by yet again transgressing, this time transgressing the very rules by means of which he in the first place asserted his humanity. Eroticism will be found in the violation of, say, the taboo on menstrual blood. 'The taboo does not change the violence of the sexual activity, but it opens for disciplined man a door to which animality could have no access, that of the transgression of the rule' (pp. 240–1).

Where does this put woman? At best, in the place of champagne. Always passive in these accounts, the object of exchange between subjects that become constituted in the exchange, she has no share either in the constitution of the structure, nor in the generosity of the gift. She does none of the self-denying that leads to essentiality. Nor can she have access to the transgression of the taboos since she had no share in their constitution. She is, be it in the Structuralist or the Surrealist account, the 'inessential' as opposed to the essential. Eroticism, though she may by its initiator, as in many Bataille texts, in its essence constitutes her as an object, not a subject. The phrase *objet sexuel* is not of the MLF making.

No use saying, as Lévi-Strauss does, that we are all human, that the scenario would have been the same had women exchanged men instead. The human sciences can speak only of what is, not what might have been. Indeed, contemporary anthropology has tended to argue that matriarchal societies were largely an invention of nineteenth-century male anthropologists, wishing to console women for what was, with the imagination of what was supposed to have been.

More follows, as the Italian anthropologist Ida Magli argued in one of the language issues of the *Cahiers du Grif*.[8] She claims that the system of communication which was established through the exchange of women was a first step towards, or continuous with, the exchange of language. Woman is the sign, the symbol, of language, 'speech of speech': destined to communication, in effect if not in essence as Bataille would have it. The gist of her complex argumentation is that woman throughout culture has been barred from any access to language as power (juridical, religious, political, etc.); from language as constitutive (initiation rites, myth-making); because she has been used as the 'guarantee of speech', the sign of communication. Perhaps also because if she had accumulated those functions she would have been too powerful, God-like.

It can easily be seen, even from such a skeletal sketch as this, how with Bataille's 'women appear essentially destined to communication . . . the sexual relation itself is communication and movement' we are on our way to Lacan, twenty-odd years later, in *Encore*, arguing that woman is excluded from the Symbolic, from language, because she lacks a relation to the phallus, lacks what organizes masculinity, that is, the fear of castration. The phallus, or 'transcendental signifier' (transcendental in that it organizes the whole structure of subjectivity), is what inscribes its effects, its effects of fear of castration and resistance to castration, and from then on the very organization of language. Woman 'is this unclassifiable feminine structure whose power to produce otherness is a power that does not return to herself'. She can speak, but not 'say'. She is, lucky she, Lacan stresses, in the position of speech, of 'le dire', which is the position of God (*dieu, dire*), the position of truth, which can only be in the place of the Other. There were, of course, sundry links between Lacan and the Surrealists, and Bataille in particular. The ideological continuities are striking.[9]

In all these discourses, woman is what guarantees communication and what cannot constitute it because of a lack of negation as it were. Or, as Hélène Cixous put it, because she 'lacked lack'. It means that she has to be debarred from powerful language: castrated, or decapitated, in the name of her supposed state of native or cultural castration. '[Her] tongue is cut and what speaks is not heard because it is the body that speaks and man does not listen to the body.[10] Luce Irigaray argued in *Speculum de l'autre femme* that it might be the fear of women, which is also a fear of death, homosexual in its essence, that leads men to deny women their essentiality.[11] She also pointed out how poor psychoanalysis was in its awareness of the importance of women's relation to their mothers, and women's relations between themselves.[12] The whole French enterprise of 'writing the body' – developing an 'écriture féminine' that would be both writing, saying, but also reinscribing the denied female body, that would make woman whole – must be understood in this context. Hélène Cixous answered Lacan's claim that 'you cannot say "la femme" without crossing *la*' by writing a book called *La*. Psych et Po stressed 'des' femmes. The Editions des femmes and their reviews and journals were in those years in the vanguard of the fight.

WRITING THE BODY/GROWING A
TONGUE/INVENTING DIFFERENCE

It is indeed as if, through many of the texts of the seventies, the three were part and parcel of each other. As if the Marie Grelard story were being re-enacted, the speaking mostly taking the form of writing. One can see how seminal was psychoanalysis, how much it was being used, turned against the founding fathers.

Freud's claim that Dora coughs, chokes, cannot speak, because she is repressing her desire for Herr K. who has kissed her, is worth quoting from not only because it will be critiqued in so many ways, but because it makes the link between sex and mouth so startlingly clear:

> Once more, therefore, we find a displacement from the lower part of the body to the upper . . . The disgust is the symptom of repression in the erotogenic oral zone, which . . . had been over-indulged in Dora's infancy by the habit of sensual sucking. The pressure of the erect member probably led to an analogous change in the corresponding female organ, the clitoris; and the excitation of this second erotogenic zone was referred

by a process of displacement to the simultaneous pressure against the thorax and became fixed there.[13]

'If it is only a metaphor, which isn't certain, it's one that functions well', Hélène Cixous points out in *La Jeune née*.[14] It isn't that Dora has been over-indulgent in infancy nor that she represses and denies her own desire, but that an array of socio-cultural repressions are at work, around and inside her. Yet in effect, as the case study shows in despite of itself, the force of Dora's desire is explosive. The Freudian notion of displacement serves to conceal the real sources of the repression, making Dora's body, with its two poles, clitoris and throat, both its origin and place. The link itself, though (between mouth and sex, speech and sex), with all it signifies, is one which is explored and critiqued in the period. For instance, Séverine Auffret's eloquent *Des couteaux contre des femmes*, in a long and imaginative enquiry into clitoridectomy, its patterns and practices, relates the various repressions and the 'feminization' of western women to the practice of excision in Africa, or foot-binding in China. Gayatri Spivak, countering Derrida, reiterates with her customary lucidity what French women writers had, through poetic texts, been saying:

> The clitoris escapes reproductive framing. In legally defining woman as the object of exchange, passage, or possession in terms of reproduction, it is not only the womb that is literally 'appropriated'; it is the clitoris as the signifier of the sexed subject that is effaced . . . [An] at least symbolic clitoridectomy has always been the 'normal' accession to womanhood and the unacknowledged name of motherhood.[15]

This is what French women were writing in the seventies. Catherine Clément:

> That is what is at stake, in feminist action: to modify the imaginary so as to act upon the real, to change the forms of language which in its structure or history has always been subjected to the patrilinear, therefore masculine, law.[16]

Hélène Cixous:

> If you censor the body, the breath, you are censoring

speech. Write yourself: the body must be heard. Then the immense resources of the subconscious will spring . . .

. . . a deed which will signal woman's taking hold of language, therefore her shattering entry into History which has always been constituted over her repression.[17]

Madeleine Gagnon, the French Canadian writer:

Like millions of women, I want to inscribe my fighting body for something tells me – and it isn't my manly science – that a great part of History, because it has neither been thought nor written by us, has become fixed in the memory of the female body.[18]

Chantal Chawaf:

Writing, for me, is seeking to allow words and sentences to escape from their arbitrary linguistic abstraction and to re-enter the dough, the muddy earth, to be kneaded and worked with the palm of the hand . . . The writing I hope for is the language of what the grammarians have deprived of a language, have censored; domesticated; castrated, chastened (why do you speak praisingly of a 'chastened style'?). The word is the stage at which there is not yet an agreed order, in which the natural order can still prevail.[19]

It would take a lot more space than is available here to show what attempts were made to create an 'écriture féminine'. It would need to start with the reminder that the French term *féminine* means, 'woman's, 'of woman', not feminine in the English sense. It would have to explain how the cut tongue/clitoris was turned into a kind of *felix culpa*; what was supposed to be a disadvantage was turned into a source of strength. Woman, it was claimed by Luce Irigaray for instance, does not have one sex, but many. She writes with many tongues (*langue* meaning both the physical tongue and language). She has tongues, is sexed, all over her body. The witchcraft, the hysteria, of which she has been accused throughout so many centuries also mean that she has had to compose with forces of nature which she is now less afraid of than man. Thus, Catherine Clément claims in *La Jeune née*,[20] Italian women dance a tarantella, a spider's dance, which both wards off and mimics the convulsions that the dreaded spider's sting can inflict. Hélène Cixous, in a text following Clément's, verbally dances a tarantella, demonstrating in the process woman's dizzying register, her multiple ability with language. Urging: the dark continent is not dark, we can explore it, we need not be afraid . . .

Even in these early days however women were wary of attaching definitions to 'écriture féminine' (and one should now beware the risk of fetishizing it, French and quotation marks and all, in English). Everything becomes recuperable as soon as it is *énoncé* by the signifying discourse which is in power, Irigaray warned. If I could say, 'This is it, this is what women are on about, this is what women's writing is', I would stop immediately, many were saying. Rapidly, there were divergences. Some feared the narcissism, the relegation to a particular register, the elimination of the social dimension. Using Kristeva's term 'the semiotic' to refer to women's writing was misleading, was paradoxical: and anyway, didn't she herself go on to say that the semiotic was always in a relation to the symbolic, and that it was at work in men's writing (as the drive to incest with the mother) just as much as in women? Didn't even Hélène Cixous claim she'd found the feminine mode in Genet? Others worried that the term itself was dangerous: yet another (inferior) thing women did. Men did writing, women 'écriture féminine', Jeanne Hyvrard snapped.[21] Yet the fiery, molten prose that she writes raised accusations against syntax, against the power of certain tabulated forms of speech (in, remember, the land of the French Academy and primary school grammar), that echoes Chantal Chawaf, intent on working on the warm fleshiness of words:

They are going to come and take me to the asylum. She will say, that's her. She does not know how to speak French. I do not know how to speak French. I cannot speak French. I do not want to speak French. I do not know grammar. She laughs at my spelling mistakes. Confident. I run, I stumble across the snares she lays for me. The agreement of the participle. Do you know the agreement of the participles? She is in a rage. She is going to choke me. No, she laughs. I answered I do not know how. Perhaps I spoke of the stars. Or of the marshes. Or the cliff. Perhaps I simply answered yes and no. She laughed. But she did not open her arms to me. She did not call for them. She said, that's her. She does not know how to speak French. I run between the walls they have erected. I run towards her. The woman in mauve, her parasol, her lace dress. My blood on her hands. The mauve woman shakes her dress and closes her parasol. I run towards her. With outstretched arms. I beg her. Teach me. Teach me the tongue they have torn away from me. Teach me the language that has one tense only. The infinitive no doubt. Mother death, teach me back the language in which I shall at last be able to tell my body that dissolves in the light.[22]

It is highly interesting, in the light of this, which is about being in trouble, straining against trouble, to reread Monique Wittig's accusatory passage in *Les Guérillères* which, whilst being concerned with the same thing (women and language), is about getting out. Waging war. It will be many years to *Virgile, non,* which refuses even metaphor (let alone bodily writing) but prospectively, with the benefit of the hindsight she has now provided, one can see how she was getting there – how opposed she could become, despite the similarity of the struggle, to Psych et Po:

They (the women) say, you wretched one, they (the men) have chased you from the world of signs, and yet they have given you names, they have called you slave, you wretched slave. Like masters they have exercised their master's right. They write about this right to give names that goes so far back that the origin of language can be considered as an act of authority emanating from those who dominate. Thus the men say that they have said, this is such and such a thing, they have attached such a sound to such and such an object and through that they have as it were appropriated it. The women say, thus doing the men have yelled howled with all their might to reduce you to silence. The women say, the language you speak poisons your throat your tongue your palate your lips.

The women say, the language you speak is made up
of words that kill you. They say, the language you speak
is made up of signs which properly speaking point to
what they have appropriated.[23]

By contrast yet again, Hélène Cixous escapes from phallocracy through sheer mobility. (The history of each woman is
different, of course; in the case of Hélène Cixous, the migrant
condition from the start, and the voyage through Joyce say
something about the closeness of her practice, at a certain
stage, to Deconstruction.) She does not denounce the murder
that is in the words, the sounds of the words. She opens them
out, like the seven colours of the rainbow. She makes words
have tongues all over their bodies, as it were, diffract, multiply.
This means that she translates badly (or that I find myself
doing an even worse job of it than of the others; I was unhappy
enough with Wittig's wonderfully unspecific *'ils'* and *'elles'* that
have, for want of pronoun genders in English, or rather of
plural gender, to be translated as 'the women' or 'the men'):

I get hold of this tongue which is also my mother and
that of all my daughters.
And with it I open the mouth of my eyes.
Then all that sees speaks and each word lights up
another knot of meaning.
. . .
For her, for the red mother in my mouth, the electuary
of pleasure: take a thousand grains of wildness, take
the grain of nakedness, the seeds of the virgin creeper
henbane horses' grass sulphur jasper the juice of water-
lily-lighthouse add electricity the night in a dream glass
the pale green water streaked with blood pissed by the
divine young girl, drink! drink my linctus of the
thousand moons.[24]

Well, I've done a lousy job of that. At least it suggests
something of the range of tones – from the biblical, hymn,
Song of Songs, to the recipe for the witches' brew, turned into
a list of delights, a night of love, celebrating menstruation,
with the feminized *nénuphar* alias water-lily turning into *ne-nu-
phare*, a not-naked-lighthouse, and *jusquiame*, henbane,
not only alliterating with 'jasper' (*jaspe*) and 'juice' (*jus*) but

87

diffracting into *jusqu'y âme* (to the very soul) or *jus qui a(i)me* (loving juice). The magic that is called into play, or called upon to play, is a veritable orchestra that creates pleasure for every sense.

> [G]reat poets do not die; they are continuing presences; they need only the opportunity to walk among us in the flesh. This opportunity, as I think, it is now coming within our power to give her. For my belief is that if we live another century or so – I am talking of the common life which is the real life and not of the separate lives which we live as individuals – . . . then the opportunity will come and the dead poet who was Shakespeare's sister will put on the body which she has so often laid down. Drawing her life from the lives of the unknown who were her forerunners, as her brother did before her, she will be born. As for her coming without that preparation, without that effort on our part, without that determination that when she is born again she shall find it possible to live and write her poetry, that we cannot expect, for that would be impossible. But I maintain that she would come if we worked for her, and that so to work, even in poverty and obscurity, is worth while.

So ends Virginia Woolf's *A Room of One's Own*. I can think of no more fitting tribute to the writing and thinking of the women whose work I have attempted to describe, and to the actions and the thinking and the writing of the women who made it all possible. Whether Judith Shakespeare is among us I do not know. But perhaps her name is many?

APPENDIX

Some of the fiction written in the period reflected upon in this chapter is listed here for further reading. Unless otherwise indicated, the publication place is Paris and the publishers Editions des femmes.

Gisèle Bienne, *Marie-Salope* (a history of a peasant childhood), 1976.
Marie Cardinal, *Les Mots pour le dire*, Grasset, 1975.
Chantal Chawaf, *Rétable: la rêverie*, 1975.
Hélène Cixous, *Souffles*, 1975; *La*, Gallimard, 1976; *Angst*, 1977; *Portrait de Dora*, play, 1976; *Préparatifs de noces au-delà de l'abime*, 1978, Ananke, 1979; etc.

Viviane Forrester, *Le Corps entier de Marigda*, Denoël, 1976; *Vestiges*, Le Seuil, 1978.

Benoite Groult, *Ainsi Soit-Elle*, Stock, 1976.

Claudine Herman, *Les Voleuses de langue*, 1975.

Jeanne Hyvrard, *Les Prunes de Cythère*, 1975, *Mère la mort*, 1976, *Meurtritude*, 1977, all Editions de Minuit; Hyvrard was later to be published by the Editions des femmes.

Annie Leclerc, *Parole de femme*, Grasset, 1975.

Denise Le Dantec, *Le Jour*, 1975; *Les Joueurs de go*, Stock, 1977.

Eugénie Luccioni, *Marches*, 1977.

Geneviève Mouillaud and Anne Roche, *La Cause des oies*, Denoël, 1978.

Claude Pujade Renaud, *La Ventriloque*, 1976.

Emma Santos, *La Malcastrée*, 1975; *La Loméchuse*, 1978; *J'ai tué Emma Santos ou l'écriture colonisée*.

Irène Schavelzon, *La Chambre intérieure*, 1975.

Geneviève Serreau, *Ricercare*, Denoël, 1973, *Dix-huit mètres cubes de silence*, Denoël 1976; *La Lumière sur le mur*, Gallimard, 1979.

Victoria Thérame, *Hosto-blues* (about a hospital nurse), 1975; *La Dame au bidule* (about a woman taxi-driver), 1976.

Christiane Veschambre, *Le Lais de la traverse*, 1978.

Nicole Ward Jouve, *Le Spectre du gris*, 1977; *L'Entremise*, 1980.

Catherine Weinzaepflen, *Isocelles*, 1977; *La Farnésine, jardins*, 1978.

Monique Wittig, *L'Opoponax*, 1965, *Les Guérillères*, 1969 and *Le Corps lesbien*, 1973, all Editions de Minuit.

NOTES

All translations from the French in this essay are my own, though several of the books or articles I quote from have now been translated into English. My intention was to convey as much of a sense of the original as I could by sticking close to the French.

1 Hélène Cixous, 'Le Sexe ou la tête?', in 'Elles consonnent: femmes et langages II', *Cahiers du Grif*, 13, October 1976, pp. 5–15.

2 'Parlez-vous française?: Femmes et langages I', *Cahiers du Grif*, 12, June 1976, back cover.

3 A necessarily brief but, it is hoped, representative list of titles from the period is given in the appendix. Details of the books mentioned here are included.

4 See Jacqueline Risset's piece 'La Traduction commence' and her interview in number 4 of the *Mensuelle*.

5 Simone de Beauvoir, *Le Deuxième Sexe*, vol. 1, Paris: Gallimard, 1949.

6 Lévi-Strauss, *Les Structures élémentaires de la parenté*, Paris: PUF, 1949, esp. pp. 52–86; for the link with psychoanalysis (Freud's *Totem and Taboo*) and with language, see pp. 608–17.

7 Georges Bataille, *L'Erotisme*, Paris: Editions de Minuit, 1957.

8 Ida Magli, 'Pouvoir de la parole et silence de la femme', in *Cahiers du Grif*, 12, pp. 37–43.

9 Jacques Lacan, *Encore, Le Séminaire XX* (1972–4), Paris: Le Seuil, 1975; see pp. 13–15, 34, 44, 65–78, 94, 108. Stephen Heath's article, 'Difference', *Screen*, 1978, pp. 51–112, remains to my mind the best in English on the question.

10 Cixous, 'Le Sexe ou la tête?'

11 Luce Irigaray, *Speculum de l'autre femme*, Paris: Editions de Minuit, 1974.

12 Luce Irigaray, *Ce sexe qui n'en est pas un*, Paris: Editions de Minuit, 1977, pp. 123–4.

13 Sigmund Freud, 'A Case of Hysteria . . .' in the Pelican Freud Library, vol. 8, Harmondsworth: Penguin, 1976 p. 61.

14 Hélène Cixous and Catherine Clément, *La Jeune née*, Paris: 10/18, 1975, p. 271. A translation now exists: *The Newly Born Woman*, Manchester University Press, 1986.

15 Gayatri Spivak, 'French feminism in an international frame', *Yale French Studies*, 62, 1981, pp. 154–84.

16 Catherine Clément, 'Enclave esclave', *L'Arc*, 61, *Simone de Beauvoir et la lutte des femmes*, 1975, p. 43 (my translation).

17 Hélène Cixous, 'Le rire de la Méduse', *L'Arc*, 61. Now translated as 'The laugh of the Medusa', in Elaine Marks and Isabelle de Courtivron (eds), *New French Feminisms*, Amherst, Mass: University of Massachusetts Press, 1980, pp. 245–64.

18 Madeleine Gagnon in Hélène Cixous, Madeleine Gagnon, and Annie Leclerc, *La Venue à l'écriture*, Paris: Union générale d'édition, 1976.

19 Chantal Chawaf, *Chair Chaude, suivi de L' Ecriture*, Paris: Mercure de France, 1976.

20 *La Jeune née*, pp. 19–22.

21 Jeanne Hyvrard, *La Meurtritude*, Editions de Minuit; quoted in 'Si l'écriture des femmes', in *Cahiers du Grif*, 23/24, December 1978, pp. 153–6.

22 Jeanne Hyvrard, *Mère la mort*, Paris: Editions de Minuit, 1976.

23 P. 162.

24 Hélène Cixous, *La*, Paris: Gallimard, 1976, pp. 112–13.

6

Hélène Cixous: from inner theatre to world theatre

The crippling combination of hubris and self-doubt in my make-up makes me want to do the big thing: produce an account of the whole of Hélène Cixous's work. Immediately I want to say that this is of course impossible and in any case I'm not up to it. Set your target too far. Fail to reach it. Crucify yourself with your failure. A characteristic female manoeuvre and one that Hélène Cixous herself has steadily avoided. Indeed, her whole work urges us to avoid it. Do not dream, then retreat. Act. Go through the gate. Do not hang around it, fashioning ghostly guardians out of your dreams and fears.

My purpose is to speak of a larger Hélène Cixous than is normally discussed in Great Britain. The translation process implies untold selections, omissions, enlargements, that have as much to do with the translating culture, its needs and projections,[1] as they have with the writing that is being translated. Only seven or eight out of forty-odd texts by Hélène Cixous exist in English: *Angst, Portrait de Dora, To Live the Orange, Inside, The Newly Born Woman*, and a few essays, 'The Laughter of the Medusa', 'Castration or Decapitation', the pieces in Susan Sellers's *Writing Differences*.[2] Among these, the theoretical essays have been the object of the more intense scrutiny, and have been more influential than the so-called creative prose. I say 'so-called', being at a loss for a word to apply to drama and fictions that are poetic, meditative, critical, sometimes autobiographical; and because the so-called theory is written creatively. Indeed, *La Venue à l'écriture* is more directly autobiographical than any of the first-person fiction, and arguably as imaginative. But in Anglo-Saxon terms the theoretical Cixous has prevailed and been perceived as the proponent of a practice called 'l'écriture féminine', the defender of a *féminité* that has to do with *jouissance* and body language. It is assumed that, as she herself is a practitioner of 'l'écriture féminine', her practice as it were illustrates her theory. That her writing is difficult, and need only be taken into account by the Francophone specialists. And that the writings, as well as the theoretical positions, are homogeneous, unchanging over time. A monolith is thus engineered, placed on the horizon of foreign theory, its clay feet dangerously planted in the marshy ground of experimental writing. Will the water seepage dissolve those feet, will the idol tumble of its own accord – or will it be toppled by the lances of Anglo-American pragmatists quixotic enough to charge it?

This, though unfair, is not meant to be negative: if translation is always a betrayal (*traduction/trahison*, as Risset says), it is a necessary betrayal, and a productive one. If each language, each culture, distorts the foreign that it takes into its midst, it is because it is different: it also casts new light on it, gives it new life, is fertilized by it. And so it is with Cixous. It was Great Britain, not France, that held a colloquium in Liverpool on her work and practice, that paid tribute to her. What I have said of the Anglo-American Cixous is not meant as an attack on a generous and enthusiastic readership. It is meant to serve as a backcloth to the other Cixous. The one that my position as a bilingual reader and friend, with one foot planted in France and the other in England, makes me perceive.

How to convey that perception?

Being simple (especially when your tongue so instinctively forks) is the most difficult thing. The most important thing. It means striving to grasp the thing that stares you in the eye and which you cannot, will not, see. Making the two prongs of that damned tongue for once act as one channel. Gathering the bridles of all the horses that are galloping through you at any minute and making them run together: as Plato's coachman does the black and the white horse in Phaedo's fable of the well-regulated soul.

Here goes.

Hélène Cixous always writes in the present.

There are two ways of writing in the present.

It can be argued that any text is in the present. In *Writing Degree Zero* Roland Barthes has described the prevailing mode of fiction, the preterite, as a disguised, idyllic and bracketted present. You could also say that any of the futuristic modes of science fiction or the present or future or conditional tenses of Nouveau Roman or post-modernist fiction include an element of the present: partly because, as Barthes and Sartre have first shown,[3] reading is always done in the present, and any text addresses itself to the reading-in-the-present of its prospective readers. Partly also because, whether you're writing a historical novel or a utopia, the process of writing itself means you're summoning what is in you as you write, which is often only brought to the fore as it is being written.

But there is another way of writing in the present, which is, as it were, writing blind. Writing as a process of projection and discovery. Not writing out of an intention or as a *projet*, nor as mimesis nor reportage nor to tell a story. Writing as surprise. To find out what you do not know but somehow know that you know. I can find no better example of this than Clarice Lispector's *The Apple in the Dark*.[4] I think that Hélène Cixous was dazzled by Lispector's gift of a truly refreshing fruit of knowledge, as she says in *To Live the Orange*,[5] because she had found that here was a woman superbly practising what she herself had in a multitude of ways striven to do for years. 'Ten years to wring from my body the strength to take another step.'[6] Such writing allows us to pass through the gate described in Kafka's fable, which is discussed in *The Newly Born Woman*.[7] Our fear of going through is what keeps the gate in place, and each step requires that the fear be conquered. Risk and surprise are continuously involved. Nothing to help you before or behind. Each step is costly, from word to word, sentence to sentence, book to book, and the unpredictability of Hélène Cixous's as of Clarice Lispector's writing is the mark of this. The sequence is engendered by the attempt, is born out of what precedes, but you hadn't seen that it could, it comes as a surprise. You have to trust to language, its mobility, the spectrum of connotations that storm and sunshine can open in it, to show you the way. 'Elle ne plante pas, elle fraie.'

She does not plant, she opens a path. You might say that

unlike man the agriculturalist, who sows *logos spermaticos*,[8] the hunter-gatherer-woman-who-writes and her sentence open paths for others, and other sentences, to follow. They do not deplete the woods, use up the earth. Yet there is abundance in the process. And each new moment involves beginning again. Such writing is hard to read, hard to translate. I see nothing wrong with reading it bit by bit, as you read poetry. Antoinette Fouque used to say that women need new forms of literacy: they need to learn to read without such reliance on habit and memory, for the weight of a cultural past that has almost always placed them in inferior positions makes habit and memory dangerous tools for women.

Such writing is in the field of paradox (though it doesn't seek paradox for its own sake, indeed confesses itself suspicious of it). Contradicting what I have just said, Cixous's writing, however much in the present mode, shows both sequence and progress: it looks to the past, and to the future. It is sequential in that the fiction at least shares in the diary-writer's compulsive need to record every single stage that is being gone through. It also has the inner logic of a psychoanalytic cure, but one that is home-made. It progresses from an obsessive innerness[9] to the elaborate construction of a confident identity. The voice gradually becomes open to others, as co-writers of the text, as people to love, as characters.[10] Until self is no longer central, and theatre begins. Theatre is selflessness incarnate. Cixous's theatre has evolved from the domestic though mythological dramas of Dora and Oedipus, to political plays on a huge scale, concerned with Cambodia and the partition of India. The titles alone express this evolution from self to the world. The preoccupation with identity of *Portrait de Dora* and *Le Nom d'Oedipe* gives way to the Shakespearian-sounding *L'Histoire terrible et inachevée de Norodom Sihanouk roi du Cambodge* and the epic *L'Indiade*. Private leads to public. Inner to outer. The link is made. It is unbroken.

The fictions written up to 1978 (up to *Préparatifs de noces au-delà de l'abîme* and *To Live the Orange*) proceed in a painstaking way towards more integrated selfhood, better self-knowledge. The thing-that-writes is in a sense the thing-that-is-being-written. The material is psychic (conscious/unconscious) and cultural (made up of mythologies, the political, etc.) The method is often associational, as with psychoanalysis. The meanings dormant in etymologies, sounds, permutations of letters, slips of the tongue, are given creative importance. All forms of subjecthood are used: *je, tu, elle, elles, vous, nous*: the whole scale. The archetypal, the relation to the Other, are all at work in a textuality that is woman-centred, not just because the sexuality at work is that of a woman, but because the enterprise is political. The body-that-writes is retrieving woman from age-old constructs.

In Valéry's 'La Pythie', for example, the Pythoness goes through appalling throes, is flooded by darkness before the god can speak with her voice. The female body has to become dormant, lose consciousness before it can be possessed by 'Saint Langage', 'le dieu dans la chair égaré', the god who has wandered into female flesh: before the 'August Voice' which is at once the voice of the poet (always male) and a disembodied voice, the voice of the 'caves and woods', can speak. The female body speaks without knowing that it speaks.

This account of creativity repeats the situation of (male) doctor versus (female) hysterical patient. Indeed, as the links between *The Newly Born Woman* and *Portrait de Dora* show, it is no accident that Cixous, a writer attempting to create a genuinely female voice, should have had to traverse hysteria, and the Dora case in particular. Writing a body-that-writes, and knows that it writes, calling a fiction *La* in reply to Lacan who had just said that you cannot write *la femme* without crossing *la*, is conquering ground, not just for the writer Cixous, but potentially for all women who write.

Recent psychoanalysis has shed interesting light on the relation between hysteria and knowledge. Peter Lomas argues that the psychotherapist has to recognize that the hysterical symptoms are both a search for a socially acceptable breathing-space and a highly condensed autobiography. The hysteric, burdened by emotional trauma, refers to it so as to 'disown the disturbing implications' of the bodily message, but yet to express 'that which is not known or socially acknowledged'. The bodily symptoms (the oppressed chest, the aching throat, the paralysed tongue – my own halting start) convey 'information about a problem, the desire to solve it, and the fear of facing it': but not 'knowledge' (which would include some conscious volition and awareness).[11] Though the term 'body language' is used to describe these symptoms, they are not language but 'iconic signs'. The task of the psychoanalyst, Szasz says, 'is to foster the self-reflective attitude in the patient towards his [her]? own body signs in order to facilitate their translation into verbal symbols.'[12] Art is precisely the domain in which symptoms can be translated into symbols. The creative imagination has the power to breach the impossible gap – to step across the gate. Writing can act as the psychoanalyst holding up a mirror to the self so that it can perceive its own bodily symptoms, the voices of the 'caves and woods' in us, that want to speak but do not know how to, and that need the self-reflectiveness to become transformed into symbols. They also need creative playing, need speculation for the trans-formation to occur, as Winnicott has shown.[13]

It seems to me that this is precisely what happens in Cixous's fictions, at least between the early seventies and *Préparatifs* . . . Writing instals a scene in which the narrative voice is at the same time patient, mirror and analyst. Part and parcel of the process of self-discovery which I described earlier as a continu-ous present is the creative play, the punning, the 'Let's have another go at this', 'Try it this way', 'What if? . . .' which according to Winnicott opens up images to interpretation and multiplicity. Identity becomes constructed through repeated acts of identification. The hysteric, the great figure of the repressed and alienated woman, ceases to be divorced from her own knowledge, only able to make sense through iconic signs. Body language does not mean writing in milk instead of ink, developing a writerly stammer or talking non-stop about *jouissance*, significant though all these might be as symptoms. It means constructing verbal symbolizations that enable the writing self to know what she knows only in the depths. To experience profound pleasure in being able to say 'I' or 'La'. That is why it seems to me so daft – I can think of no better word – to talk of Cixous as Toril Moi does, as somehow stuck in some pre-Oedipal Imaginary state, or as gathering 'all the contradictions within the plenitude of the Imaginary'.[14] The whole problem instead is how to make that repressed Imagin-ary find ways of reaching forms of symbolization. Eventually, because self has reached self-knowledge and self-love, which is the basis of all love, the world opens up. The multiple voices that contribute to the single text are recognized as multiple, in *Limonade tout était si infini*. Love appears, timidly in *Préparatifs . . .* , powerfully in *Le Livre de Prométhéa*. The thieves of language, Cixous and the women who have become sources of inspiration to her and are sung by her texts, reclaim a woman's voice.

Three women in particular play Promethean roles in Cixous's mythologies: in the late seventies and early eighties, Antoinette Fouque with the Editions des femmes, her publishers and collaborators in what was then felt to be a joint venture. Then, from 1978 onwards, Clarice Lispector, the giver of the orange, showing the way to the lost springs of the self: 'I wandered ten glacial years in over-published solitude, without seeing a single human woman's face, the Sun had retired . . . and behold, it was Clarice, the writing.'[15] And then, from about 1985 on, the collaboration with Ariane Mnouchkine and the Théâtre du Soleil opens out Cixous's writing to yet another form of body language. It is through the bodies of the actors, their long training, inspired from the theatres of the East, in mime, dancing, meditation, make-up, costume, that the text now speaks, is communicated. Performance is a live present in which the body is more complete than in the written text, since it is there as flesh, spectacle, music, movement, speech. Through theatre, the voice that was once threatened by hysteria, that had to articulate itself out of its inward-looking state, becomes many voices talking to many. From the self-knowledge grown out of a long struggle against the forces of death in the body, in the psyche, is born the capacity to imagine and body forth the struggle between the forces of life and the forces of death at large in the world. The two major plays to date, done by the Théâtre du Soleil, the play on Cambodia and the play on India, are about how the forces of war and hate prevailed over the forces of life and love: how Cambodia turned from the gentle Khmer kingdom into a place of fanatical holocaust, sucked as it was into the East–West maelstrom of the Vietnam war; how India became partitioned at independence, how flesh was torn from flesh, land from land. They tread a fine line between fidelity to history, recreation of the facts as they can be known, and a rereading of the facts in the name of the 'impossible': Gandhi, being Khmer. Forces which might have prevailed, to which theatre gives form.

L'Indiade, the epic of India, of a fratricidal war, avoidable perhaps like the war between Greece and Troy, is subtitled 'L'Inde de leurs rêves'. There might have been, Gandhi and Nehru dreamt of, an unpartitioned India. The play explores what complex forces, political, tribal, religious, international, psychological, made for division, embodying them in symbolic characters as once the symptoms of the hysterical body were made conscious through verbal symbolization. In other words, the drama, however grand and public, is born out of, is continuous with, the work of self-discovery and healing of the fiction. This is writing which aims at producing at least the dramatic dream of a cure: discovering a principle of life, of healing, in the very process of showing how hate and death prevailed. Utopian perhaps, but more than utopian, in that it does not bring news from nowhere. It brings, together with news from the actual Cambodia and the actual India, news of what might have been, what should be, what could and can be if each of us were to work in and around ourselves to make those life-forces prevail which the writing, the theatre, bring into symbolic existence.

Another progress, almost mystical, runs throughout Cixous's work alongside the personal and political progress, the progress from inner to outer theatre I have just tried to describe. Taken over time and from book to book, the writing has the character of a *Divine Comedy*, a long journey through the Other World.

Strikingly like Dante, the fictions traverse a variegated hell, ascend a mount of healing if not a mount of Purgatory (the wedding beyond the abyss, the gift and curative power of the orange). A variety of figures (Kafka, Lispector) are there as guides. Then, at the top of the mount, very much as in Dante, Eden is reached. A state of innocence which is art, not ignorance. The taste of the fruit, which has the freshness of childhood tastes: *With, ou l'art de l'innocence; Limonade tout était si infini*. Here the resemblance to the *Divine Comedy* ends. Cixous's recent writing does not reach out towards the spheres of paradise beyond the Earthly Paradise. It chooses to return to earth, to history more precisely, bringing back as gifts what it has glimpsed of paradise: the possibility of a better world.

The last book I have seen, *Manne pour Mandelstams pour Mandelas*, has a title that says it all. It attempts to make the imaginative gift of loving poetry, food from heaven, Manna, to two couples who in reality, having suffered all the agonies of the desert, exile, separation, imprisonment, are beyond retrieval. No one can alter the fate of the Russian poet Mandelstam, dead in Siberia in 1938 for his opposition to Stalin. No one can give back to Nelson and Winnie Mandela the life they might have had as a couple, had they not been partitioned by apartheid. Only Manna from heaven, the gift of a writing inspired by and continuous with the love of the two wives, Nadezhda Mandelstam and Winnie Mandela, the gift of a writing that is celebratory and poetic and never tries to exploit the tragedy of its characters for its own purposes, writing that is of woman for both men and women, can make the 'impossible', like Gandhi, 'smile upon' them. And upon us.

NOTES

1 As I tried to argue at greater length in chapter 3, which also contains some quotations relevant to the question of 'écriture féminine' and body language.
2 Susan Sellers, *Writing Differences: Readings from the Seminar of Hélène Cixous*, Milton Keynes: Open University Press and New York: St Martin's Press, 1988.
3 Roland Barthes, *Writing Degree Zero*, tr. Annette Lavers and Colin Smith, Boston: Beacon Press, 1970, first published Paris: Gonthier, 1964; Jean-Paul Sartre, *What is Literature?*, tr. Bernard Frechtman, New York: Harper & Row, 1965, esp. chs 2 and 3.
4 Clarice Lispector, *The Apple in the Dark*, London: Virago, 1985.
5 Hélène Cixous, *Vivre l'orange/To Live the Orange*, Paris: Editions des femmes, 1978.
6 Hélène Cixous, *Angst*, tr. Jo Levy, London: Calder, 1985, p. 190.
7 Pp. 101–3.
8 See Christine Battersby's most interesting discussion of theories of the genius as male throughout the ages, in *Gender and Genius: Towards a Feminist Aesthetics*, London: The Women's Press, 1989.
9 For example in titles such as *Les Commencements, Neutre, Dedans, Souffles, La*.
10 *Illa*, Latin for 'that one there', takes over from *La*.
11 Peter Lomas, *True and False Experience: The Case for a Personal Psychotherapy*, London: Allen Lane, 1973, p. 117 and p. 120.
12 Thomas Szasz, *The Myth of Mental Illness*, New York: Harper & Row, 1974, and London: Paladin, pp. 226–42; D. W. Winnicott, *The Maturational Processes and the Facilitating Environment: Studies in the Theory of Emotional Development*, London: Hogarth Press, 1965, and *Playing and Reality*, Harmondsworth: Penguin, 1974, ch. 2.
13 I am deeply grateful to Marie Addyman for having drawn my

attention to this particular line of thinking in her Ph.D. thesis 'The character of hysteria in Shakespeare's England', York, 1989. Chapter 4 is the one from which I have drawn. I quote this most relevant passage: '[For] Donald Winnicott, fantasy is, like brute fact for Coleridge, entirely fixed and dead. As the factual world is an inflexible state of affairs in which the person moves passively and uncreatively, not seeing action therein as the possibility of self-expression; so the non-functioning, split-off part is given over to the dead process of fantasising – apart, unproductive, something which "happens immediately, except that it does not happen at all", and is therefore unavailable for interpretation, identification and authentic existence in reality. Conversion symbolisation, like a record stuck in a groove, corresponds to the fantasying process . . . Quite contrary is the activity of the imagination in which, instead of dislocation, "conflict and coalition" within the person subjectivity and objectivity come together as the realm of urgent and immediate possibility, of "what if . . . ?", to enrich life. In Winnicott's vocabulary, this is creative playing . . . for we are again talking about the artistic process'; op. cit., p. 92.

14 Toril Moi, *Sexual/Textual Politics*, London: Methuen, 1985, p. 121.
15 Cixous, *To Live the Orange*, p. 48.

7

How *The Second Sex* stopped my aunt from watering the horse-chestnuts: Simone de Beauvoir and contemporary feminism

Gentle or brutal reader, if, misled by my subtitle, you expect an authoritative survey, skip this. It's not going to flow from a biro held by Superbrain, a hermaphrodite as all snails are. I shall write out of what I am, what life has made me. And I don't like definitions, or definiteness. I'm suspicious of why I should suddenly be writing on Simone de Beauvoir: is it that she's just popped off? That I have a pious reverence for the dead, feel that I must turn up with my little wreath? Others may do it for me when I in my turn go to 'manger les pissenlits par la racine' or settle quietly, bones and ash, in my little urn. Or do I share the general feeling that when the dead can no longer surprise us with new books and prove our theories wrong we may at last safely bottle and label them? Neither the genie, nor the wizard and his daughter the witch, are going to escape any more. Only Scheherazade knows that even after centuries the deep smoke may still erupt from the uncorked urn, and assume the gigantic proportions of an *efrit*.

Comparative Criticism have complicated stakes in what they've asked me to do (i.e. review books in the field of feminism in the light of Simone de Beauvoir's death and her own achievement in the field). I don't think they like feminism. At the same time, they must feel that it's become such a literary industry, has gone so far with the production of a field of theoretical knowledge, that they must do something about it. But why ask me? They know my position is an eccentric one: I'm French, and most interested in the 'feminine' perspective which, though it is the occasion for many a book or article in this country, tends to get short shrift when it comes to judging it. The answer, I feel, may be interesting. Perhaps they hope that some of my little grey matter will be salt on several sparrows' tails, i.e. that I may be good at demolishing a lot of the stuff that is doing well here at present. Alternatively, I may so infuriate the people I shall criticize that the line of argument I may wish to present will be sure of meeting with a hostile hearing. Divide and rule, as Caesar did with the Gauls he got at each other's throats so thoroughly that he only needed one legion and a half to keep the country down. I may also make a complete fool of myself, in which case I will discredit everybody. Whichever way they play they win. (Also, they have the reserve position of deciding that what I write is unprintable because it's not academic enough.)

What I retain at any rate from *Comparative Criticism* commissioning *me* at this particular juncture is an alternative: either feminist theory is here to stay, something that must be now reckoned with; or, it may not be in a very good state. Is our Moses still looking for Tablets on that particular mountain-top, or are our leaders beginning to cast longing glances towards the Golden Calf? In France certainly, feminism is said by many people to be 'finished', or 'pas fameux'. Of dozens of publishers and collections of women's books, only three, I think, remain. Women's Studies, however, are being created or continuing to function, though not at the rate they do in this country, and with nothing like the dynamism to be found in the USA or Australia. Anglo-Saxon countries are certainly holding out better. Publishers, collections, etc. are thriving, the subject sells beautifully. To a large extent it's owing to all that fine work put in by people like Virago and The Women's Press, and others after them. Also, Anglo-Saxon women have been in the main, at least in the past 150 years, stronger and better organized than the French: they *earned* the vote almost twenty years before their French sisters did. (Which was *two* years before *The Second Sex* came out.)

But a curious phenomenon is taking place. In the past two or three years, so-called French feminism(s), *as theory*, has become immensely fashionable, and the debates it is spawning are buoying up Anglo-Saxon critical debates (A metaphor which holds water if you imagine the spawn of French feminism as of the dolphin kind.) What annoys me about this is that debates tend to be reductive. Books and articles get written, which take up and *summarize* and *clarify*, while they're at it! particular *positions*, then explain what is wrong about them. Alas! many of us like playing skittles, in the academic world. Makes you feel you're somebody when you've bowled a particular alley clean. Can move on to the next one. Well, skittles are being put up, bowls are rolling at a great rate, and the people who've been at the game for a long time, who've even quite amorously polished the skittles they'd set up, which they then thought were beautiful, the new totems, are getting impatient, saying, OK, OK, we know it all, let's move on to other things. We're now in the era of post-feminism. There's even a Chatto collection of post-feminist women poets. It seems that, at least in part, we owe this notion of post-feminism to Kristeva herself. Well, Kristeva ought to go and blow her nose somewhere else. She's a wonderful lady and like everybody else I adore her cleverness but on occasion she ought to stop and feel a little. Know then yourself, etc. What am *I* doing when I write about love or faeces? Who was it that wrote those lovely things about supposedly endless progress turning into regression? The more a monkey climbs up a tree, as my hubby keeps reminding me, the more he shows his arse. We'll be in the era of post-feminism when we, of the two sexes, are a great deal wiser than we are now.

Indeed, as far as theory goes, what will come after post-feminism (as after post-modernism)? Post-post-feminism, post-post-modernism, then post-post-post-post, the farting of a motor-bike? Or antiquarianism? (Why not, Walter Scott was wonderful too, and at least he knew what he was doing.) Will women go back to the corset, or demand excision on the National Health? I hear Chinese women are getting their eyes operated on as in the good old days of, was it Pearl Buck? – so that the slant is attenuated.

When Arthur Symonds wrote *The Symbolist Movement in France* (1899), he put his own gloss on what he was writing about. But he had met the poets who were still alive, Mallarmé, Verlaine in his decay but still Verlaine. He himself was a poet, perhaps not a very good one, but passionate about poetry. His book inspired *poets*, Eliot and Pound and Yeats. When Stephen Heath wrote his article 'Difference' in *Screen* (1978), the psychoanalysts and writers he was presenting, Lacan, Luce

Irigaray, Michèle Montrelay, Eugénie Luccioni-Lemoine, as well as Cixous and others, were at it. Some of their books had just come out. It was a live issue. What is increasingly happening now in the literary market *re* feminism is rather like what happened in Cambridge when they got rid of Colin McCabe on the ground he was a Structuralist (so the story went in the media). We were treated to Sunday papers' summaries of this breathtakingly disturbing new thing, Structuralism – was it *thirty* years after Lévi-Strauss had published *The Elementary Structures of Kinship* – a book, incidentally, the consequences of which for women Simone de Beauvoir had discussed in *The Second Sex* in 1949! Talk about Making it New! I don't wish to suggest this is an Oxbridge phenomenon, for I know several people in Cambridge at least who have long been genuinely interested in, and kept in close touch with, French women's writing, theoretical or otherwise. But I do see it as a market (and perhaps institutional) phenomenon, that excitement is being generated about things which are in a sense *passé*, which have lost some of their momentum. And the further effect of vulgarizing them, making them fashionable as a supposedly cogent field of theory and/or research, is that it makes them unreal, bland – safe. And so perhaps, the phenomenon of 'capitalistic' recuperation of the subversive so often meditated upon by people like Raymond Williams and Frederic Jameson has here also set into motion. There certainly is capitalizing by academics of a younger generation on the work of their – foremothers. The 'Dora' case, for instance, had made the rounds. But it was placed centre-stage again in 1975–6 by Hélène Cixous's play *Portrait de Dora* and the Cixous/Clément book *La Jeune née*. Dora has this year come to us via the USA as a brand-new collection of articles ranging from the 1920s to today, but with neither Cixous nor Clément in it – though, to anyone who's followed the interest in hysteria, they're the ones who've given the debate its salt. Worse, Cixous, whose texts are never 'theory', not in those terms, which are generally oral to start with – and who has changed enormously year after year, book by book (is now writing Shakespearian history plays about Cambodia and India for the Théâtre du Soleil) – is having articles she wrote in the mid-seventies stolidly discussed as pure theory, as what she stands or falls upon, as what she is to be criticized and discarded by. So we get a digest of the real thing, instead of the real thing. Which would be: women (or men) making theory out of what they *actually* think about difference or gender or sexuality in the light of their *own* experience, of what and who they are, the very thing that Cixous did and does, or that Luce Irigaray also did. Theoreticians would be much better inspired taking to Plato *et al.* what Luce Irigaray begins in *Speculum* in her meditation on the famous cave, and on whether philosophy is gendered, than in summarizing what Irigaray says in *Speculum*. But then, it is costly to try and think with the whole of oneself, of one's life, rather than with one's (hermaphroditic, snail-like) brain. Helps if you can mount it on stilts.

(I should have this article illustrated by a cartoonist.)

So. The 'grande question' (as Candide's friend Martin would have said) is whether the present commercial vogue of feminism is the sign that it's become established, or that it's being smothered by means of academic respectability. Is it rising into the intellectual sky to become a constellation, a female Castor and Pollux, since at least French theory is double ('féministes' and 'des femmes') though there is no love lost between its twins? Is the wheel turning, are the gurus looking for new ways of being gurus, and is the last surviving revolution from the sixties in its last pangs? I find that hard to believe, not only because a large number of people have had their consciousness altered, if not their lives. Economically and socially, *some* changes have taken place, some laws been passed – though, as Christine Delphy keeps reminding us, women still own only 1 per cent of the world's wealth. But there are the signs, the increasing hostility, the triumphant vogue of both pornography and romance, the impatient daughters, the exasperated sons, the young old men, the New Right, the continuing recession, the 'you've never had it so good' and, 'look at women of the Third World' (as if quite a number of women's presses didn't), the Doris Lessing argument, 'such a small thing compared to the threat of the nuclear holocaust' or to world poverty, the 'after all there have always been strong women, remarkable women, but they didn't make such a song and dance about it'.

There is a French study on Virginia Woolf ('Les Ecrivains par eux mêmes'), written in the early 1950s, in which the lady author says of *A Room of One's Own* and of *Three Guineas* that they have stood the test of time badly. Progress has made them invalid. I have sometimes wondered what the author must have felt in the seventies, when *A Room of One's Own* in particular was spawning such a progeny. And how could she have written what she did? After all, it was only three or four years after *The Second Sex*, five or six at most since French women had been given the vote. Did she think such giant strides had now been taken that, give or take a few more years, and half the French National Assembly and ministers and big businessmen and professors would be women? Or did she just think she'd done well, she was educated, she was writing a book on Virginia Woolf, what more could women ask?

It took over twenty years for *The Second Sex* to sink in, or re-emerge, largely via the USA. It's taking about another twenty for it to sink again. And so it goes, with larger or smaller expanses of time, throughout western history. There are good periods for women, at least the women of the dominant class, and then there are bad periods. You have the French Précieuses and the ladies of the Fronde and Poulain de la Barre and the lady pamphleteers of the English seventeenth century – and then you have the shrinking curricula taught to the eighteenth-century bourgeoises and aristocrates, the impact of Rousseau's Sophie – then a glorious re-emergence with Olympe de Gouges (whom they didn't take long to behead) and Mary Wollstonecraft and Mme de Staël – another 'bad' period, the French Restoration, The 'Biedermeier' mood that forced Walter Scott to make un-pregnant the pregnant lady-knight of *Robert Count of Paris*, the Romantic Angels and Muses – and then there is 1848, and then the trial of *Madame Bovary*, and then there is 1871 and the Commune and Louise Michel and the debates between socialism and feminism – and so on. And when you read what the debates were about, what was said about women, it's mind-boggling how the same things return, again and again. Indeed, you could find the root of almost all the books I have mentioned in my, quite literally, sub-text, in *The Second Sex*. Theory: philosophy, anthropology, pyschoanalysis, biology, in the introduction and the first chapter. Then come history/ies, then myths, images, representations, then biographies, studies of education, fiction, even poetry. It's all there. The lady already had her famed genius for covering all the available space.

Feminism is like the worms in *Dune*, it keeps disappearing under the sand then resurfacing, and perhaps while it's deep under, it churns the magic powder that is the wealth of the empire. But in periods when feminism is buried or dormant, then presumably women find it normal not to be able to get jobs or education? Do they grumble individually, and that's about it, as Maggie Tulliver does in the Red Deeps or as Mrs Quest alias Doris Lessing's mother does with her female friends in unnamed Rhodesia? Or are they happy, better fulfilled, do they develop strengths and wisdoms that their rancorous or rebellious daughters lose, keen as they become to make it as women rather than as 'human beings'? In short, how is it that with the condition of women mutating and varying enormously, of course, but some basic things like power repeatedly evading them, there should be periods in which large or small numbers of women of one class or another become *aware* of this, and others when they don't? Is it a question of economics, and does the women's movement of the late sixties and the seventies 'signify' the novel access of unprecedently large numbers of middle-class women to the labour market, and the tensions built by this? The wise ones got on with it. The less wise jumped on horses and went through all the ideological hoops and got tired. The young ones are raking the sawdust and describing the show as the greatest on earth or just a bit of circus. Is it just that the pendulum will swing, or that the public appetite for what's new will make it tire of anything, regardless of its relevance? Are things so much improved? Do three hundred women sit in Parliament? What *is* fascinating is how, through what process, do people go back? How did women whom the French Revolution had freed from stays and *paniers* and high headgear and high heels you had to learn to balance on, having got used to flowing robes and comfortable slippers, decide one day that yes, corsets and crinolines that took at least half an hour and the help of a maid or companion to get laced into and that prevented running and even taking long walks were adorable garments they all wanted to wear? Is fashion so powerful as to be irresistible? Is it female narcissism? Eternal feminine giddiness? Oh dear, let's not be essentialist. Any more than biological. We all know that, like nets under trapezes, they're only for the faint-hearted.

How was it, to finally home in on Simone, that it not only took twenty years for *The Second Sex* to have its impact, but also that Simone herself, Simone who'd done it all, didn't somewhere know what she had done, and that she had done it? For she forgot. Left it behind. Then in the late sixties remembered. And yet, she had put as an epigraph to the second part:

> What a misfortune to be a woman! and yet the worst misfortune of all for a woman is not to understand that she is one.
>
> Kierkegaard

She had added another epigraph, Sartre this time: 'Half victims, half accomplices, like everyone else.' Perhaps she thought the very fact of having been able to write *The Second Sex* meant she was not a victim; and the fact of having written it, that she had ceased to be a blind accomplice in the victimization of women, herself included. And so, the misfortune Kierkegaard speaks about had been vanquished.

I well remember when *The Second Sex* came out. It made enough noise to reach the women of my family, which must have taken some doing, as it was not their kind of book. We were in the country house where the entire *gens* spent their vacation, grandparents, old relations, parents, uncle, aunt, cousins, my brothers, myself. And the maids. That's what provincial middle-class families used to do. My aunt read the book first, then my grandmother, then my mother. I don't think I was allowed to read it that time round, but I certainly read it not all that much later, and bits stuck. Or was it the bits the women of the house were discussing. As for men, perhaps my uncle read it, he was up to anything, he even read De Sade for medical reasons, but certainly my mother must have said, 'I mustn't let André see this, it'll upset him.' Which is also what she said after I'd taken her by mistake to see *Last Tango in Paris*. Discussions took place on the gravelled terrace where the women sat in the afternoons, knitting, mending, sewing, embroidering, by themselves or with the frequent visitors from the town, and we children played around, or scampered to the neighbouring pinewoods. The consensus was that it was an outrageous book, the work of an unbalanced woman, who wasn't a real woman in any case, who couldn't know what it was like, for she was not a Mother. Being a woman was being a Mother, and Simone's bit on that was ill informed and hostile. I remember my grandmother being half-indignant (she was big on Motherhood) and half-amused (she enjoyed anything bawdy and had no doubt spotted some juicy quotations). My mother was half-seduced but dared not say so, she was just limp in her attacks. My aunt was raucous, and eloquent. An intelligent woman who made a career out of the skilful deification of an imperturbably macho husband (an engaging fellow all the same), she must have been deeply aggravated to find all that she knew was best left unsaid, said. 'On ne naît pas femme; on le devient.' One is not born a woman; one becomes one. But of course! what need you go and let them know, you idiot! she must have thought. Years later, when I got married, she explained to me that all the art of being a wife lay in knowing how to boost your husband's ego. And I, poor fool, was contemptuous! Anyway, what particularly exasperated her was the discussion of a German attempt to build *pissotières* where women could pee standing, and it hadn't worked. Women, it was said, envied men for their ability to pee standing, to direct the jet as they pleased, and it was out of such envy that they so liked to play with hoses when they watered their gardens. My aunt used to enjoy watering the terrace in the evenings, when the Provençal heat abated, and direct the hose up and down the trunks of the horse-chestnuts that were the pride of the upper garden. She couldn't forgive Simone for having done that to her, and her delight in watering was impeded for some time.

It was a time when I used to write poems for the *males* of the family – my father, my grandfather, my uncle – my offerings for their birthdays. I wrote an ode about Adam, Eve and the apple and gave it to my uncle. It was to the effect that men were wrong to think themselves superior, the superiority was based upon the legend that Eve had made humanity fall. Not so: Adam had been the one. He'd rushed on the apple, snapped it from Eve and taken the first bite. The piece had stuck in his throat, and that was why men were branded, had a bulging Adam's apple on their necks, while women, who had simply followed suit, were smooth-necked. I don't know why I remember this. Not very startling, you might say, but it does make it clear that I resented being made to feel inferior because I was a girl. Not wanting to hit at my beloved father, whose power over me was almost infinite but not of the disciplinarian kind, and not wanting to beard any lions in their dens, I chose to be flippant, but went all the same for the most flamboyant male of the pride. And yet as I grew up I forgot I had felt this. Rather, I came to feel that it was best forgotten, a piece of puerile behaviour I had now left behind. As I was successful in my studies, I assumed I was 'human', was being allowed into the paradise of the intellectual elect, and I didn't see it was gendered like everything else. I now would love to know what Freud would have said to me if I had been born fifty-odd years before and had been sent to see him after Dora. I'm glad that in my scenario I wasn't the one left choking . . .

But Simone. She fought. She emancipated herself, bit by bit, as the *Mémoires d'une jeune fille rangée* (*Memoirs of a Dutiful Daughter*) narrate so lucidly, from the bourgeois values they had tried to instil into her. She chose a career. She entered Literature. She didn't become a wife and mother. Was that why she could write *The Second Sex?* And why, though she had fought like a wildcat, but also wisely, did she wait till she was turned forty to write it? And that, *after* Sartre had suggested it ('nobody's done it'), and at a time when she had been thinking of writing her autobiography. It was Leiris's *L'Age d'homme* which had given her the idea. *L'Age d'homme.* (Sartre's) *L'Age de raison. The Second Sex.* Second. Autobiography. Yet she's free. Is she writing about the others, then? A man suggests the title. *Le Deuxième Sexe.* 'La Seconde' has already been taken as a title by Colette. Who means something quite different by it. The second woman in Farou's life. They're equal, the first and the second, Fanny and Jane, just different. They're equal to Farou too. And it's also the second in which the infidelity is discovered by Fanny. But for Simone, second means second to first. 'The Other' to 'The One'. Yet she's a free woman. And she's doing it *in the place* of autobiography. Sartre's encouraged her. Sartre has sent his indefatigable beaver to chomp trees and pile trunks in the Bibliothèque Sainte-Geneviève. His beaver is building a dam, and he doesn't think that what she says about men thinking they're the ones etc. etc. concerns him at all. He's just intellectually interested. And in a funny way, while she feels concerned, all her reading is coming together, all the books she's read as an adolescent, Margaret Kennedy and Rosamond Lehmann and Colette, are all making a different sense suddenly, and what about Tolstoy, and look at Sophie Tolstoy; she, Simone, will do it all, go to the end of the road as she always does, as she will even with her mother's death and Sartre's death and, I am sure, she was a brave woman, her own, and all the time she is somehow writing about the *Others*. For she is no longer down among the women, she's escaped the condition, and her lucidity, her daring to go to the end and be so exhaustive is a sign of this. So she ceases to be 'second' while she writes *The Second Sex*. And, in doing so, she adopts the valuation of woman as 'second'.

And so, my aunt, and the other women in my family, were right to feel resentful. Wives and mothers all, submissive and yet powerful each in her own way, and the maids also, the maids who were of course much more oppressed (beside being the maid, one of them was there with her baby from a married man who had promised he would divorce his wife for her and then . . . and then she slaved at every kind of job to bring her son up, still reading the picture-strip romance magazines, *Intimité* and *A Tout Cœur* that had fascinated her as a young girl) – the maids, who had *not* read *The Second Sex*, and who were also powerful and brave women, how could they accept to see their entire existence read as a 'mystification' – the mystification that Simone felt followed her mother to the grave, that she even got to be an accomplice in, when by her mother's bedside she pretended to believe her mother would get better (*Une Mort si douce – A Very Easy Death*). For yes, the women of my family were right, not in the way they meant, but all the same: it had to do with motherhood. Not just becoming or being a mother, but one's relationship with one's mother, and the type of relations one is capable of.

For Simone, her mother meant claustrophobia. Repetition. Meaninglessness. She is eloquent in her vision of her mother in her cramped kitchen of their cramped Paris flat, when she sees her mother's life as an infinite series of identical little grey boxes. She, Simone, chose space, open space. Chose progress, which means diversity: her feeling of claustrophobia is repeated when she lies in a field of grass as an adolescent, and is horror-struck by the infinite series of blades of grass. Writers like Colette or Giono might have written many books out of such a field: repetition and a bad infinity may be in the eye that fails to perceive differences. But Simone chose to devour space. Project herself forward. When she worked as a teacher in the prewar years in Marseilles, my native city, she went on Sundays for mammoth walks through the neighbouring countryside. I was torn by mixed feelings when I read those sections of *La Force de l'âge* (*The Prime of Life*). I admired the phenomenal fitness ('Sartre and I were bursting with health', she keeps repeating, as he joined her on occasional visits and later when, during the war, they cycled a complete 'tour de France' on stolen derelict bikes). I admired the energy, the memory of the spaces she's covered – and I resented her feeling that she'd somehow got to know them and 'pass on' ('passer outre', as Gide's Theseus says). She doesn't know them at all, I thought. She just thinks that because she's covered the ground she knows them. And there is something ruthless about such walking. She describes how she leaves the companions that cannot keep up with her, another school-teacher in love with her, her own sister, exhausted, in local monasteries or inns, and pursues her intended course. Once a dog follows her, she's given it a piece of her *brioche*, but she has nothing else, no water despite the scorching sun, for her eight-hour walk. So the dog that keeps following her grows desperate, it begins to foam at the mouth, and she feels it's about to attack her as if it had contracted rabies when they luckily hit a village. Later, it is Olga, and the likes of Olga, young enough to be her daughters, and in love with her, who follow her. She is both attracted to them and exasperated. Once she throws Olga out and finds her in the morning asleep on her doormat. In *L'Invitée*, it is Françoise, her fictitious alter ego, who murders Xavière, Olga's fictitious double, to get rid of her. It isn't the dog that, in the end, bites.

Stride on. Read on. Go on learning, talking, doing it all, thinking. Write on. Thousands of pages later, at the end of *La Force des choses* (*Force of Circumstance*) there is an encounter with a mirror, and her own aged face. And several wonderful pages. Perhaps I was so moved by them, more moved than by anything else I have read by her, because that ageing image in the mirror is the one I'm grappling with at the moment. Also reading Colette's *La Naissance du jour*, it has struck me that it would be good to emerge the other side of the night with something like grace. But there it is. With Colette the end of the struggle coincides with a new dawn. The image she's inherited from her mother, an image she uses as a *model*, something ahead of her that age will enable her to approximate, is an image that turns ageing into a state that can be progressive, a succession of dawns. For Simone, ageing is that beginning of the end, the appearance of death. A little grey box from where a greying self beckons, when her whole life had been lived as progress, demanded an open future. Oh yes, she'd enjoyed herself, she'd had a wonderful life, a lot of pleasure of every kind, and yet somehow somewhere her body has been forgotten. She'd never liked her own looks. How can such a beautiful woman have liked her looks so little, I wonder? Did her mother never tell her she was beautiful? (Unlike Colette's mother, Colette.) Did Sartre never do so? Did she pay so little attention to her own beauty because he, being an ugly man, might have felt she had sources of pleasure he had not, and she wanted to have nothing he did not? Was she above narcissism because she was so bright, so projected forward? And yet, the projection still led her to the mirror. It led her to Villon's question, 'Where is it gone', 'le temps de ma jeunesse', where has my face gone? And there is the terrible final sentence, the statement that 'she's been had': 'J'ai été flouée.'

I feel she had estranged herself from herself. She wanted higher things, and she left behind the sex she thought of as second. She rejected her mother's state, her mother. She refused motherhood, in the spirit as in the flesh. Olga could sleep on the doormat. Xavière had to be killed. No one was going to come between her and her 'authentic' male counterpart, Sartre. How galling it must have been, how galling it was, when Sartre went for fatherhood or was it motherhood, and adopted a young woman for his daughter. 'J'ai été flouée.' Yes indeed.

What do I mean by 'her sex'? In a sense it is impossible to tell. Lacan has a point, though not necessarily the one he means. You cannot say '*la* femme'. To arrive at 'woman' within the field of logical thought, you've got to write another *The Second Sex* which making it second from the vantage-point of both writer and reader will preclude that she be *'la'*. But you can make suggestions in irreverent little ways. Such as, I love peeing crouching. Outside, in woods or fields or wherever. It smells lovely, the heat and the flow release the smells of ferns or moss or thyme or whatever. You see the details of leaves. You see the liquid run into the earth. It's just as interesting as, but of a different character from, directing the jet in playful arcs. And don't tell me this is biology. For these distinctions between 'biology', which is supposed to be deterministic, and 'culture', which is supposed to be fluid and amenable to human action, seem to me to be fatuous. There is nothing 'deterministic' about any of the human functions, in the sense that the range of experience they can release is infinite. *Vide Ulysses* for a good try at that kind of infinity. Or Cixous's *La*. There is also nothing biological that is not cultural in human kind, and vice versa.[1] Gypsy women and South American Indian women pee standing. I like to pee crouching because in my 'culture' that's what girls did. But the thing is, whatever you do, *do* it. Close to the earth, if that's what's you're used to, like the girls at the beginning of Wittig's *Les Guérillères*. Not inferior. Different. Reclaim peeing crouching, which doesn't mean you shouldn't enjoy playing with a hose, in the same way as Lawrence dares to make a male character, Birkin, roll in the primroses. You've got to break through the – call it 'logos' – to speak that thing called 'femininity', and doing it is not unlike what the Romantics or the Surrealists were after, except the borders are different, since gender, with all it entails, is here at work. But in my opinion, only *writing* that is in touch with the complete 'gendered' self is able to articulate it. Which is why approaching feminism as unifiable theory seems to me so counter-productive.

' "Of all the theories concerning women, none is more curious than the theory that it is needful to make a theory about them . . . We are driven to conclude . . ." that while men grow like trees "women run in moulds, like candles, and we can make them long-threes or short-sixes, whichever we please." '[2]

It is a symptom of the suppression of women that they have been cast into so many moulds, and have often (like my aunt) been more than glad to fill them. It is also a sign of their dynamism and power that they have made so much of the situation, so often ended growing inside their moulds, filling them with life and breaking out of them, not at all like candles but like the plants in the narrow-necked green bottle friends gave me last Christmas. It is perhaps equally a symptom of the surreptitiously continuing suppression of women that theory about women should be so welcomed by the powers-that-be, and that it should be again casting them into moulds: Anglo-American feminism, French feminism, gyno-critics, semiotic versus symbolic . . . We should do everything to break the moulds, break out of them, remember that what counts is growth, growth within as well as without. 'La femme' cannot be said. Women cannot be thought, and we should be glad of that: it does not mean that women cannot think.

NOTES

1 I am struck by the anecdote that old Amalia tells Colette, upon rereading *Le Pur et l'impur*. She tells how Loulou, Lucienne's brow-beaten lesbian lover, finally abandons Lucienne for her man-lover Hector, with a parting shot that is 'the most hurting' that she can find: 'he can do something that you can't . . . it isn't what you think. When we go out together as a pair . . . everybody takes you for a man . . . But for my part, it humiliates me to be with a man who can't pee against a wall' (quoted in Catherine van Casse-laer's lovely book, *Lot's Wife: Lesbian Paris, 1890–1914* Liverpool: 1986, p. 126). What they call 'la petite différence et ses grandes conséquences'.

2 Frances Power Cobbe, 1869. Quoted in Judith Lowder Newton's *Women, Power and Subversion: Social Strategies in British Fiction*, repr. in paperback, New York and London: Methuen, 1985, p. 2.

Part III

FORGING A FEMINIST AESTHETICS

8

Doris Lessing: of mud and other matter – *The Children of Violence*

I say I. I am going to say I. I claim the right to say I. Since I, a woman using language, am going to say what I find wrong with the language of a woman I admire, I will not shelter behind the anonymous array of third-person modes 'crrrriticism', by tacit agreement, requires. I will be no puppeteer of my own sentences. No ghostly judge arraigning my betters in the name of some assumed (fatuous) moral right. If I 'pass' 'judgement' (rather, it suddenly occurs to me, as one passes water, or a motion), I will also lay my own head on the chopping block. Then (to go on with what's turning out to be in worse and worse taste) my judgement may appear due to fear.

For my own life.

My own language.

The logic of the sequence: from mud to the void

The Children of Violence: what 'happens'

Martha Quest, 1952	Martha, born in Rhodesia of first-generation, ineffective English settlers, leaves home (in the 1930s) and goes to live in the city – Salisbury (though neither Rhodesia nor the city are ever
A Proper Marriage, 1954	given their actual name). Proceeds to search for herself, search for truth, justice, freedom, racial and sexual and social harmony (the four-gated city), periodically allowing her bewilderment,

A Ripple from the Storm, 1958 *Landlocked*, 1965

The Four-Gated City, 1969 (timespan: from post Second World War years to the year 2,000)

good nature, liberal convictions or peculiar passiveness to snare her into unwanted situations (her two marriages, the birth of her daughter, Caroline), but always escaping in the end without doing too much damage: not remaining trapped in what for instance she sees as the unreality and paltriness of her friend Marjorie's marriage. Proceeds through communism, committee activities during the war, the odd affairs with RAF officers posted near Salisbury, a deep involvement with a radical Jewish/Pole settler, Thomas, more committee militancy for racial equality, till she finally leaves for England. Once there, goes at an accelerated pace through every struggle of the liberal intelligentsia from resistance to the Cold War witchhunt to Aldermaston marches, caring for the drop-outs and the mentally sick, and surviving nuclear war. As she wends her way through cause after cause, there is an increasing feeling of unreality. Martha realizes that she, and everyone else from youth to age, spend their time stepping from one preordained role to another. A combination of breakdown and interest in mysticism finally delivers the vision that they all, not just the characters in the novel, everyone in England, in the world, are children of violence, acted upon by wave after wave of forces no one can control. Everyone is a succession of parts. Lives a partitioned, inauthentic existence. One can only escape from the violent impulses by plugging on to creative forces, developing new, mystical skills. Ceasing to play the game of violence. Withdrawing into a wise passiveness. The way for *Memoirs of a Survivor* is open at the end of *The Four-Gated City*.

The first thing to say about the sequence is that it is strongly autobiographical. In two ways: it is close to the 'events', the pattern, of Doris Lessing's own life; and the way Martha's vision of life evolves roughly corresponds to Lessing's own

120

evolution. That it is so need not be established by biographical research.[1] Strong evidence shows it: internal evidence – one feels the 'factual', the documentary quality of the novels despite the disguises, despite the (wavering) fictionalizing intention (at its strongest in the first two novels, where Martha tends to be entered into as a 'character'; at its weakest perhaps in *A Ripple from the Storm* and in most of *The Four-Gated City*, where Martha, instead of functioning as a mirror of the self, is much more of a (near transparent) window to look out of). There is also corroborative evidence from the other books: the documentary (*In Pursuit of the English, Going Home*) where one recognizes the veld, the house on the veld, the parents (their quality, the father especially, as 'grail-seekers' strongly confirming the 'quest' element of Martha),[2] and the fictional: Anna Wulf's African experience, her German husband, are very similar to Martha's; the visions of Emily's childhood in *Memoirs of a Survivor* spell out many things about Doris Lessing's family complex which are only half-expressed in *The Children of Violence*.[3]

There is nothing wrong or even unusual of course about novels being so strongly autobiographical. One could name scores of great novels which are. But a question immediately arises here, because of the *universal* significance which attaches to the factualness, the documentary 'truths' which are being presented: how does the 'fictional' form and the overall significance attached to it grow out of the 'documentary', the 'individual' 'truth'? And, in particular, how does the concluding position, the late Martha's wisdom, tally with Martha's earlier sense of life?

For she starts from mud. Warm African mud. Which is what at the start 'signifies'.

> The bush lay quiet about her, a bare slope of sunset-
> tinted grass moving gently with a tiny rustling
> sound . . . her flesh was the earth, and suffered growth
> like a ferment.
>
> (*Martha Quest*, pp. 61–2)
>
> This naked embrace of earth and sky, the sun hard
> and strong overhead, pulling up the moisture from
> foliage, from soil, so that the swimming glisten of heat
> is like a caress made visible . . . this frank embrace
> between the lifting breast of the land and the deep

blue warmth of the sky is what exiles from Africa dream of.

(*Martha Quest*, p. 252)

Mud. Sex. Mud is where Martha defends herself, her strong body, against the inroads of convention – clothes, marriage: propriety.

[H]e was agitatedly dancing on the steps, saying, 'Matty, Matty, do be careful'. There was something about that shrill and helpless exhortation which turned her mood into defiance. She looked calmly about her: there were six feet of muddy water between her and the gate. 'To hell with it', she [the text has 'he' – which must be a misprint] remarked; and fell all at once into her element. She lifted her crisp white skirts in a bunch around her waist, and composedly walked in her gold shoes, the water lapping cool around her ankles, to the sidewalk, saying, 'Oooh, it's lovely, it's lovely, Don', like a child paddling . . . She lifted her feet and examined them. The gold leather had dulled, and was crinkling; there was a faint brown tide-mark around her ankles. She could not help looking at them with satisfaction; the elegant, cool white dress seemed quite remote from her, a mere surface to her body, which continued strongly upwards from those reckless strong ankles.

(*Martha Quest*, p. 165)

She began taking off her clothes, with rapid clumsy movements. Martha did the same. They held the door half open, for a last look for any possible invaders, and then plunged across the road into the long grass on the other side . . . [Martha] almost ran into a gulf that opened under her feet. It was a pothole, gaping like a mouth, its red crumbling sides swimming with red water. Above it the long heavy grass almost met. Martha hesitated, then jumped straight in. A moment of repugnance, then she loosened deliciously in the warm rocking of the water. She stood to her knees in heavy mud, the red thick water closed below her shoulders . . . In the jelly spawn were tiny dark dots of life. She could see a large snail tilting through the

grass-stems . . . Then across the white-frothed surface
of the pool, she saw an uncoiling in the wet mat of
grass, and a lithe green snake moved its head this way
and that, its small tongue flickering. It slid down over
the red pulpy mud, and, clinging with its tail to a clutch
of grass, it allowed itself to lie on the surface, swaying
its vivid head just above the water.

(*A Proper Marriage*, pp. 153–4)

Mud comes into its own – the strong, healthy body finds
fulfilment ('Lawrentian' fulfilment, one cannot help but think,
since in a way and at this moment this seems to be very much
where the novels are going) in the brief affair with Thomas:

a young woman . . . lay face down on a rough bed,
dipping her arm in and out of the greenish sun-lanced
light below her as if into water . . . Martha turned on
her back to stretch her body's happiness in cool, leaf-
smelling warmth.

(*Landlocked*, p. 102)

Yet – yet, if one excepts this section of *Landlocked*, it is as if
mud disappeared from Martha's universe after the end of *A
Proper Marriage*. Strangely, in *A Ripple from the Storm*, mud,
grass, lush 'singing' African grass, is given to a passing character, Jimmy, *not* Martha: and the 'tiny dark dots of life' swarming in it are experienced as horrifying, not beautiful:

The grass behind him was a solid wall, grown to its
July strength, the sap no longer running, each stem
taut and slippery as fine steel, massed together in a
resilient antagonism [the text has 'antagonist' – which
must be a misprint] to his back. He swung himself
slightly; away from it and back again, and found
himself laughing out loud out of a deep startled pleasure
because of the toughness of the resisting grass . . .
And again his nostrils filled with a sweet sharp breath
of scent. His mouth fell open, his eyes stared and
glazed a little, his body was tense, trying to absorb
noises, scents . . . he had stared too long at the fine
black outline, because it had clotted, on the delicate
feather was a black knot. He blinked, hard and sharp,
hearing, just above him, a sudden outburst of noise, as

loud as machine-gun fire. And from behind his back,
in the grass-stems, another. He shifted uneasily, his
blood pounding, his nerves tight. He looked and
waited. All of a sudden he realized that the *black* knot
was an insect . . . My God, they were all over him,
large, horny beetle-insects, clumsily moving their feelers
and moving up over him. He let out a yell of fear, and
brushed them off with frantic hands.

(*A Ripple from the Storm*, pp. 150–1)

By the time of *The Four-Gated City*, Africa's of course been
left behind, there's no mud left anywhere. Anyhow. The disappearance of mud from the universe of the novels is bound up
(runs parallel with) the disappearance of the home. The mud
house. The childhood house. 'Roots'. They of course appear
most strongly in the prose of the directly autobiographical
Going Home:

the wall that faced my bed was not flat.
When the workmen had flung on the mud, naturally
it was a little bumpy because no matter how you
smooth on mud over poles, if there is a knot on the
pole where a branch was chopped off, or if the pole
had a bit of a bend in it, then the mud settled into the
shape of bump and hollow . . .
I knew the geography of that wall as I knew the lines
of my palm . . . The grain of the wall, like a skin, was
illuminated by the clear light. There were areas of light,
brisk graining where Tobias the painter had whisked
his paint-brush from side to side; then a savage knot of
whorls and smudged lines where he had twirled it
around. What had he been thinking about when his
paint-brush suddenly burst into such a fury of
movements? . . .
A young tree used to shoot up under my bed every
wet season. There was a crack in the mud there; the
linoleum began to bulge upwards, and then split; and
out came a pale, sickly, whitey-yellowish shoot which
immediately turned a healthy green. We cut it off; but
it sprouted up once or twice every wet season . . .
It was the ants, of course, who finally conquered, for
when we left that house empty in the bush, it was

only a season before the ant-hills sprouted in the rooms
themselves, among the quick sprouting trees, and the
red galleries must have covered all the walls and the
floor. The rains were heavy that year, beating the
house to its knees. And we heard that on the kopje
there was no house, just a mound of greyish, rotting
thatch, covered all over with red ant-galleries.

(*Going Home*, pp. 51–5)

This is also Martha's house (the kind of connection that makes
one realize how deeply autobiographical *The Children of Violence*
novels are):

[The house] was built native style, with mud walls and
thatched roof, and had been meant to last for two
seasons, for the Quests had come to the colony after
seeing an exhibition in London which promised new
settlers that they might become rich on maize-growing
almost from one year to the next. This had not
happened, and the temporary house was still in use . . .
The roof of the house too had sagged, and the walls
had been patched so often with fresh mud that they
were all colours, from dark rich red through dulling
yellow to elephant grey . . .
     In the middle of the floor was a pole of tough
thornwood, to hold the end of the ridgepole. It had
lain for weeks in a bath of strong chemicals, to protect
it from ants and insects; but now it was riddled with
tiny holes, and if one put one's ear to it there could be
heard a myriad tiny jaws at work.

(*Martha Quest*, pp. 20–1)

Martha is never described as being deeply attached to this
house. Yet, once mud is left behind by the novels, once the
mud house is lost, all sense of *home* is lost. I think that by
that, I mean the ability of things, people, to *signify*. Certainly,
nothing has a real *pull* upon Martha. Nothing is ever too much
for her: no house ever again has any weight of meaning:

That flat was bright, modern, compact . . . Coming into
it was a relief; one enters a strange place feeling, To
what must I adapt myself? But there was nothing
individual here to claim one's mood, there was no

need to submit oneself. In this country, or in England, or in any other country, one enters this flat, is at home at once, with a feeling of peace. Thank God! There are enough claims on us as it is, tugging us this way and that, without considering fittings and furniture; who used them before? What kind of people were they? What do they demand of us? Ah, the blessed anonymity of the modern flat, that home for nomads who, with no idea of where they are travelling, must travel light, ready for anything.

(*Martha Quest*, p. 178)

For me all houses will always be wrong; all bungalows, cottages, mansions and villas will be uncomfortable and incongruous and confining. I only like blocks of flats, the most direct expression of crammed town-living. I did not understand why this should be so for a long time, until I took to dreaming nightly of the house I was brought up in; and then at last I submitted myself to the knowledge that I am the victim of a private mania that I must humour . . . In order to find a place I live in tolerable, I have not to see it . . . If, in an unguarded moment, I actually see it, all of it, what it is, then a terrible feeling of insecurity and improbability comes over me. The fact is, I don't live anywhere; I never have since I left that first house on the kopje.

(*Going Home*, pp. 36–7)

True, a new home is temporarily re-created for Martha by her love for Thomas; it saves her from compartmentalization, that curse of the four notebooks: from the separate rooms:

She had complained that her life had consisted of a dozen rooms, each self-contained, that she was wearing into a frazzle of shrill nerves in the effort of carrying herself, each time a whole, from one 'room' to the other. But adding a new room to her house had ended the division. From this centre she now lived – a loft of aromatic wood from whose crooked window could be seen only sky and the boughs of trees, above a brick floor hissing sweetly from the slow drippings and wellings from a hundred growing plants.

(*Landlocked*, p. 103)

But soon that loft, what it signifies, collapses, while the old house on the kopje falls to bits: an image of Europe in ruins two years after the war; a warning of the future collapse of the city Martha is contemplating:

> Nearly a hundred miles away, in the red earth district, the old house had sunk to its knees under the blows of the first wet season after the Quests had left it, as if the shambling structure had been held upright only by the spirit of the family in it . . . It was wet and sultry on that hill, because of the heavy growth, although a thousand winds poured over it, and so walls and roof had rotted years ago in a fierce compost. The wet heat spawned, and the undersides of rafters sprouted fungus, and mosquitos bred in old shoes.
>
> (*Landlocked*, p. 196)

Thus, mud, home, are lost. Irretrievably lost it seems. Indeed, the apocalypse which closes *The Four-Gated City* simply fulfils what has already happened to the mud house, what is 'envisoned' as happening to Salisbury: 'Yes, this city could be like the minute, brittle, transparent cases that have held insects and now lie blowing about on the sand. It would be like the carcass of a stick insect.' Mud is lost. Leaving the orphaned, the children of violence, a prey to violence, the 'forces' of two world wars, the splitting of the atom, the Cold War, madness. The empty anonymous shells of London tenement flats where they learn in their turn to shed their shells, the flats whose walls fall off or open in vision, the people who, limb after limb, lose their 'personality', their illusions of selfhood. For evidently what happens to 'home' – alias mud, alias significance – in these novels is also what happens to 'character'. The tree at the beginning of *The Four-Gated City*, on a London bomb-site, has lost all 'tree-ness':

> This object had been a tree. For some days now Martha had been pausing by it, trying to make it out. Because it was hard to imagine it as a tree. Its surface was not smooth: if it had ever been planed, that smooth skin had been worn away long ago. Touching it was not touching wood, but nearer to water-eaten stone. It was almost spongy. Damp had swollen and filled every fibre.

Wood had meant a hand on a trunk under which sap
ran; wood had meant the smell of bark; wood had been
the smell of oiled surfaces where grain showed
patterns. Wood had never meant a great baulk of
greyish-brown substance that smelled of wet, of damp,
of rot, and of the gas which must have soaked
everything in this street since everything smelled of it.
(*The Four-Gated City*, p. 19)

The people are exactly like the tree; they have lost all 'people-
ness':

There were very few people indeed, in, or near or
associated with these columns of walking people
whose lives did not have a great gulf in them into which
all civilization had vanished, temporarily at least. There
was probably not one here whose life had, or could, be
[*sic*. proper syntax would have been: 'whose life had
been, or could be . . .] remotely like that one once
described by Thomas as 'being born under the elm
tree, living, courting, marrying, dying, being buried
under the elm tree.'
These were people who had all been stripped.
(*The Four-Gated City*, pp. 428–9)

Martha's voyage has its own sullen, uncompromising logic.
She goes from the complex mineral-vegetable-animal-and-
human 'life' of the mud house on the kopje to the anonymous
shell of London flats. From 'the individual to the collective,
from the personal to the communal, from the female to the
global, consciousness'.[4] The effort to make contact with world
reality takes the form (among others) of having the space of
one's room entirely plastered with 'world' information:

In his study he had put up two enormous maps of the
world . . . When Martha asked what they were for, he
said: Well, he thought perhaps it might be an idea to
see what was really happening – you know, *really*
happening.
One wall was soon devoted to atom bombs, hydrogen
bombs, large bombs, small bombs (what one committee
in the States had christened 'kitten bombs') and the
establishments which developed them, made them,

128

and sold them. Soon the wall was covered with little
red flags . . . With black flags, on the same map, were
marked the factories and laboratories which researched,
made and sold, materials for germ warfare . . . With
yellow flags, on this map, were marked areas of air, soil
and water contaminated by bomb blasts, fall-out, the
disposal of radio-active waste . . . Mark soon learned
how very little indeed was known by the men who
used these various techniques. For instance, the
movement of the air around our globe, which might
carry poisons of different kinds into the lungs and flesh
of humans and beasts, was not well understood.
Therefore this map could never be anything more than
approximate and rough.

(*The Four-Gated City*, pp. 308–9)

Whatever the complexities which the context of this passage
creates,[5] Mark's (and Martha's) attempt to relate to a 'world'
reality is part and parcel of, the means of furthering, Doris
Lessing's own evolution towards a collective voice. It is a
stage in that evolution equivalent to Anna's obsession with
newspapers, except that it is presented as more systematic and
less insane (the encounter with insanity is left to the Lynda of
The Four-Gated City:

Anna found that she was spending her time in a curious
way. She had always read newspapers, journals,
magazines in large quantities; she suffered from the vice
of her kind, that she *had* to know what was going on
everywhere. But now, having woken late and drunk
coffee, she would sit on the floor of the big room,
surrounded by half a dozen daily newspapers, a dozen
weekly journals, reading them, slowly, over and over
again. She was trying to fit things together. Whereas,
before, her reading had been to form a picture of what
was taking place all over the world; now a form of order
familiar to her had disappeared. It seemed as if her
mind had become an area of differing balances, she was
balancing facts, events, against each other. It was not
a question of a sequence of events, with their probable
consequences. It was as if she, Anna, were a central
point of awareness, being attacked by a million

unco-ordinated facts, and the central point would
disappear if she proved unable to weigh and balance
the facts, take them all into account.

(*The Golden Notebook*, p. 623)

Although the attempt nearly sends Anna mad it remains
that it is in some way a necessary stage, that it corresponds
to what Doris Lessing is trying to do herself, both in *The Golden
Notebook* and in *The Four-Gated City*, over the space of the novel.
Anna's endeavours mystically to 'conceive', open herself up
to, the world, are continuous with her creator's:

something from my childhood. I used at night to sit up
in bed and play what I called 'the game'. First I created
the room I sat in, object by object, 'naming' everything,
bed, chair, curtains, till it was whole in my mind, then
move out of the room, creating the house, then out of
the house, slowly creating the street, then rise into the
air, looking down on London, at the enormous
sprawling wastes of London, but holding at the same
time the room, and the house and the street in my
mind, and then England . . . then, slowly, slowly, I
would create the world, continent by continent . . . until
the point was reached when I moved out into
space . . . Then having reached that point, with the stars
around me, and the little earth turning underneath me,
I'd try to imagine at the same time, a drop of water,
swarming with life, or a green leaf. Sometimes I could
reach what I wanted, a simultaneous knowledge of
vastness and smallness.

(*The Golden Notebook*, p. 531)

In *The Four-Gated City*, the attempt simultaneously to know
vastness and smallness takes a different form, becomes a kind
of 'atmospheric' or 'biological' mysticism.[6] It has to do with
the lack of world knowledge Mark notices when pinning his
little yellow flags: 'The movement of the air around our
globe . . . was not well understood.'

'. . . where do the ideas come from?'
  'Oh', he said smiling, 'that's easy – I'll show you if
you like.'
  'Other space fiction', said Martha.

130

'Oh no', said Lynda, 'it's everywhere – all round you
if you can look, from the Bible to poetry to every
edition of every newspaper or if it comes to that how
one is oneself . . .'

'. . . you assume that to think something is the end
of that – a thought being self-contained, an end. Well,
it isn't.'

'. . . The only way that would be of some use would
be, not just throwing a pebble into a pool anyhow, so
that ripples go out, but one doesn't know how, but
knowing how to throw it so that the ripples go out
exactly as one foresaw'.

(*The Four-Gated City*, pp. 457–8)

Of course, Lynda's idea is as old, if not perhaps as the Bible,
at least certainly as Romanticism.[7] But within the context of
The Children of Violence, it consecrates the breakdown of the
personal. The self is a permeable place where impulses upon
the air reach and in their turn pass out. The self is a void: no
longer rooted, feeling the need to burrow into warm mud. The
Martha of the early novels has disappeared, leaving room for
the new Martha, a transparency, a porous medium.

Ah, you could say. But there are links between the old and
the new Martha. The 'old' – the young – Martha is presented
from the word go as playing the 'role' of a young girl against
two 'impersonal' 'matrons' – as she later, in *The Four-Gated
City*, will play the role of matron against two young girls. And
think back to your first quotation from *Martha Quest*. In her
end is her beginning:

The bush lay quiet about her, a bare slope of sunset-
tinted grass moving gently with a tiny rustling
sound . . . There was a slow integration, during which
she, and the little animals, and the moving grasses,
and the sunwarmed trees, and the slopes of shivering
silvery mealies, and the great dome of blue light
overhead, and the stones of earth under her feet,
became one, shuddering together in a dissolution of
dancing atoms. She felt the rivers under the ground
forcing themselves painfully along her veins, swelling
them out in an unbearable pressure; her flesh was the
earth, and suffered growth like a ferment . . . during

that space of time (which was timeless) she understood
quite finally her smallness, the unimportance of
humanity . . . it was as if something new was
demanding conception, with her flesh as host; as if it
were a necessity, which she must bring herself to accept,
that she should allow herself to dissolve and be formed
by that necessity.

(*Martha Quest*, pp. 61–2)

But the similarities are notional. For, in this passage, it is the
strength of the contact with the earth which is the bearer of
the mystical flight. In *The Four-Gated City*, it is the completeness
with which Martha, like everyone else, has been 'stripped',
which brings about the possibility of plugging into universal
forces. Martha the young girl is a fully fledged being, richly
rooted in a particular location. The young girls of *The Four-
Gated City*, barely exist as characters. A change occurs, not a
growth. What strikes me about it, is how compulsive and
repeated a change. One finds it spanning the whole of Doris
Lessing's work, exemplary: her first novel, *The Grass is Singing*,
is the most rooted in detailed loving knowledge of people and
landscape and things and social relations. *Memoirs of a Survivor*,
and beyond it *Shikasta*, the most detached, gutted. The 'transcendent' vision which is given to Mary before her death, in
The Grass is Singing, literally springs from, has been earned by,
the painstaking enquiry into the petty, the multifarious details
of Mary's life:

The idea of herself, standing above the house,
somewhere on an invisible mountain peak, looking
down like a judge in his court, returned; but this time
without a sense of release. It was a torment to her, in
that momentarily pitiless clarity, to see herself . . . And
time taking on the attributes of space, she stood
balanced in mid-air, and while she saw Mary Turner
rocking in the corner of the sofa, moaning, her fists in
her eyes, she saw, too, Mary Turner as she had been,
that foolish girl travelling unknowingly to this end. I
don't understand, she said again. I understand nothing.
The evil is there, but of what does it consist.

(*The Grass Is Singing*, p. 207)

DORIS LESSING

In a sense, Mary too is a child of violence: but the violence
that has made her into a bitter, petty, frustrated and ultimately
defeated and self-defeating racialist is the violence of white
Rhodesian society and beyond that, of western imperialism;
our understanding of Mary, of the 'impersonality' of her racialist hatred and violence and fear, are thoroughly informed by
the novel. The 'transcendent' visions of the narrator in *Memoirs
of a Survivor* may be informed by Doris Lessing's own childhood, and if they work it is because we feel a pressure of
untold things.[8] But in the explicit framework we are given,
they spring from nothing, they are gratuitous.

And this change, from rootedness to the void, repeats itself
inside *The Children of Violence*. Time and time again, not just
from the first novels to the last, but inside the novels themselves, the texts seem to feel the need to root themselves again
in Martha's body – then move, more and more, towards the
void. In a sense, it's all perfectly logical – all of a piece: once
you've lost mud (once you've moved from Africa to London?),
all you can do is pursue the void. Make yourself the void.
Burn through everything that promises significance, as Martha
does in *The Four-Gated City*, so as to be able to discard it. It's
all perfectly logical – even though one thought at first, as
perhaps Doris Lessing alias Martha Quest herself believed,
that a 'Lawrentian' rather than a 'Sufi' fate awaited the strong
healthy yearning girl.

My pole is full of ants. My mind is swarming. A myriad tiny
noises.

'Is there really no mud left four years before 1984?' I think.
Bitterly fighting it, the mud. Is there really no mud left in
London? Has Dickens's mud, the mud of *Bleak House* and *Our
Mutual Friend*, all gone? The Thames, after all, is now clean.
So clean, it seems, that all the 'matter' the London intelligentsia
has got left to dream about, is the Apocalypse.

Darling, you may think there is mud left, because you live
in some provincial backwater. But we do live in the age of the
nuclear deterrent, black holes, and silicon chips, you know.

Has the prose which could be mud, which *knew* about
matter, gone the way of all flesh? (and no grass singing).

What are you trying to say? This. The books that make up *The

133

Children of Violence go in one particular 'logical' direction: from 'mud' to the 'void'. Well, not quite so clearly as I have suggested: I have privileged 'mud' in my account; and there is no denying that Doris Lessing would not agree with my labelling Martha's wisdom, at the end of *The Four-Gated City*, a choice of the 'void'. However, the general direction is evident. It is also evident that the experience conveyed through the agency of Martha is meant to be 'representative' in a most ambitious way. We feel it is 'typical', the only honest vision possible; not just the results of temperamental, nor even moral, options. Proof of this, if any were needed, is that all the other 'wise' or 'representative' characters Doris Lessing created in the period roughly corresponding to the long-drawn writing of the sequence, from Anna Wulf to Kate Brown, go the same way as Martha.

From 'I' to 'We'.

Lessing obviously believes that 'I' has gone rotten:

> Some sort of a divorce there has been somewhere along the path of this race of man between the 'I' and the 'We', some sort of a terrible falling-away, and I (who am not I but part of a whole composed of other human beings as they are of me . . .) feel as if I am spinning back into a vortex of terror . . . and it is towards a catastrophe, yes, that was when the microbes, the little broth that is humanity, was knocked senseless, hit for six, knocked out of their true understanding, so that ever since most have said, I, I, I, I, I, I, I, and cannot, save for a few, say, We.
>
> (*Briefing for a Descent into Hell*, p. 120)

The 'jelly spawn' full of 'tiny dark dots of life' where Martha 'loosened deliciously' has become ludicrous: a collection of 'microbes', 'the little broth that is humanity'. It can no longer be celebrated as 'life'; it's got to be saved. The ambition informing Lessing's work, and especially the last volumes of *The Children of Violence* is absolute. It is to evolve from 'I' to 'We', carrying into 'We' all the old 'I's of the *Bildungsroman*.

Supposing, for the sake of convenience, I made a ladder – not a neo-Platonic ladder, a ladder rising from the particular to the universal – and saw where *The Children of Violence* fitted. It would be a pretty shaky ladder, of course, with more holes than wood, like all ladders. But it should help me see what tradition stands behind Doris Lessing, and what kind of ambition was hers.

Martha, unlike, say, Colette's Claudine, does not have a 'particular' fate.[9] She is not 'just' a girl who grows up, becomes a 'free' woman, moves from one kind of exile to another. She is that, of course, but is meant to be much more.

The next 'step' is the 'progress' of a Rastignac, or a Moll Flanders. They are 'typical' in that they 'represent' a particular class ethos at a particular time in the development of capitalism or of French history. Other young men can identify with Rastignac, learn from him, etc. But, though Balzac's novels may exhale a 'terrible *moralité*',[10] Rastignac's fate is not meant in itself to be 'universally' valid in 'moral' or 'existential' terms. Martha's clearly is.

So are the fates of a Julien Sorel, a Jane Eyre or a Maggie Tulliver. They have the particularity, the 'class' and historical 'typicality' of a Balzac hero. But it is also implied that they are bearers of values, that the values their creators construct by means of them are, however modestly and particularly these values may be expressed, and whatever the individual failures of the characters themselves, absolute and universal. Yet Martha is meant to be more universal than that.

A further degree in generality could be found in *A la recherche du temps perdu*. There, the narrative process, and the attempt to know, are the object and the agency, the end and the beginning, of the narrative itself. The contrast is extreme between the apparent 'means' and the 'end': between the obsessional, brilliant particularity of every piece of observation, every moment of time and turn of sentence, and the fact that a whole society and a considerable, continuous moment of history are actually being portrayed; between the eccentric, perverse, sickly, failed persona of the narrator and the universality his voice achieves.

And yet Martha is claimed to be more than that.

Resurrection could be regarded as going one better in that the wisdom achieved through – yet again – the particularity of Nekhùdov's experience is more mystical, and more propagandist, than anything in the novels evoked so far. The insight into 'life' is more pantheistic, roots the author more firmly in the Russian soil, the peasant soul, has therefore more – fluid

– extra sensory – implications, than are to be found in Stendhal or George Eliot. Yet it still all remains mediated by the particularity of Nekhùdov, his problems as land-owner versus peasants, etc.; there is no escaping from 'life' as 'we know it'. And that a certain kind of 'rootedness' should be implied anchors the novel in the specific. What, however, is striking about Martha Quest is that *she's been born uprooted*. That the metaphors that ultimately become significant for her are *weather* metaphors. 'A ripple from the storm'. The universality she is seeking, or her author through her, is one that wants *to get rid of the particular*.

By journeying through experiences and relationships (the sum total of her experience as woman, as lover, as political militant, etc.) Martha is meant to grow into a being who achieves a universal, absolute wisdom *through* access to the universal, not through development of the particular. It is through their *specificity* that Jane Eyre, Julien Sorel or Jude Fawley as individuals and members of a class, gain access to, or are the means of establishing, a particular but universally relevant, view of life. Martha, who seems to start with the 'particular' too, is presented more and more as a 'child of violence' like all the other 'children of violence'. And that comes to mean that all the particularity that the early novels have created comes more and more to be seen as irrelevant. It is implied for instance that the trouble in the affair with Thomas is 'determined' by mass forces – a ripple from the violence of Europe at war, racialism, etc., spreading to every consciousness. 'Usura steppeth between the bride and the bridegroom.'[11] The sequence is informed, or becomes informed, by a notion of the individual lost in the mass – as no more than an item in the series, basically. She/he achieves wisdom by coming to recognize this semi-scientific, semi-mystical, fact. By evolving from a 'mud' to a 'void' view of life. From fertile 'spawn' to a 'broth' of 'microbes'.

What I am trying to say is this. Not just that Doris Lessing wants to go 'one better' than the tradition of the *Bildungsroman* has done. But her subject-matter is 'modern' (or 'modernistic' – not everyone would agree to her view of consciousness) in that it becomes the discovery of twentieth-century 'mass' phenomena, and their interaction with the individual consciousness: world wars, totalitarian states, concentration camps, gulags, the cultural breakdown of relations between men and women, and the nuclear threat of universal holocaust.[12] *Yet* the novels are centred on the consciousness of a character which is largely portrayed like a nineteenth-century character. The social 'background', in Rhodesia as in London, at least at the start, is rock-solid. The adolescent Martha goes through fits of moodiness and rejection which are written about as if she were Emma, or Maggie Tulliver.[13] She's got all the baggage of the traditional fictional heroine. A distinct physique, a temperament, a very decided character, clothes, a family. She is located in all possible senses – socially, geographically, racially, historically – with the utmost precision. You name it, she's got it. She's got to have it all, because her author wants to 'do' it all – objects to all that Virginia Woolf leaves out.[14] The one thing she's got little of, but more about that later, is childhood.

Well, you could say. She's got it, and learns to shed it all, bit by bit, to arrive at wisdom. To actually understand what's been the matter with her. In *The Four-Gated City*, Martha, dealing with a household of troublesome teenagers, and informed by a new realization of the forces of violence, comes to see her own adolescent throes (or the reader can choose to see them retrospectively) as (a) produced by uncontrollable universal forces, and (b) the particular skin, role, every adolescent has to wear and shed.

Question is: can you use one mode to establish another? Can you *move* from the particular *to* the universal? (Rather than, as the nineteenth, etc., century had done, posit the universal *through* the particular.) Or move from the universal particular to the universal universal within one framework and equipped with the same language?

Can paddling in the mud – creating 'traditional' characters, using a prose that solidly establishes the 'existence' of a particular kind of social realist world – ever lead you convincingly to the void?

In other terms: I don't *believe* that the logic at work in those novels is right. And I think, if these texts created a truly *compelling* logic, I would be more inclined to believe them. And I think that all sorts of gaps and unresolved contradictions occur throughout.

Hold. What gave you in the first place the confidence to try to read *The Children of Violence* as a whole? To sum it up, in the first place, as if it were *one* novel?

Well: they follow from each other chronologically; in terms of recurring, 'realistically' presented characters; their time-span corresponds to 'historical' time (there is all the 'chronological' weight of world events to give authority to private events and individuals in them); and each novel is presented as yet another (a further) stage in the evolution of Martha. They have an overall title, *The Children of Violence*, which suggests they are moving towards, or informed by, an overall vision. That vision is being investigated through a central character whose surname is *Quest*. Furthermore, not only, as I have said, does the material of the experience of Martha Quest correspond roughly to Doris Lessing's own experience (geographical, emotional, political), but all the novels have been written quite some time after the event. By which I mean the author (like Proust) was not only in a position in which she could 'see it all' from a distance, but also decide (as she obviously did) that she was going to tell it all in the light of the wisdom gained after the event. Decide to narrate the search for, not so much 'temps perdu' as meaning, in the light if not of 'temps retrouvé', then time ahead. The experience that is presented in the first four novels was over and done with by the time Lessing started writing the sequence (by 1952 she had been in England already for some time). And most of the experience in the last volume, *The Four-Gated City* (if one excepts the final year–2,000 section) was also quite some time 'behind' by 1969. She did decide to organize her experience into a sequence rather than try to present it through a series of different novels.

What this account of course excludes is that there might have been a change of heart, a change of vision, in between the writing of the first few volumes, and *Landlocked*, and, even more, *The Four-Gated City*. Perhaps even between the first two and *A Ripple from the Storm*. But then, there we are. Precisely. How do you reconcile the existence of a claimed overall logic (manifested by all I have just said, the novels being written *as* a sequence) and the author changing her mind in the course of the writing?

One could go about it that way: show what the difference in the subject-matter and organization of each volume does to the overall logic (e.g. *A Ripple from the Storm* is much more concerned with general political issues, much more 'impersonal' than *Martha Quest* or *A Proper Marriage*). But this is so obvious as to be hardly worth doing. Furthermore, in itself it would be no argument against the existence of an overall 'logic'. *La Prisonnière* is different, in all sorts of ways, from *Le Côté des Guermantes* or *Un Amour de Swann;*[15] yet each contributes to the 'logic' of the whole.

I could try another line of argument, which would be equally concerned with form. To a large extent, the 'vision' which Martha throughout is striving for, is an *existential* one. Indeed, the meditation on the tree on the London bomb-site which I quoted earlier reminded me, while I was writing it down, of Roquentin's own meditation on the root of a tree in Bouville public garden, in *La Nausée*.

But. From the word go, in *La Nausée*, all the 'realistic details', from pebble on the beach to Roquentin's contemplation of his own face and the Autodidacte's 'humanism', are suffused, made unstable by, the phenomenon of 'nausea'. So that the process of 'discovery' of the fundamental alienness of *'pour-soi'* and *'en-soi'*, mind and nature, is continuously being catered for by the text. This is not so in *The Children of Violence*. The writing on the mud house is informed by a different sense of reality than the writing on the bomb-site. It is because experience has changed (Martha is older, she's left Africa, the war has occurred and destroyed parts of London) that the vision is different. Not because a more exact or deeper reading of reality has been arrived at; nor because life's caught up with itself. And yet that is what we are implicitly asked to believe.

Come on. All you've said is that *The Children of Violence* are not an 'existential' novel as you had thought (wrongly), or that if they are, they are so in the sense that they show the evolution, the capacity for change of the human being, the capacity to adapt to new circumstances, to be part and parcel of the great process of *surviving* (no mean art after all these days). And who says 'consistency' is a good thing? Who is the writer worth his salt who has not claimed the right to contradict him/herself? Take the nineteenth-century novel: it is full of the most strident, artistically unresolved, but *exciting* contradictions: from Scott to Anne Brontë to Mrs Gaskell to Dickens not to mention Balzac. There is a whole critical industry that thrives off theorizing on them. Doris Lessing's changes of heart, as you call them, are justifiable, praiseworthy even. All the more justifiable as the novels were written over such a long period: she herself must have changed very much. She did change: she owns as much in the preface to *The Golden Notebook* (1962), which was written in between *A Ripple from the Storm* (1958) and *Landlocked* (1965):

> At last I understood that the way over, or through this dilemma (there was no way of *not* being intensely subjective), the unease at writing about 'petty personal problems' was to recognize that nothing is personal, in the sense that it is uniquely one's own . . . The way to deal with the problem of 'subjectivity' . . . is to see [the individual] as a microcosm and in this way to break through the personal, the subjective, making the personal general, as indeed life always does.
>
> (*The Golden Notebook*, pp. 13–14)

The fact that Lessing should have chosen to embody these changes in the same heroine – Martha Quest – makes a lot of sense, too. We're not just dealing with the tradition of the *Bildungsroman*, you know. Change – the picaresque – is ingrained in the very notion of questing. And Lessing did – does – believe in the necessity of a reconciliation between change and coherence.

> Literature must not capitulate and succumb to an inability or a refusal to fit conflicting things together to make a whole; so that one can live inside it, no matter how terrible: the refusal means one can neither change nor destroy; the refusal means ultimately either death or imprisonment.[16]

You haven't understood. I'm not saying that change is not a good thing. That age, sorrow, war after peace, do not change you. Nor am I saying necessarily that one should abandon the struggle for coherence, be it 'formal' or existential'. What I am saying is that you cannot have it both ways. You can't posit a structure in which everything follows from everything else and wisdom claims to be, as it were, logically deducible from the whole, and have actual *change* occur inside it. Or you only could if you did it. I mean, if the overall structure, the voice,

had the capacity of integrating, the all-inclusive capacity it *says*
it has, instead of proceeding as it does from hand to mouth.
You can't make a compelling whole unless it is an actual
whole. It is, I suppose, a question of *form*.

But who says the 'whole' is not there? Who says the end is
not in the beginning? We've already had this one out, but you
haven't convinced me. Elements of Martha's late 'mysticism',
her understanding of 'role-playing', are there from the start.
There are signs of what is going to happen. In the same way,
as at times, for instance when they enjoy solitude on heights,
Stendhal's Julien Sorel or his Fabrice have intimations of the
'contemplative' state that will ultimately satisfy them, though
when these states first occur, they are intent on Tartuffe-esque
or Don Juan-esque ambitious careers. They have not got to the
stage when they can catch up with themselves. Understand
what they 'want'. In the same way, you could say, Martha's
final discovery of the futility of the 'personal'; Doris Lessing's
attempt, in her later novels, to show the shallowness of
'psychological realism', could be read in the tradition of the
'philosophical' novel. The self discovers itself to be elsewhere
than it thought it was – and the discovery is all the more
impressive as it has been achieved at the author's deeply felt
cost, as well as at that of her heroine.

Sorry. That argument is not really tenable. It makes sense
theoretically, but the texts don't bear it out. The *fact* that
changes of heart are shown to occur in the course of the
sequence means that they are not integrated. And they are
not, cannot be, integrated, because the voice from the start
claims to be inclusive. There is a totalizing intention written
into every line of the prose. And it is because of this that one
cannot allow the contradictions and lapses to go their own
way. Or to signify in the way that, say, gaps would signify in
a Balzac, or a Stendhal novel. In the famous passage in which
Julien Sorel goes to kill Mme de Rênal and in which nothing
whatever is recorded of his state of mind, the very absence of
verbal matter acts as infinite wealth. Whichever way you
choose to interpret it, you know that the truth of the character
lies also in what cannot be made explicit – in the non-written
as well as in the written. But then Stendhal's prose, his way
of jumping from chapter to chapter, of moving across time,
has made that kind of interaction between the written and the

141

non-written, black and white (or red), possible. There is an abundance of absence, of 'more'. Nothing remotely like this occurs in Doris Lessing's prose. You are never given to understand that there is more to Martha than the text gives you – because whenever there is going to be more, or there has been more, the text is going to tell you. Reread any of the passages quoted so far: as you read them you know that the authorial consciousness, either through, or in default of, its characters, claims to be complete.

And this is why it cannot afford contradictions. The changes of heart flaw the coherence which the confidence of the tone and the progress forward parade. It cannot allow gaps to exist: they might pull the text some other way than it is intended to go. That is perhaps why all of Martha's dreams are so clear, readily and totally interpretable. Darkness, unintentionality, are not allowed in.

Yet they are there. The gaps, the contradictions, are everywhere.

ROOTS: CHILDHOOD, AFRICA, THE BODY

Childhood

The baby was desperate with hunger. Need clawed in her belly . . . She yelled inside the thick smouldering warmth . . . She twisted and fought and screamed. And screamed – for time must pass before she was fed, the strict order of the regime said it must be so: nothing could move that obdurate woman there, who had set her own needs and her relation with her baby according to some timetable alien to them both . . .

Perhaps I would have done better to have begun this chronicle with an attempt at a full description of 'it'. But is it possible to write an account of anything at all without 'it' – in some shape or another – being the main theme? Perhaps, indeed, 'it' is the secret theme of all literature and history, like writing in invisible ink between the lines, which spring up, sharply black, dimming the old print we knew so well.

(*Memoirs of a Survivor*, pp. 135–6)

Martha Quest, most bizarrely for a fictional heroine who is

given five volumes over 2,000 pages – more, if one counts *Shikasta*, etc. – has virtually no childhood. What there is of it is the passage on the mud house, which I have quoted earlier; and there are a few, very few, reminiscences, generally of clashes with the mother. Now there are all sorts of excellent extraneous reasons why this should be so. The best, which I can easily sympathize with,[17] is fear of offending one's parents or close relatives by writing about them, a taboo which for all sorts of reasons seems to be felt by women even more than men. It is surely no accident that Lessing's first *actual* foray into infancy and early childhood should be in *Memoirs of a Survivor*, the work of a 'mature' woman, where one feels that perhaps through the deaths of loved ones she has left a great deal behind, has been somehow released. In any case, that's none of my business. But the absence of a childhood *signifies* in Martha Quest's progress in ways that the text, because it claims to be inclusive, does not cater for. There is no getting out of this: writing in invisible ink only functions successfully in a text if that text is prepared to allow absence, silence, to function.

As it is, there are two – related – areas where the 'gap' seems to me to show. The first is Martha's quite 'specific' temper; her combination of daring and passiveness, of generous courage, recklessness even, and bad temper; the contradictory ways she allows herself to be trapped – and yet never to be trapped; her strength of feeling and continuous cool observer's detachment: what makes her into a writer, of course, except that she's never allowed to become one.[18] It is all 'rooted' in a specific childhood and parentage, but we're never allowed to look far into that: our attention being instead concentrated on the fact it's all 'roles', impersonal. And it becomes more and more so, Martha finally having most of her 'character' ironed out of her in *The Four-Gated City*. Yet there is an area which does not allow itself to be quite so easily ironed out. It's Mrs Quest, the awful, hopeless, exasperating Mrs Quest. For me, she is the most alive of the characters of *The Children of Violence*. And I think this is because the text somehow feels repeatedly compelled to give her passages of her own, passages which are rather unsuccessfully controlled by the author – and are presented as outside Martha's consciousness. It's as if the author wanted to be 'fair', to be 'sympathetic', but could not help showing Mrs Quest to be really as exasperating as Martha finds her. And the tension that is set up (which I, and probably many other readers, feel must be informed by Doris Lessing's own tussles with her mother, seething areas of frustration and resentment) comes to a pitch in *The Four-Gated City* when news of her mother's threatened visit to England precipitates a breakdown in Martha. Mrs Quest's 'point of view', her inner world, is presented there, her maiming youth and experience, her neurosis, her evolution towards 'wisdom': her own discovery of 'role-playing' (on lines parallel to Martha's own discovery of the same thing) which, it is suggested, makes it all the more ironic that Martha and she could not communicate, but that's yet another face of the 'violence' syndrome, the text goes on to suggest: evading its own neurosis in relation to the mother. For me, that neurosis makes it the most real 'relationship' of the whole sequence. But neither Martha nor her author are, of course, prepared to accept that that is where significance lies – more, perhaps, than in reading six daily newspapers and twelve weeklies at a go, or in watching Aldermaston marches. Marguerite Duras knew it, who felt Hiroshima on her own pulse, through a love story. And Virginia Woolf, of course, who explored the impending violence of war through a country-house play, in *Between the Acts*.

Politics aren't necessarily in the newsreel.

Africa

But perhaps Martha's lack of childhood represents the colonial situation. The white settler's point of view: the passing implantation of an English family in an African landscape. Martha is doomed to the nomad's flat because she's been *born* uprooted. Doris Lessing herself could only write about the childhood house once she'd left Africa, was settled in London, and briefly revisited her native country: in *Going Home*. The passages on the house in *Going Home* are much better realized, as I think should have been obvious when reading them, than the passages in *Martha Quest*. Peculiarly, it is only in *Going Home* that, through the passing figure of Tobias, the painter, an actual *labouring* African appears. The first four volumes of *The Children of Violence*, though they are preoccupied with racial issues, though the existence of the many white characters who appear is based on the *labour* of the black Africans, ignore that labour. Only the odd 'house-boy' or cook or nanny or waiter is shown, but hardly ever in a *working* situation. Even in *A Ripple from the Storm*, where the 'Marxists' go visiting black townships and distributing pamphlets, actual encounters with blacks are kept to a minimum. *Africans*, in the four novels that take place in Rhodesia, are there like children, who ought to be seen and not heard: worse, they are barely seen at all. Oh yes, they are occasionally perceived from the corner of the eye: a black driver, a child crossing a street, people crowding in at a meeting. They are crusaded for, with a wide-eyed realization of the futility of white liberal efforts. Racial prejudice is neatly caught on many occasions, all shades of it; from the landlady who lives in paranoiac terror of her house-boy murdering her, to Judge Maynard's infiltration of the leftist group by the only black member, who happens to be his spy. But if you reflect that the proportion of black people to white in Rhodesia is of more than ten to one, it becomes slightly surprising that the proportion is the reverse in the novels: surprising, not perhaps in itself (this must be how it was: blacks and whites just did not, could not, mix), but because of the 'totalizing' ambition of the texts, because you feel all along that it is some kind of all-inclusive statement that is being made. Also, the blacks in those novels are nearly always presented as ideas, as causes. Hardly any of them have any individuality at all. *Yet* in the period in which Doris Lessing was writing *The Children of Violence*, she was also producing the volumes of African short stories (to my mind, some of her finest work). Why did she thus have to partition the material? And how could she hope to represent an inclusive consciousness in the character of Martha when all the time she made her blind – I don't mean *ideologically* blind, I mean blind where it really matters. For instance, the whole 'sexual' dimension which haunts *The Grass Is Singing* is totally ignored, bracketed, in *The Children of Violence*.

The partitioning is not simply between the African short stories (or *The Grass Is Singing*) and *The Children of Violence* sequence: it is there in the novels themselves. Those extracts now about 'mud', and 'grass'. On reflection, it is no accident at all which gives Jimmy the only 'real' 'mud' experience after

145

A Proper Marriage; which makes two *men*, Jimmy, then Thomas, take over what, until then, had been Martha's susceptibility to 'mud'. Jimmy's experience of course is *the* white man's experience of Africa: the drive to explore, to surrender, the sense of, yes, this is it, followed by terror, 'the horror', at the life that is discovered there; and rejection by the life that is there: soon after the discovery of the myriad beetle in the grass, there is the awfulness of the African township, the squalor; the poverty; and the exclusion of Jimmy. He is white, he is the enemy. Despite all his fraternal socialistic goodwill, there is no way in which the Africans can accept him. Thomas goes to the extremes of that exclusion, he goes to die among Africans. But why did Doris Lessing keep this on the outskirts of her novels? Why did she have to give this central experience to one of her most peripheral characters, Jimmy, or make Thomas die in a way that is not shown, simply reported? Why give the experience to *men* rather than to Martha? Because women could not have it? Obviously they could: Mary Turner dies of it. Martha survives because Doris Lessing survived: left, *chose* something else. But then Martha should not be presented as having somehow exhausted the potential of the situation. Doris Lessing survived because she wanted to become a writer, because experience was for her a means to something else which is the only possible key to Martha's redirection. In fact, the African short stories and *The Children of Violence* are written from a position that is partitioned into rooms, notebooks – that very position which *The Golden Notebook* denounces.[19] Presumably the author is not herself aware of this particular partitioning, for if she were, how could it still affect *Landlocked*, published three years after *The Golden Notebook?*

In fact, choices are continuously being made, but they are not acknowledged as choices. For instance, if you think about it, you realize that Doris Lessing has two ways of writing about beetles: the way of the Jimmy passage, and the way of 'The Sun between their Feet'. Beetles can be the strange, horrifying creatures they are to Jimmy; or, as the dung-beetles in the African short story, beautiful, obstinate creatures, lovingly observed, battling on uphill, the shade of Sisyphus across their path, the very image of ongoing life. Maybe Jimmy is horrified because he is English, not used to this nature. But what about

Martha? She's been born there. How come, after her immersion in the red mud hole in *A Proper Marriage* it never occurs to her to wonder if there is no significance for her in this land? For instance, there could be two ways of looking at Marjorie. As Martha does – sympathetically, or course, and with an awareness of the futility of sympathy, as a fool who has allowed conventional pressures to trap her into a soul-destroying marriage. Or as the narrative voice of 'The Sun between their Feet' does – as the obscure heroine of everyday life, battling on with the mud she rolls uphill between her feet: the dung-beetle which is also a sun-beetle. But that contradiction is not allowed to appear. You know that if you want to think about Marjorie in other ways than Martha does, you're extrapolating. And yet I feel that the sense of life offered in 'The Sun between their Feet' ought to have been allowed to clash with the other, the sense that significance is elsewhere, in Europe, that you're getting near it by selling leaflets about the Red Army.

One must return to it – to Martha – Doris Lessing having been *born* uprooted, to her 'world view' springing directly from the white settler's situation. Among other things, he/she has no roots in Africa because his/her 'past' there is so small: he/she has little historical or cultural relation to the land and its people. Of course, the people themselves, the black Africans, have in a way no 'culture' either. They have no 'history' that could be 'written', and they, or at least those who are shown in the sequel, have lost touch with any tribal/oral traditions they might have had. One of the most interesting moments is when Johnny Lindsay attempts to record working-class experience in South Africa, by 'telling' it to people who *write it down* for him. Only, it is *white* working-class experience. There is nobody to tell (let alone write down) black experience, and when black Africans come to the whites for education, for 'culture', it is only white culture they can be given. *Sense*, therefore, necessarily, is *elsewhere* for the white: in Europe largely. It is also elsewhere for the blacks. Awareness of this is brought to the white people – to Martha and her 'liberal' friend – by the distrust and distance of the black people: but we are not shown the relation as 'happening'. There is no consciousness in the novels which is *shown* as *experiencing* estrangement, as Mary Turner is in *The Grass Is Singing*. We are shown people – Martha, mainly – having an *awareness* of estrangement, of political impotency. But the core of Martha's experience is not what it *ought* to be, in the sense that it *is:* her *relation* to the Africa of her birth.

This 'white settler' position is also, of course, the source of Martha's – of Doris Lessing's – strength. Belonging, in terms of 'sense', nowhere, her relation to the world of sense, to language, is one of absolute freshness. People have often remarked on the extraordinary thing that happened when Olive Schreiner first used English words to convey the presence of an African landscape. The words of a faraway culture were suddenly alighting upon a veld that had for thousands, perhaps millions of years, existed without them. This is also relevant to some extent to Doris Lessing writing about Rhodesia: the bush, the house on the kopje, even the towns, were also largely innocent of 'English' writing. But it is also true in relation to 'English' as a European 'culture' – medium of culture. She was (she still is?) outside it. She was born an exile from it, as much as from Africa. This has turned out to be a prodigious source of strength for her. It has given her the freshness of an outsider in relation to traditions of writing. She has come in particular to the language of 'realistic' writing without the weight of an inheritance. The nineteenth-century novel, as she discusses it in the preface to *The Golden Notebook*, is for her ageless. As if time were spatialized, the 'tradition' a panorama towards which she could reach out at will. Joyce and Kafka are no closer than Tolstoy. (Yes, there will be Musil later on, but for different reasons).[20] Time has no depth[21] at least until *Memoirs of a Survivor*, and she, Lessing, is in some strange way innocent of meaning. She is equal to anything. A natural nomad, she can take anything on, for she belongs nowhere, and sense is always elsewhere: she does not have to contend internally with it. Hence, perhaps, those crystal-clear dreams. She has chosen herself as a being without a subconscious. Estranged equally from the dark continents of childhood, of Africa and of an inherited *incorporated* culture.

But this is because a *choice* has been made. She could have chosen to belong. Perhaps, of course, that would have meant choosing to die, like Mary Turner or Thomas. Perhaps that would have made writing impossible. But there is no denying there was a choice. She chose to leave. The text of *The Children of Violence* chooses to ignore that it is informed by detachment rather than rootedness. It claims to be inclusive when it is exclusive. Like its heroine, it chooses exile, and claims there is only truth in exile. There is truth in exile. The *only* truth? Martha chooses to become a grail-seeker. A Quest. She chooses the way of the father.

Of the body, the female body

I can smell you from a mile. Stinking to high male heaven. You're going to speak of the 'feminine sentence'. Virginia Woolf. Fluidity. Tradition passing on through the mother. Etc. Etc. Lord preserve us. All right. You've won. I won't. The way of the father, you say. Come come. Only of the father? *Both* parents are referred to as 'grail-seekers' in *In Pursuit of the English*.

Yes. But isn't the father's eccentricity so much more heart-warming than the mother's? Isn't the father, *not* the mother, recognizable as the source of the daughter's – I was going to say, 'eccentric' – centrality? And I don't think one can deny the point I've made earlier – that Mrs Quest pulls like unease, neurosis even, at the text. The mother is never chosen: she is avoided, rebelled against, fled from, even when she is actually closest.

'We relate to tradition through our mothers.'[22] This is not true of this particular daughter.

The Golden Notebook, because it was received by readers and critics as being essentially about 'women's liberation' and because the central character there is a *woman writer*, poses the question of femininity more directly than other works by Less-ing: 'this attempt on my part assumed that that filter which is a woman's way of looking at life has the same validity as the filter which is a man's way.'[23] But the assumption is taken to be right. The preface, written over ten years later, in the full swing of the women's movement, is impatient of the attempts made to drive the novel into the 'women's' fold. Yes, dearies, it implies, I beat you to it by ten years and straightaway saw beyond it, how paltry it all really is. On to higher things.

Spite. Nasssty. OK. I'm sorry.

And yet. Are women writers altogether free to 'choose'

between a 'feminine' style and a (presumably to be called so, since there are after all only two sexes) 'masculine', 'freer' one?

> [*The Trinket Box*] . . . – intense, careful, self-conscious, mannered – could have led to a style of writing usually described as 'feminine'. The style of *The Pig* is straight, broad, direct; is much less beguiling, but is the highway to the kind of writing that has the freedom to develop as it likes.[24]

I'm not trying to be prescriptive. I don't know any of the answers. And they're all necessarily dependent on what Luce Irigaray says: 'For in fact, we do not exactly know what "masculine" language is. As long as men claim to say everything and define everything, how could we know what the language of the male sex is?'[25] And all efforts to define a 'feminine voice' come up against the fact that the search for a *different* voice characterizes all 'modernist' or 'avant-garde' texts – which are being written by men as well as women: 'I do not find it easy to define a masculine or feminine specificity when I think of the great aesthetic experience of the decentering of identity,' Kristeva says. If that formidable theoretician can't, not many can.[26]

Yet women who want to write are, whether they know it or not, confronted by formidable taboos: I use this particular bit of Lacan as examplary of all that Simone de Beauvoir sums up in *Le Deuxième Sexe* as well as of a great deal of what has come out of Freud and Structuralism:

> There is no woman but excluded by the nature of things which is the nature of words, and it has to be said that if there is one thing about which women themselves are complaining at the moment, it's well and precisely that – it's just that they don't know what they are saying, which is all the difference between them and me.[27]

Those women who – think they know what they are saying? – have taken stock of this:

> This is precisely what is at stake, always, in feminist action: to modify the 'imaginary' so as to be able then to act upon reality, to change the forms of language

which through its structures or through history has
been subjected to the patrilinear, therefore male, law.[28]

through writing herself, woman will return to that body
which has been, worse than confiscated, made into the
disquieting stranger in the place, a sick or dead
being . . .
Write yourself: your body must make itself heard.
Then the immense resources of the unconscious will
spring . . . it will be an act which will signal the *Taking
Word* of woman, therefore her deafening entry into
History which has always been constituted *on her
repression.*[29]

Like millions of women, I want to inscribe my fighting
body for something tells me – and it is not my man's
science – that a great part of History, because it has
neither been thought nor written by us, has become
fixed in the memory of the female body.[30]

Certainly, it would be over-simple to suggest that working
to modify the 'imaginary', writing from inside the 'body' as
the place where an identity can be created, a spring released,
or where censorship, the law of the 'logos' can best be evaded,
are specifically female procedures. It would also be wrong to
claim that women *have to* start from there in that it would trap
them inside yet another prescriptive circle.

I would, of course, not refrain from playing the devil's advo-
cate: recalling that this is where *The Mill on the Floss* starts
from: George Eliot's arms go numb on the arms of her chair,
like the arms of the little girl on the stone bridge who is
looking down into the water – the little girl who is both George
Eliot as a child and the Maggie that's just been given birth to.
I would also stress that *Jane Eyre* and *Villette* are anchored in
the intensity of childhood sensations – that Virginia Woolf's
novels never allow narrative mastery to go outside a bodily
hold upon the text – and that it is not for nothing that Joyce
has put Molly Bloom in bed (though that particular remark
invites trouble rather than brings water to my mill). Counter-
arguments no doubt would sprout like the dragon's teeth. I
would be reminded that *A la recherche du temps perdu* also starts

in bed, from inside the sleeping/walking body. That there are, as Woolf herself acknowledged, 'feminine' male writers as well as 'masculine' women writers. Indeed, that George Eliot herself is frequently described as one of the latter. It would further be said that if I had been about to say that Doris Lessing had 'bracketed' her 'femininity' because she writes such lucid, 'masterful', logical prose; deals with 'externals'; is preoccupied with all that the world has to show from politics to racial issues to mysticism, I was going to speak nonsense, and it is just as well I have been stopped in time. That in any case the particular 'situation' or 'position' of women is continuously at stake in her novels. That that is why so many women identify with her heroines. Martha's wise passiveness at the end of the sequence, her 'Tolstoyan' acceptance of 'life forces', her finding more wisdom in the 'mad' Lynda than in all the supposed sages, are arrived at through specifically 'female' kinds of experience.

Yes. Yes. I'm not denying that that's what 'happens', what the narrative *tells* us. What I'm wondering about is, where do Martha's sentences come from?

And how come the text is haunted by the presence of Martha's *body?* Of her body as a source of *knowledge?* How come it keeps anchoring itself in that, touching it as if it were Anteus and Martha's body were the earth – and yet reneging on it, abandoning it, shedding it bit by bit as if that body were a series of skins (personality itself a set of chinese boxes), and, in its own favourite image, it was peeling it like an onion?

For it is very striking how again and again new chapters or sections start from Martha's *sensations*. There are, to return to them once again, the 'mud' passages I have quoted at the beginning of this essay. There are others, dying out virtually through *A Proper Marriage* and *A Ripple from the Storm*. In *A Proper Marriage* the 'body' passages are nearly all connected with child-bearing (like the time when Alice and Martha take a mud bath in a pot-hole) or being with a child. Yet she is – especially in the second passage – in a state of boredom and gloom:

The two rooms at the top of the block of flats were filled with light from the sky as soon as the sun, splendid, enlarged and red, swelled up over the horizon of suburb-clotted hills, pulling behind it filaments of rose-and-gold cloud. By half-past five, fingers of warm yellow were reaching over the big bed, over Caroline's cot. Martha lay warm in the blankets, listening to Caroline wake.

(*A Proper Marriage*, p. 222)

Above, trees: the glossy dark masses of the cedrelatoona, the sun-sculptured boughs of the jacarandas, and, between, those small stiff trees the bauhinias, with their pink-and-white blossoms perched on them like butterflies. It was October, and the jacarandas were purple and the streets were blue, as if they ran water or reflected the sky, which was unrelievedly blue and pulsing with heat.

Inside the gate was a large tree, under which Martha stood looking out. Behind her was a rough lawn, where Caroline was playing.

(*A Proper Marriage*, p. 273)

In *A Ripple from the Storm*, perhaps because Caroline has been left behind, and the focus is on 'politics', the 'sensations', the body-anchorage are all given to Jimmy. The only moment when Martha's body is used as a source of knowledge is her illness, in the early part of section II: but it is not really a knowledge of *place* that the body then registers: it is more a symptom of unease of self. Martha's body comes back very strongly in *Landlocked*. From the opening of the book its resurgence as a medium of awareness of place seems to herald the affair with Thomas:

The afternoon sun was hot on Martha's back, but not steadily so: she had become conscious of a pattern varying in impact some minutes ago . . .

Areas of flesh glowed with chill, or tingled with it: behind heat, behind cold, was an interior glow, as if they were the same . . . And, since the patches and angles of sunlight fell into the office for half of its depth, and had been so falling for three hours, everything was warmed – floors, desks, filing cabinets, flung off heat; and Martha stood, not only directly branded by sunlight and by shadow, her flesh stinging

precisely in patterns, but warmed through by a general
irradiation.

(Landlocked, pp. 9–10)

The heat of a stormy day had drained into the scarlet
flush that still spread, westwards, under bright swollen
stars only intermittently visible. Hailstones from the
recent storm scattered the street and lay on the dirty
windowsill . . . It would be winter soon, the ice
seemed promise of it. Martha's calves sweated slipperily
against the wood of the bench, and she sucked a bit
of ice as an ally against heat.

(Landlocked, p. 48)

Etc., etc. Obviously, the renewed frequency of such passages
shows the return of Martha's sexuality. But they don't only
serve that purpose, they bizarrely act as 'stills', a camera's
fixed effect, that then allows movement – and what is the
significance of this? What further contributes to making this
problematic is that the very sensuality of the affair with
Thomas is meant to be shot through with political implications:
somehow rotten because of the evils in Europe, because also
of the racialist evil in Rhodesia: but what relationship does
the writing of the 'sensation' passage bear to that political
rottenness?

Perhaps, when Thomas and she touched each other, in
that touch cried out the murdered flesh of the millions
of Europe – the squandered flesh was having its
revenge, it cried out through the two little creatures
who were fitted for much smaller loves . . . It was all
much too painful, and they had to separate.

(Landlocked, p. 167)

But what relationship does the writing of the 'sensations' passages bear to that stated political rottenness? Take the opening
of part II, from which I earlier on quoted in part, when discussing 'mud':

Six inches of marred glass in a warped frame reflected
beams of orange light into the loft, laid quivering green
from the jacaranda outside over wooden planks and
over the naked arm of a young woman who lay face

down on a rough bed, dipping her arm in and out of
the greenish sun-lanced light below her as if into water.

(*Landlocked*, p. 102)

Now there recur here some of the elements of the other passages: the chequered heat – the sun-drenched African trees –
the sunlight like water.[31] But what are we to make of 'marred'
and 'warped'? Are the glass marred and frame warped because
Martha's and Thomas's love is already spoiled by the violence
from Europe, or are they simply humble sources of the sensual
bliss – 'Martha . . . [stretched] her body's happiness in cool,
leaf-smelling warmth' – all the more touching, like the frail
shed in which the two lovers meet, with its 'crooked' window,
because they are humble and awry? I can't help but think that
it's the latter: the first reading is hard to sustain. But isn't it
rather *risqué* to allow words like 'warped' and 'marred' and
'crooked' to be present in a passage describing a love that's
going to turn out to *be* marred if they are not *intended* to convey
this?

The point I am trying to get at is this: there are two kinds
of knowledge acting as sources for the text: the 'bodily' knowledge, which I shall with all the reservations and queries made
earlier call 'feminine', and which is certainly feminine in the
sense that we have a woman writer using the closely autobiographical medium of a female character to convey her sense
of place; and the 'abstract', political, knowledge of politics at
large: manly, in that its simple sentence structure and the 'free'
generalizing possibilities such a structure permits are regarded
by Lessing herself, as her remarks about *The Pig* and *The Trinket
Box* testify, as 'masculine'. It seems to me that Doris Lessing
resorted to the first kind of knowledge when she returned to
the writing of *The Children of Violence* after a gap in which
The Golden Notebook and *Going Home* were produced. Now the
positions reached in *The Golden Notebook* demanded that *Landlocked*, itself looking forward to *The Four-Gated City*, proceed in
a 'trans-individual', 'abstract', ('male') direction, towards
which in any case *A Ripple from the Storm* was fast going. I
don't know whether the experience of returning to Rhodesia
(*Going Home* was published in 1957, a year before *A Ripple from
the Storm*, but seems, emotionally at least, not to have affected
it at all) had anything to do with it. But it seems to me clear

that what gets *Landlocked* 'started' is what I described earlier as what gets *The Mill on the Floss* started: a 'Proustian', a bodily memory revived, at least imaginatively, by a return to place. The place of childhood and youth. Immersion within Martha's world of sensations is what makes the return to the place and theme possible.

But that bodily memory, although it permits the return of Martha's sexuality, is neither trusted nor made fully significant. The narrative voice does not really care about being 'there' since it wants to move on and wants Martha to move on, too. One of the reasons it wants to move on is that somebody there wants to 'write' about the experience: there is something analytical about those passages, showing Martha to be the 'detached observer'. But also, the pull of 'elsewhere', of Europe, is being felt. The pull of the 'trans-individual' consciousness that becomes prevalent in *The Four-Gated City:*

> [Iris] knew everything about this area, half a dozen streets for about half a mile or a mile of their length; and she knew it all in such detail that when with her, Martha walked in a double vision, as if she were two people: herself and Iris, one eye stating, denying, warding off the total hideousness of the whole area, the other, with Iris, knowing it in love . . .
>
> Iris . . . had lived in this street since she was born. Put her brain, together with the other million brains, women's brains, that recorded in such tiny loving anxious detail the histories of window-sills, skins of paint, replaced curtains and salvaged balk of timber, there would be a recording instrument, a sort of six-dimensional map which included the histories and lives and loves of people, London – a section map in depth.
>
> (*The Four-Gated City*, p. 20)

Martha has got to where her author wants her: where her author is. Instead of 'living', of paying a bodily price for her own knowledge, of seeking for 'History' inside her own female body, she is ready to *use* the bodily knowledge of others – use Iris as her other eye, her source of knowledge: but for a wider quest. A bit like Scott who, having used, transcribed, 'written', 'oral' material (a lot of it got out of *women;* see preface to the *Waverley Novels*), talked – playfully – about mechanizing the whole enterprise of *The Waverley Novels*, and of weaving them like damask,[32] Doris Lessing alias Martha seems poised here to computerize the whole process of female bodily knowledge of places. (A new age wants improved methods. We're on our way to the galactic files of *Shikasta*.) Martha wants a section map in depth without having to pay the price Iris and the other million women have paid for depth: living.

Ah. Henry James & Co. But there we are. Precisely. If you're not going to 'pay the price' in 'living' you've got to pay it 'imaginatively'. In the relations you establish with your 'subject-matter'. In your readiness to be immersed inside it.

And that's where the gaps seem to me to be. In the passage from *Landlocked* which we were considering, the fact there is a tension between the bodily knowledge which has impelled and to a certain extent keeps impelling the text, and the 'general' knowledge the text is moving towards, means that the language does not control and organize sufficiently its range of significance – terms like 'warped' and 'marred' carry an uncertain load; the 'water out of sunlight' image appears equally in a gloomyish passage about suburban Salisbury in *A Proper Marriage* (p. 273: 'the streets were blue, as if they ran water or reflected the sky') and in a passage of sexual ecstasy ('dipping her arm in and out of the greenish sun-lanced light below her as if into water'). It is as if the text had no memory of itself at a deeper level – a metaphoric or unconscious level: and yet it is entirely concerned with continuity. It is as if it did not try to envisage on the level of language the questions it is posing on a theoretical level – what is the relation between sex and politics, between the feel of the body and the economical or political infra-structure at work, determining (or not) each individual life.

LANGUAGE

It's all a question of how the text is imaginatively produced. Of the relations that exist between the authorial voice and the heroine who is devised as a mirror for authorial experience.

Martha Quest, A Proper Marriage and *A Ripple from the Storm* all start from *two* women – like *The Golden Notebook*, interestingly – before homing in on Martha (she is looking at the two in *Martha Quest;* she is one of the two, in the others).

Landlocked, as discussed above, starts inside Martha's body. So does *The Four-Gated City:*

> In front of Martha was grimed glass, its lower part
> covered with grimed muslin. The open door showed
> an oblong of browny-grey air swimming with globules
> of wet. The shop fronts opposite were no particular
> colour. The lettering on the shops, once black . . . was
> now shades of dull brown. The lettering on the upper
> part . . . said *Joe's Fish and Chips* in reverse and was
> flaking like stale chocolate.
> She sat by a rectangle . . . Her cup was thick . . .
> Across the room sat Joe's mother . . .
> For a few weeks she had been anonymous, unnoticed
> – free.
>
> *(The Four-Gated City,* pp. 13–14)

Relentlessly, sentence after sentence, subject verb object with as unique complements location ('In front of Martha', 'opposite') or time ('once black', 'for a few weeks'). All the perceptions are Martha's, the locations from Martha's own situation ('Across the room sat . . . Joe's mother'); she is inside the cafe, so she sees the lettering on the door in reverse. Yet the book is written in the third person, which allows, among other things, the authorial knowledge to be greater than that of the character: occasionally to transcend it.[33] What is striking in this opening is the solidity and unflinchingness of the knowledge that is being registered and imparted: the author knows and tells us, without a shade of doubt, who Martha is, what she sees, what the quality of what she sees is (all rather dingy, dull colours that must be striking for someone just come from Africa, fresh from the memory of sunlight and jacarandas) where it is, what she feels, how long she's been there, etc. Neither the author nor the character doubt the descriptive power of language, nor the amenability of perception to order: first we're told what's 'in front', next paragraph what's she's sitting 'by', 'Across the room', then the characters are gradually introduced with added information (that is, what Martha knows from previous acquaintance with the characters is slipped in to help the reader find out even more clearly where 'we' are. God's in his heaven, all's right with the world.

Subject verb object, and precise, undoubtable locations in place and time.

Ah, you could say. But Martha here, in this last volume of the sequence, has fully developed her tendency of the 'detached observer'. That tendency has been there from the first – from the beginning of *Martha Quest:*

> if she was often resentfully conscious that she was
> expected to carry a burden that young people of earlier
> times knew nothing about, then she was no less
> conscious that she was developing a weapon which
> would enable her to carry it. She was not only miserable,
> she could focus a dispassionate eye on that misery.
> This detached observer, felt perhaps as a clear-lit space
> situated just behind the forehead, was a gift of the
> Cohen boys at the station, who had been lending her
> books.
>
> (Martha Quest, p. 14)

Whether one thinks this 'detached observer' is a gift of the Cohen boys or the sign that Martha is a born writer (which the text does not envisage), it is seen as a specific product of the 'modern' world – a 'weapon' against 'violence'. Is it, in the opening of *The Four-Gated City*, also meant to be a symptom of the modern disease? A disease in the eye, a split in the personality? Perhaps the very syntactical simplicity is a ruse: perhaps what's happening is that the kind of maniacal observing detachment that the narrator of *La Jalousie* shows is also at work here, demonstrating that all we can know are man-made dimensions, measure and number and place? But that's simply not tenable: how could such a stance be compatible with the fourth paragraph: 'For a few weeks she had been anonymous, unnoticed – free. Never before in her life had she known such freedom.' This is the free indirect speech, speaking of easy intimacy between author and character, the very reverse of the non-committal mode of Robbe-Grillet.

In Robbe-Grillet, all the certainty ultimately leaves you with is a state of absolute uncertainty. The opposite occurs here: everything is protectively, reassuringly, exhaustively significant. As you read (unless of course you're a fool, a hypothesis not to be excluded, since Doris Lessing often complains of the way her novels are being misread), you *understand* everything.

You read, 'In front of Martha was grimed glass, its lower part covered with grimed muslin', and you know that that's all there is to it. You know you can hang on to Martha, she won't let you down. You immediately picture to yourself that particular shop window with its halfway-up net curtain. You know that 'grimed' says a lot about the dirt of the place, its working-class, end-of-the-war dereliction, soon confirmed of course by the other details. And no more. No Mr Grimes hiding in the cupboard. You know the character is in a bit of a trance, thus intent observing it all, but that you've got nothing to fear, she isn't going to go mad, she'll move from her bench within a suitably short number of paragraphs, you won't get stuck, there'll be plenty more 'action' to keep you busy. That kind of clarity is deeply comforting. Of course, that's got to do with the A to Z principle, which requires the continued 'illusion' of action. What's perhaps most comforting of all is the sense that there is *no more* than what there is. The clarity, the subject-verb-object routine, also ensure this. For instance, it's rather unlikely that you should have to read 'flaking like stale chocolate' as *more* than a precise visual indication. An ample one, certainly, London of course *is* in a derelict state, and the dingy state of the fish shop expresses, or partakes of, that dereliction; but you know that things aren't going to become metamorphosed (as they might in Marquez, where the chocolate might become literal, and escalate into God knows what); you also know that they aren't metaphors for Martha's state of mind: you know, because the language operates in such determined grammatical ways, that nothing is going to happen from *inside* the language; that the process of writing itself is excluded, except as a tool, from the operation that is taking place. Even if you take the most crisis-like passages, Martha's breakdown towards the end of *The Four-Gated City*, they are hemmed in as an insurance against their running away with the text:

Here Martha succumbed again to the Devil.
Hell (one of them?) is hot. It has a harsh light. There is a sticky clinging feel to it. MOST IMPORTANT OF ALL it has a beat. Both regular and irregular. Like a mad clock, like the way paraffin lamps flare up before going out . . . Faces like embryos, half-formed. A gallery of faces of people. Devils.

Ordinary people . . . Hate, envy, greed, fear, slide over
people's faces so fast you can only just catch them.

It was at that stage that Martha was conducted
through the Stations of the Cross by the Devil. She
knew nothing of this ritual, had never been instructed
in it, nor had known well enough to affect her people
who performed it. Yet it was as if she knew it, knew
its meaning.

(The Four-Gated City, p. 566)

The very fact that the more broken-down syntax (which
remains, however, perfectly intelligible and syntactically correct) should be italicized and bracketed between the comforting
indications 'Here Martha . . .', 'It was at that stage that
Martha . . .', takes the sting out of the breakdown. The prose
never really confronts you with the *experience* of madness (any
more than I think it does in *Briefing for a Descent into Hell)*
unlike, say, the prose of Nerval or Poe or Artaud or Jeanne
Hyvrard. It never fully actualizes the crises it is about. This is
because Martha, as at the beginning of the sequel, has a
'weapon' against crises: she somehow knows it all in advance,
perhaps one could say she is dual (hence perhaps those beginnings of books with *two* women together). The experience is
only for the statement of it. Everything that happens serves
one purpose, and one only: to contribute to the 'plot', which
is the achievement of a certain wisdom about 'life'. The prose
is interested in saying, *not* in doing. Less and less in doing as
the 'detached observer' takes over in the later novels. The texts
are, in more than a chronological sense, A to Z texts.

Are they? And are there no significant gaps between the
narrator and her protagonist? Well, when I read more closely,
I do feel there are. But I am not sure that they are *intended*.
This for instance:

Martha turned her face away; her lids stung with tears;
she felt the most rejected and desolate creature in the
world. It occurred to her that the Cohen boys might
have felt like this when she (or so it had appeared)
rejected them; but she dismissed the thought at once.
The possessors of this particular form of arrogance may
know its underside is timidity; but they seldom go on
to reflect that the timidity is based on the danger of

thinking oneself important to others, which necessitates a return of feeling.

(*Martha Quest*, p. 45)

This is a subtle 'psychological' remark, not infrequent, especially in the early novels of the sequence. It reminds one of Jane Austen, or George Eliot perhaps: the author in her superior wisdom stepping back from her character to comment in a 'general' way about the failings of that character or to draw a universally valid moral/wise lesson from the experience presented. Thus, when Sir James Chettam, at the end of chapter 6 of *Middlemarch*, hears that Dorothea is going to marry Casaubon, he is bitterly disappointed but decides to put a good face upon it when he goes to see the Brookes:

> He really did not like it: giving up Dorothea was very painful to him; but there was something in the resolve to make this visit forthwith and conquer all show of feeling, which was a sort of file-biting and counter-irritant . . .
> We mortals, men and women, devour many a disappointment between breakfast and dinner-time; keep back the tears and look a little pale about the lips, and in answer to inquiries say, 'Oh, nothing!' Pride helps us; and pride is not a bad thing when it only urges us to hide our own hurts – not to hurt others.

Such comments – what would be called 'meta-language'[34] by Colin MacCabe – besides soaring above the immediate experience of the characters, being beyond what *they* are capable of thinking, weaves a relationship between author and reader. Often, too, when the remarks are made about the heroine or hero (as in *The Mill on the Floss* or *Pride and Prejudice* or *Daniel Deronda*) it is implied that the heroine/hero, though not yet or never quite capable of the kind of wisdom shown by the authorial voice, is still moving towards it throughout the novel in that she/he is 'learning' all the time. The novel is coaching him/her out of prejudice, selfishness or naivety. And we are being coached along too.

To this must be added that, be it in Jane Austen or George Eliot, the language of each text elaborately produces the mental operations it wants its readers to become involved in: Jane

Austen being more concerned with 'judgement',[35] George Eliot, in *Middlemarch* at least, with knowledge: the concept of a meta-language is in fact too simple to represent the multiplicity of manoeuvres[36] and areas of language which are being resorted to; the novel is continually producing processes of knowledge, and staging them as processes.

Now, the remark about Martha makes the book seem to belong with 'classic realist texts', texts with a meta-language. But if one then begins to wonder whether the overall language of *The Children of Violence* is concerned with *processes* of knowing, the answer must be negative. The novels are interested in questing for sense, yes, but by means of what *happens* to the heroine. The remark about Martha is *odd*. The only reason I can see for its presence is that the author underwent a change of heart whilst writing the sequence (we're back where we were earlier). Martha was *intended* to have a different fate from the one she turned out to have.

Indeed, if I think of this remark in the light of what I have said earlier (that everything in the text contributes to Martha's progress towards 'wisdom'), I straightaway realize that this reflection does not. Martha is no Emma who would learn that you have to be kind to the Misses Bates, the Cohen boys, of this world. In fact, she never solves her bizarre conflict, attraction to/revulsion from Solly and Joss, though Joss turns out to be better than his brother: it is even suggested Martha could have had an affair with Joss; if the sequence built up into the novel it seems to set out to be at this point, she would. A *personal* commitment to others is not what Martha learns to make. We are never made to feel that Martha's *human* shortcomings matter, nor that she ever does anything she should feel guilty about (not even leaving her child). We are not in a *moral* world. We are not even in a world in which 'classical' psychological wisdom would help. Thus, when Martha watches Thomas come up a ladder, there is a sharpness to her perception of him which does not belong to the rest of what is happening: 'His face was thoughtful, held the moment's stillness that accompanies wonder – which in itself is not far off fear' (*Landlocked*, 103).

Nathalie Sarraute's ironies about Camus's Meursault.[37] She argues that we are surprised as we read *L'Etranger* by some deep psychological remarks, which suggest that this estranged and distanced man has fished deep in 'human' waters. And that our unease at a wisdom which jars with Meursault's professed detachment, his implied claim that there is no sense, that there are no 'values' in life, is finally dispelled by Meursault's outburst at the end – his declaration of love for life. That outburst, she says, confirms that here indeed was a man who had a deep understanding of 'life'. It is a 'return' of the 'psychological'.

Well, the passing remark from *Landlocked* has the reverse effect on me. It seems to belong to a *past* fiction, a fiction that might have been, rather than to the novel the sequence is becoming. It belongs to a world in which 'psychology' matters, in which observing other people acutely matters in itself, is a self-justifying activity even. But that world is, from *A Ripple from the Storm* onward, in the process of disappearing:

> She thought: and it was a moment of illumination, a
> flash of light: I don't know anything about anything
> yet. I must try and keep myself free and open, and try
> to think more, not to drift into things.
>
> (*A Ripple from the Storm*, p. 186)

> She recognized Marjorie's dry and humorous tone, and
> thought: Why is it I listen for the echoes of other people
> in my voice and what I do all the time? The fact is,
> I'm not a person at all, I'm nothing yet – perhaps I
> never will be.
>
> (*A Ripple from the Storm*, p. 279)

Sure enough that remark is followed up in the epigraph to the following volume, *Landlocked* – the Sufi fable about the Mulla saying to the shopkeeper who thinks he has seen *him* walk into his shop, 'How do you know it [was] me?' We are on our way to the man – the woman – without qualities – to the Musil model that is used for one of the epigraphs of *The Four-Gated City*. On our way to the 'children of violence' vision, a *plural* (therefore impersonal) vision arrived at through the single consciousness of Martha:

> Every fibre of Martha's body, everything she thought,
> every movement she made, everything she was, was
> because she had been born at the end of one world war,

and had spent all her adolescence in the atmosphere
of preparations for another . . .

The soul of the human race, that part of the mind
which has no name, is not called Thomas and Martha,
which holds the human race as frogspawn is held in
jelly – . . . was twisted and warped.

(*Landlocked*, p. 202)

(See what I mean about 'warped'? It's as if she reused the word
because it was 'there' but she, who yet knows everything, does
not know this is why.) Impersonality – the discovery of it – is
soon to prevail:

She sat looking at the blank television screen. As far as
she was concerned, the scene they had just played out
was no more real than what they could see on that
screen by turning a switch . . . Oneself, or Paul, had
to be, for as long as it was necessary, screaming baby,
sulking adolescent, then middle-aged woman, whose
eighteen hours a day were filled with a million details,
fragments, reflected off the faceted mirror that was
one's personality, that responded all the time, every
second, to these past selves, past voices, temporary
visitors.

(*The Four-Gated City*, p. 369)

'Make love'. 'Make sex'. 'Orgasms'. 'Climaxes'. It was
all nonsense, words, sounds invented by half-animals
who understood nothing at all. Great forces as
impersonal as thunder or lightning or sunlight or the
movement of the oceans being contracted and heaped
and rolled in their beds by the moon, swept through
bodies.

(*The Four-Gated City*, p. 510)

To sum up: the texts act (especially the first two volumes)
as if the authorial voice had a knowledge and wisdom superior
to Martha's. But in the end, they have no use for that knowledge and wisdom. They are in excess of what the writing can
make 'signify'. Not simply in the 'psychological' remarks I
have quoted: when Anton is first introduced, he is presented
in much more merciful and sympathetic terms than when he
gets to be known to Martha, and seen through Martha's eyes

(*A Proper Marriage*, 326) – there is, of course, the Jimmy epi-
sode, the account given of Mrs Van, which shows that Martha
doesn't understand her. Now these gaps between the author's
knowledge and Martha's have different effects. Some – the
piece about Anton – suggest that the author changed her mind
about what to do with this character: why present him sympathetically if he was going to turn out to be so unattractive
and limited? To show that 'from the outside' he could have
sounded appealing to Martha, and justify her marrying him?
But obviously, there is no need to justify the marriage, Martha
is open-eyed and generous in marrying Anton (she wants to
preserve him from expulsion), there is no need to justify that.
To suggest there is more to Anton than Martha ever sees?
Now that would be interesting, but again that is not tenable,
since more and more we are asked to take the novels as
Martha's, her vision is more and more the central, the acceptable vision – nowhere more so than in *The Four-Gated City*.
And yet, had the kind of remarks I underlined been given
more scope, it could have been so. Mrs Van is a different case;
she comes home to roost in *The Four-Gated City*, in that Martha
sees herself finally as turning into another Mrs Van, and this
gives her retrospective understanding of the old woman. But
I think the point has to be taken: despite the claimed smooth-
ness of Martha's progress, there are gaps inside the text which
are not all recuperable by the 'totalizing' intention. They reveal
a change of heart in the writer, and perhaps more.

It all comes back again and again to the same question: Is
Martha the author? To what extent is the narrative voice
Martha in her 'superior' wisdom – later on in life – presenting
Martha's experience 'live'? If so, in what way and to what
extent does the later wisdom colour the present-day experience? There must be – there is – a gap between *how* it happened and how it is being 'totalized' when it is shown as
happening this way or that. This is evident if, reading for
instance the following passage from *Landlocked*, one keeps
wondering *who* knows what is being told. For it supposes
previous or extraneous knowledge; it also implies overall
knowledge, knowledge of what is going to happen, since the
hotel which lies on top of massacred black bodies is going to
be the place where Thomas will confront Sergeant Tressell,

and consciousness of the opposition of black Africans will finally become intolerable to him – wrecking his relationship with Martha. Reading this, gaps also appear if one wonders who is seeing, and who is speaking from *where*:

So heavy with memories was this land that people building houses here had been known to run away from them. They were unable to forget the painted warriors who walked for all to see with assegais and shields through the dark hours. The hotel, Parkland Hotel, had been such a house . . .

Does Martha know this as she drives in? Did she (did Lessing) learn of it afterwards? Does Lessing choose to have the scene occur there on account of it or did such a scene just 'happen' there in 'real' life?

As usual there was a long line of about fifty cars, although it was mid-week. It was just as well the six had booked a table.

Who knows 'as usual' since the six have never been there? Does one of the six say this? Martha? General thoughtful remark?

The hotel was half-way up a sharp hill. In front the ground fell away to a small river from which rose a wraith of white mist and a smell of stagnant water. The building was long and low, across the hill. All its front was glassed in to make a dining space. Behind this was a long, low-ceilinged room with a platform for an orchestra. Very different, this place, from those where Martha had danced, in another epoch, five years before. Then, the city's young people moved from place to place, as if they owned them all; everybody

Is Martha perceiving this? Or official description?

Same precision (journalistic?) as in opening of *FGC*. Why? So we can visualize the scene?

Here we get back to Martha.

She is remembering, presumably – stream of consciousness, or is the author telling us?

knew each other, and the managers knew them and greeted them by name. Now, as the six went through the dining tables, and then stood waiting for a moment to cross the dance floor, there was no face they knew . . .

. . . then came Martha and Thomas, not touching: it was enough to walk beside each other across the sprung wooden floor that sent up a smell of wood and fresh beeswax . . .

. . . Maisie held out a big white arm into the light of the flames to show – what of course they could not see in the shifting light – gooseflesh because of the frosty table. They sat exclaiming and enjoying the cold – one of the sharpest pleasures of living in hot countries is this – to savour the vivifying degrees of cold on a winter's night.

(pp. 141–2)

No, it's not just Martha, it's the six. Except of course that it can't be, because at least Anton, Athen and Thomas, never participated in that life, and therefore cannot share in the memory.

Does Thomas feel this as well as Martha? Or does Martha assume this is what he is feeling? Or is she as author remembering the scent?

Who sees Maisie's arm as big? Not Maisie, certainly: Martha? everybody? Does Maisie say, look at my gooseflesh, which no one can see? What is the point of making everyone, reader included, look at gooseflesh no one can see? Obviously, to make the reader imaginatively participate in the pleasure of the cold. But the text pretends to exclude relationship with the reader.

The passage, confident as it looks, is full of uncertainties: you can't say who is seeing, nor what for. The only way in which you can make the whole thing cohere is if you give it to Martha, but in a near-Flaubert-like perspective: the author as *deus ex machina* is all over the option, moves in and out of one or several characters at will. Without of course having to pay the price Flaubert pays for his omniscience and omnipresence, the continuous undermining of the text by itself, the authorial solitude, the renunciation, to hope, to sense. But can that be?

One has a well-organized piece of 'realism' here, which

convinces because of the speed with which it skates over the surface; also, because the 'tricks' are so recognizable, one thinks one knows where one is. In fact, the narrative is gliding over contradictions ingrained in the nature of the ground it is covering. Time has been ironed out, lived time, the relation between the time of writing and the time during which the events are made to occur. The text is informed by *retrospective* knowledge (the scene with Sergeant Tressell, the 'black Africa' issue; even knowing that feeling the cold is one of the pleasures of hot countries implies one should have left them to appreciate it: Martha has not been out of Rhodesia yet): but it nowhere acknowledges that it is; it uses that smooth preterite which is the assumed present of fiction. The *recherche du temps perdu* element, the actuality of the autobiographical process is erased. And the process of the writing itself is erased.

Yet time and time again, the text stumbles across a consciousness of the actuality of language: 'but these are words, and if she understood anything it was that words, here, were like the sound of a baby crying in the wind' (*Martha Quest*, 62); 'It was as if she were afraid of the power of language used nakedly' (*A Proper Marriage*, 69).

Here, 'language used nakedly' is Mr Maynard being able to say with relief, in 'this country' (coming from the circumlocutions of the English), 'The blacks need firm treatment.' Before this, the more 'liberal' phase, he could even have said, 'The kaffirs are getting out of hand.' Now, if this is so, naked language is language that expresses economic/social and, in this case, racialist, positions. You would have thought that with this perception firmly in hand, Martha's next step would be to wonder what is her *own* 'naked' language, what sort of language, that is, could express her true position; and is there a place in language where one could achieve something better than 'naked' language – a place of 'values', where not only you wouldn't be a 'salaud' (which Mr Maynard, dislikeable as he is, is not), but would become positively – free. And yet the writing continually operates from a supposed position of 'innocence'. The solid concatenation of the texts is achieved at the cost of actual exploration, even when the apparatus for the insights is there. You never lose your moorings. The bird's-eye view, the eye of God vision, even, since it sees in hearts as well as exhibits an unfailingly clear sense of location, is achieved at the expense of any actual immersion in reality.

There you are. Back in mud. You've been going round in circles. Try to get hold of it again. You've gone too far away from yourself.

My quandary: the same again and again when I read or reread Lessing. There is no doubt she is a great lady. No doubt that it is a blessing, in an age in which so much shit is being written and acclaimed, that for once a thoroughly serious, honourable and deeply concerned writer should be popular. There is no doubting either Lessing's prodigious flair for the topical, her energy, her power. Perhaps one should not doubt either that her vision of a dismal future and her belief in the need for a new humanity to evolve if humanity is going to survive may be right. Time may reveal her to have been a prophetess.

And there I am, carping about 'aesthetic' issues (am I?). Just being a petty and irresponsible lout.

Shikasta: in her young girl's diary, Rachel meditates on the strange understanding of her brother George. George is in fact an 'incarnation' (literally) of Johor (the archangel Gabriel turned into a twentieth-century Christ who has had a 'special' relationship when he was seven with a Jewish woman called Miriam). Benjamin, the earthly brother, has refused the 'special contacts'. Rachel fears she has too:

> I am thinking about it, and there is something so *awful* there I don't know what to do with myself, because of course I am thinking, what have I refused? I have always been offered everything too, but I always had some good reason not to. Like loving Mrs. Jones and wanting to be in the kitchen cooking with her and feeding the chickens. (*Shikasta*, p. 222)

Now that sentence hit me. I am like Rachel, I thought (which of course was what I/the reader was supposed to think). We're all capable of living our lives in this 'trans-individual' way Lessing suggests, open to 'we' or 'cosmic' forces, and I choose not to. I have chosen myself immersed, tied and gagged by the passionate details of trivial daily living, of ordinary relationships. A thick network of people and things which take up, joy or despair, most of my consciousness. I have chosen myself loving Mrs Jones and wanting to be in the kitchen. We're back to the dung-beetles. Back to the mud issue yet again. The reason why I 'object' to Doris Lessing's evolution to this detached trans-individual vision, why I like her short stories, the African ones especially, *The Grass Is Singing*, the early novels of *The Children of Violence* (despite the problems I find there), Rachel's journal (part of which – the best – is written while the girl is, surprise surprise, living in a Moroccan *mud* house) in *Shikasta*, the anguished passages of *The Golden Notebook* rather than the framework or the 'wisdom' which is meant to emerge, is that they feed my own choice of life. Because being *submerged* and struggling seems to me to be where life is. Depth. Thickness.

My choice. I remember a story my father (my own 'voice of the father'?) used to tell me when I was little, which always impressed me. It's about St Louis de Gonzague, a child in a religious school. The young boys are playing ball, there is a lull in the game, and one of the boys says, 'What would we do if we knew that in one hour's time it was going to be the end of the world?' One boy says, 'I'd go to my room and kneel and pray.' Another, 'I'd try to recall my past life and have it with me when I face God.' Another, 'I'd go to confession and repent my sins.' And St Louis de Gonzague says, 'I'd go on playing ball.'

That's the point of dissent, I suppose. I'm not persuaded that one cannot work towards 'sainthood' (meaning by that working with the forces of 'peace' rather than 'violence', or writing so as to make 'sense', writing towards 'truth', whatever that be) by staying in the kitchen with Mrs Jones just as well as by conversing with galactic forces. I'm not convinced that the way to trans-individuality is in disregard of, or contempt for, individuality, rather than *through* individuality. That the fate of Mary Turner is not more 'universally' relevant *because* so narrow and precise in its unfolding than the fate of the late Martha, or the various people who flit across *Shikasta* and can be catalogued as number 3 or number 8 terrorist. Evidently, Lessing is of the opposite opinion. So my criticisms only amount to a statement of my own difference or my own political and moral backwardness.

You have only devised these arguments, I was saying to

171

myself, in order to give authority to your dissent – to your immaturity.

But – perhaps precisely because I was – am – immature and individualistic and petty bourgeois – I could not accept this. I did not accept it because, genuinely, I felt uneasy. Not just because I felt on the spot. It did seem to me that there were some genuine contradictions and impossibilities where I had tried to describe them. But I had not got to the core of the matter: which was, why can't such writing *do today?*

I was stuck.

Oh, of course, theoretically, I knew the answers. All the post-Joyce-Proust-Kafka, post-existentialism, post-*nouveau roman*, post-*Tel Quel*, post-Saussure, post-Freud, post-Marx, post-Barthes, post-etc., etc., arguments: 'We now know that language cannot pretend to "imitate" reality.' 'Language as production.' 'Language that pretends to be mimetic is ideological language.' But somehow that sort of talk got on my nerves. It did not click, where it matters. I had read hundreds of things that ought to have helped me formulate my difficulties, and if I were to try very hard for theory I could have formulated them, but I didn't want to. It would have been like giving *The Children of Violence* the kiss of death by means of the Establishment. A high-brow Establishment kiss of death. The tidy bundling and posting to no-man's-land of texts into which life and faith had gone. If I was going to come to terms with my dissatisfaction with these texts, it would have to be from the depths of what had meaning for *me*. The whole of me. In any case, I often felt that it was at the expense of the actuality, the dimensions of the so-called 'classic realist text' that the theories were arrived at.

While I was musing upon this, I found myself in front of Saint-Sulpice. I had twenty minutes to spare before a rendez-vous. I remembered the Delacroix, and went into the church.

As when I go to Saint-Sulpice I normally look at Jacob's fight with the angel, I concentrated for once on *Héliodore chassé du Temple par les anges*.

How fantastically convenient, I thought. To have a subject-matter. A biblical story behind it, that enables you to *read* the shapes in a particular way. An ordered world, heaven above earth, so that the upper part of the picture, the draught created by the descent of the angel, can be *read* as heaven; that some forms can be read as *super*-added forms, the flesh and draperies of the winged angel, the angelic horse and his rider, different, separated from, of another order than, the flesh of the humans. What a blessing for a painter, I thought, to have a framework of belief (or convention) that helps him organize his space, give it an up and a down and multiple levels of conflicting significance. Why can't we have it anymore, I thought. Of course we can. I can still look at this picture. I have my own way of believing in heaven.

Ah, but something whispered, do you believe that heaven is up?

Shut up, I said. I am sure it must be possible. I can understand 'imitative' writing. I like chronological stories. Just because people now like messing up the order of things just for the sake of seeming original I don't see why . . .

Ah, but something whispered. Are *you* chronological? Has *your* existence taken place in chronological *order*?

That evening I was having dinner with a friend, who is a painter. I spared him till after dessert. 'Louis', I said, 'why can't you paint figuratively?' *Il en resta assis.* 'You've got a way of asking questions,' he said. 'Why don't you ask me who made the world?'

He is a beautiful man. He actually took the trouble of answering. 'Because,' he said, 'on ne peut plus répercuter son moi à l'univers.' '*Grosso modo,*' he said. In Balzac's time, the world of an individual could be put into correspondence with, *represent*, the world. The vision an individual had of the world, the fate of an individual, could act as a *valid model* for what was happening at a universal level. But now, because of what's happened, you know just as well as I do, as everybody does, the sciences, the 'sciences humaines', the discovery of the unconscious, politic . . .

Yes yes yes. Everything gelled suddenly. Of course. No more polymath figures after the beginning of the nineteenth century. Cassirer describing how all the sciences begin to pull apart, arguing that Comte is the last man to have tried for a global, a cohesive theory of knowledge. Specialization. In factories, as in the sciences. End of the frontier. Relativity. Speed of communications. Break up of communications. The impotency of 'totalizing' reason. This book by Feyerabend I was reading.

> We must therefore conclude that even inside science, reason cannot, and must not, have a universal relevance; it must often be overstepped, or eliminated, and other principles resorted to. There is no one rule that remains valid in all circumstances, and not one principle to which one can always appeal.[38]

In other terms: there is no single organizing formal principle fiction can hope to rely on; there is no one syntactical mode that will do to account for contemporary reality.

In Balzac's time, Louis said, it was possible for an author to hold a privileged position. A position of authority. Both to know his characters, and to know better. To know how your characters fitted into the world; because you could know the world. Now, all we can do is what Lévi-Strauss says. Use a *sharp angle*. Work on it, get it to work, so that it releases the largest possible point of view. Construct models. Individual models. Hope our individual models will have some relevance.

A Hundred Years of Solitude, I was thinking. The 'model' of Macondo. The 'universal' reached there because the particular, the extraordinary too, rather than the 'average', the 'typical', are being sought. The 'model' with a modest dimension. Couldn't care less that he doesn't have the ultimate word to speak about universal wisdom, Hiroshima, or Marxism: he has the Flood in Macondo, or the strike of the banana plantation.

Van Gogh, Louis said. Van Gogh knew that the sky could be at the bottom of a picture. He knew that putting the sky only at the top of a picture was projecting on to the world an anthropomorphic ambition that had ceased to be tenable.

Chronological sequences, I thought. Chronological sequences the equivalent in fiction of up and down, or left and right, in pictures. The development of certain fictional sequences (the history of a private individual; born in such a time and such a place), stretching in chronological order, youth being regarded as the key-moment, the moment when real choices are made, corresponds in time, '*grosso modo*', to the Industrial Revolution, the development of the sciences. Why? Is it because that type of sequence makes possible a certain form of rationalized 'progress'? Or represents the conditions in which certain forms of (financial or mechanized) progress can occur? It would be interesting to find out. But then, how is it that people – Doris Lessing for one – can go on writing like this once those conditions have become altered, or have escalated into monumental and divisive complexities? Well, forms after all go on reproducing themselves long after they are *actually* dead. People went on writing imitations of *La Princesse de Clèves* late into the eighteenth century, when the fabric of power at the French court and in the aristocracy had changed. Even now, nearly two centuries after Scott, when conceptions of history have radically altered and the conditions which gave rise to the historical novel have largely disappeared, popular writers go on churning out historical fictions.

Claiming that human life, that consciousness, goes from A to Z and can at all times be both aware of all there is to it (including those transparent dreams that always tell Martha, in perfectly intelligible language, what her 'deeper' state is) as well as of all there is to the world, is like continuing to put the sky at the top of the picture. It perpetuates a fiction that we like, of course, and *recognize* because that is what we are used to, what we need to feel 'at home', but that is truly a fiction: that no longer relates to reality. Martha may at the end of *The Four-Gated City* discover that her consciousness of reality had been false: but the manner in which she is led to make that discovery in itself perpetuates that falsity.

The time-span in *A Hundred Years of Solitude*, I was thinking. Perpetually taking off, speeding up, escalating, yet things endlessly repeating themselves (yet not repeating themselves): circular in the end; above all, the circularity containing the awareness, the fact, too, of the writing of the book. That book knows, among others, the relativity principle.

Martha's fate. In *fact*, what the books are really giving us is a portrait of the artist as a young woman. What other justification at bottom is there for Martha's 'observer' moods, her detachment, her will to freedom? What else *really* is she keeping herself free for? Yet Martha never writes a line. Never thinks about language, even. The autobiography goes far enough to include a great deal of personal experience, but the most important aspect of that experience, the one that is part and parcel of the *writing* of the books, that was part and parcel of the getting to the stage when the books could be written, is erased from them.

All that can happen to me, Louis said, is that I am haunted by figurativeness. 'Hanté par le figuratif.'

Martha, discovering emptiness with her customary painstaking honesty, discovers what is at the basis of the kind of writing which has been given to her. She also discovers the fundamental truth of her character. The truth: that the mud house once gone, she ceased to belong. Rather, decided that she would not belong. The nomad's flat, anonymous, empty. Naked language.

Ah yes, but it is not really naked, as we have seen. It only pretends to be. It pretends, with colonial simplicity, that because you're not really 'involved', you are, you can be, 'objective', 'all-knowing'. Which is yet another, unrecognized fiction.

Nomads belong to nomadism. To movement. How many writers this century have been exiles, of one kind or another? James, Eliot, Pound, Joyce, Beckett, Jabès . . . Berger even claims that to be an artist is to be an exile.

Was the only language open to them 'naked' language? The language of the 'detached observer'? . . .

Nomads. The Scythians. Small transportable art forms. Gold handicraft. Carpets.

If you have to flee, you put your values into movables. Jewels, for instance – ingots.

The language of circulation.

The kabbala. Esoterism. You belong to a secret, a spiritual society.

'Rome n'est plus dans Rome, elle est toute où je suis.'

They did not think they had to plaster the world – nothing less – all over the walls of their tents.

Martha's mammoth ambition. For the ultimate.

If you want the ultimate and you want to be able to *transport* it you carve in gold.

It is Martha's refusal to relate to the Africa that is there, that could be there, as the African short stories show, that makes her into a spiritual globe-trotter.

That the authorial stance, the all-knowing, all-encompassing voice, the confident voice, is false. Unreal. Or represents exactly what it is, 'news'. What is good about it is precisely that: the social world that is being portrayed, in Africa above all, but in London, too. The truth those novels offer is documentary.

That Martha, because she is questing for some kind of truth or freedom or self or whatever it is, because she is *voyaging*, becomes a tourist of life; she discards more and more, needs more and more people, experiences, to burn through. So that what she grows to perceive as the ultimate truth – the unreality, the comedy, the 'roles' of it all, people being activated by impersonal forces – is in fact her understanding of what her choices have made her into, of what the prose has made her throughout. The novels as they proceed become aware of something false, a vacuity, which is the falsity of their own fictional mode. It is a mark of the profound honesty of their author that they do so. Except where all the 'heart' goes into the 'mud' of experience, or when that 'mud' catches up with Martha, in the form of Mrs Quest, Doris Lessing fails to give herself the means of a reality principle. Perhaps if it is purely freedom you are after, you deliver yourself into the void. Mud, or the void. Hence probably the unease the reader feels in relation to Martha. One admires her as a thoroughly esteemable person – courageous, honest, disinterested, uncompromising, strong, competent, even at times loving – yet one feels a sneaking dislike for her, as though one was being conned by means of her: the sense that she is neutral, bland, whatever it is: a consciousness that fails to spring into full life because it is not rooted in life.

The 'philosophical' truth the sequence of *The Children of Violence* unearths is simply the principle of its own articulation. All that Martha can discover in her efforts to come closer to herself and to reality, to 'conceive' the universe, to 'roll it into a ball', is the emptiness of the universalist fictions that have been used to mimic the relation of the individual consciousness to the world. There has not been enough language there, not enough 'body' as opacity, as presence, as a place, the only place, where a *model* of knowledge could have been born.

NOTES

1 See Dee Seligman, 'The autobiographical fiction of Doris Lessing', Ph.D., Tufts University, 1975, and 'The four-faced novelist', *Modern Fiction Studies*, 26, 1980.

2 'My parents were, now I come to think of it, grail-chasers of a very highly-developed sort. I cannot even imagine a country in which they would have been definitely ready to settle down without criticism . . . I would, of course, be the first to blame my parents for my own grail-seeking propensities.'

3 See Dee Seligman's paper, 'The autobiography of a new consciousness', p. 28 (unpublished).

4 Elaine Showalter, *A Literature of Their Own*, London: Virago, 1977, p. 309.

5 The context makes this a quite complex moment: more than can be discussed within the framework of this essay. Mark's fanatical 'mapping' concern, which sends Martha researching and filing rather as she had done in Africa for Mrs Van Der Bylt on an anti-racialist campaign, is regarded by his communist friends as 'reactionary'. It is no longer 'socialist realism' but a search for individual vision on a world-scale. Yet, for Doris Lessing alias Martha, the decision to transcend the personal springs from communist convictions. 'The personal is by definition a private possession and may represent for the former communist a form of selfishness, a capitalist hoarding of emotional territory' (Lynn Sukenick, 'Feeling and reason in Doris Lessing's fiction', in *Doris Lessing: Critical Studies*, ed. Annis Pratt and L. S. Dembo, Madison: University of Wisconsin Press, 1974, p. 115). Anna, in *The Golden Notebook*, is convinced that the personal is political, that 'if Marxism means anything, it means that the little novel about the emotions reflects "what's real", since the emotions are a function and a product of society' (p. 43). It would be interesting, therefore, to work out why the steps Mark and Martha and Anna take towards transcending the personal are so suspect to their communist friends.

6 The epigraphs, e.g. pp. 11, 165, 301, make this abundantly clear.

7 Goethe, Poe, Gautier, Baudelaire among others:

> as no thought can perish, so no act is without infinite results. We moved our hands, for example, when we were dwellers on the earth, and, in so doing, we gave vibration to the atmosphere which engirdled it. This vibration was indefinitely extended, till it gave impulse to every particle on the earth's air . . . It is indeed demonstrable that every such impulse *given the air*, must, *in the end*, impress every individual thing that exists *within the universe*.
>
> (Poe, *The Power of Words*)

On this, see Georges Poulet's article on Gautier in *Etudes sur le Temps Humain*, Paris: Plon, 1949, pp. 278–307, and Nicole Ward

Jouve, *Baudelaire: A Fire to Conquer Darkness*, Basingstoke: Macmillan, 1980, pp. 280–4.

8 As if Lessing, through the voice and persona of her narrator, and that narrator's relation to her/Emily's infancy and childhood, carried out her own analysis.

9 Of course, in a sense there is no 'particularity'. A great deal of Colette is invested in Claudine, and Claudine's whole sense of life carries its own 'universally relevant' value. Yet there is a modesty and irreverence in Colette's creation of her heroines that makes them less obvious candidates for 'universal' status than others.

10 Baudelaire said this of his own *Fleurs du mal*. But he says very similar things in a discussion of Balzac, 'Les Drames et les romans honnêtes', in *Oeuvres complètes*, vol II, Paris: Pléiade, 1976, pp. 41–2.

11 After Pound's *Usura Canto*.

12 Ultimately, in *Shikasta* (in so far as one can call any recent work of such a prolific writer 'ultimate'), it's God's vision she is interested in through the medium of the archangels Gabriel *et al.* (Johor, etc.) and of Heaven's files.

13 The connection with Maggie Tulliver has been noticed before. See Walter Allen, as quoted in S. J. Kaplan, *Feminine Consciousness in the Modern British Novel*, Urbana: University of Illinois Press, 1975, p. 153.

14 'I find [Virginia Woolf] too much of a lady . . . I feel that her experience must have been too limited, because there is always a point in her novels when I think, "Fine, but look at what you've left out".' Quoted in Nancy Joyner, 'The underside of the butterfly: Lessing's debt to Woolf', *Journal of Narrative Technique*, V. 1974, pp. 204–5.

15 See on this Malcolm Bowie's inaugural lecture for Queen Mary College, 'Proust, jealousy, knowledge', delivered 24 October 1978, published by Queen Mary College.

16 Preface to the African short stories.

17 See Elaine Showalter's discussion of contemporary (and Victorian) women novelists' fear of hurting their families or offending their friends, pp. 302–3.

18 In *A Literature, In Pursuit of the English*, there is a revealing incident. Rose, the narrator's young friend, cannot understand why the narrator continues to meet the 'spiv' after it's become quite clear that he *is* a 'spiv':

> 'He's like that', she commented. 'He was always like that. That's why he frightens me, see? So don't you have nothing to do with him.'
>
> 'He said he was going to take me to see a flat tonight.'
>
> She let her hands drop away from my arm. 'You didn't say you'd go?'
>
> 'Yes, I did.'
>
> She was silent. 'Why?' she asked at last timidly. 'You don't believe what he says. I know that.'

'Well, it's because I've never met anyone like him before.'
When she didn't reply, I said: 'Why don't you like that?'
She thought. Then she said: 'You talk like he's an animal in a zoo.'

(pp. 72–3)

The narrator's reply – that she's interested because it's new to her – convinces neither Rose nor the reader – and is probably not meant to. Rose's suspicion is right: the narrator's interest *is* treacherous, *is* exploitative, *is* novelistic. She's fishing for material. Martha is fishing, too. But she is never acknowledged as doing so.

19 'The essence of the book the organization of it, everything in it, says implicitly and explicitly, that we must not divide things off, must not compartmentalize' (preface to *The Golden Notebook*, p. 10).

20 *The Man Without Qualities* is used for one of the epigraphs of *The Four-Gated City*. But it is the combination of a stripped self and a sensitivity to 'biological' or 'atmospheric' pressures that makes the book attractive to Lessing: not the writing itself.

21 See Margaret Scanlan, 'Memory and continuity in the series novel: the example of *The Children of Violence*', *Modern Fiction Studies*, Doris Lessing number, 26, 1980.

22 'We think back through our mothers if we are women', Virginia Woolf, *A Room of One's Own*, London: Panther, 1977, pp. 72–3.

23 *The Golden Notebook*, p. 11.

24 Lessing's own statement, quoted in Sukenick, 'Feeling and reason', p. 99; see also Showalter, *A Literature*, p. 309.

25 Luce Irigaray, *Ce sexe qui n'en est pas un*, Paris: Editions de Minuit, p.127.

26 'It is becoming more and more difficult today, confronted by the experiments of modern art, not to question along with the identity of the subject the very principle of a sexual identity, which is nevertheless claimed by feminist movements. I do not find it easy to define . . .', etc. 'L'Autre du sexe', *Sorcières*, no. 10, p. 37, tr. Stephen Heath. Kristeva is actually full of contradictions in this respect. She had tried to define a specific 'femininity' in an article for the *Cahiers du Grif* and moved towards it, both in *Des Chinoises* but above all in her location of the feminine as the 'pulsational' in texts: see *Polylogue*, Paris: Le Seuil, 1977, and *La Révolution du langage poétique*, where she argues that femininity can be located in the breaks and pulsions of the text; it acts as the limits, '*les bords*', or the 'trans-symbolic' questioning of the text (see especially discussion of Mallarmé's 'Prose' and 'Coup de dés'). But when woman resorts to the making of a text so as to constitute her own identity (i.e. text as child-substitute – as penis-substitute) she participates in the 'general fetishism' (*La Révolution*, Paris: Le Seuil, 1973, p. 614). I'm not sure I follow this in that it seems to me that texts can always in some ways be seen as attempts by the writer to constitute his/her identity: is woman not to write then? or

only those texts which are, *like* the texts of men like Mallarmé, Lautréamont, etc, 'pulsational'? Which lands one right back in the 'no-difference' area. For translations of Kristeva or discussions of her work, see *M/F*, 5/6, 1981, pp. 149–57 and 158–63; also J. Kristeva, *Desire in Language*, Oxford: Blackwell, 1981, and Mary Jacobus, 'The difference of view', in *Women Writing and Writing about Women*, London: Croom Helm, 1979.

27 Lacan of course, from *Encore, Séminaire XX*. Translation borrowed from Stephen Heath, 'Difference', *Screen*, XIX, 1978, p. 68.

28 Catherine Clément, 'Enclave esclave', *L'Arc*, 61, *Simone de Beauvoir et la lutte des femmes*, 1975, pp. 13–19 (my translation).

29 Hélène Cixous, 'Le rire de la Méduse', *L'Arc*, 61 *Simone de Beauvoir et la lutte des femmes*, 1975, p. 43 (my translation).

30 Madeleine Gagnon, in Cixous Gagnon Clément, *La Venue à l'écriture*, Paris: 10/18, 1977, p. 63 (my translation).

31 I wonder, given the *Waste Land* source of the epigraph and title for *The Grass Is Singing*, whether there is a reminiscence here of the 'water out of sunlight' passage from 'Burnt Norton'?

32 See preface to *Chronicles of the Canongate*.

33 Of course, when it happens, it is 'significant' in more ways than are meant; but certainly the authorial voice never ceases to be analogous to Martha's.

34 Colin MacCabe, *James Joyce and the Revolution of the Word*, Basingstoke: Macmillan, 1978, esp. pp. 16–23.

35 Obviously these points ought to be fully argued: they are well put in David Lodge's *The Language of Fiction*, London: Routledge & Kegan Paul, and New York: Columbia University Press, 1966.

36 Even the notion of 'free indirect style' (see Roy Pascal, *The Dual Voice*, Manchester University Press, 1977) fails adequately to represent the way the narrator in *Middlemarch* uses languages whose sources are in the personality and culture of the character concerned, but which are still in excess of the consciousness of the character and outside his/her range or readiness for self-knowledge.

37 *L'Ere du soupçon*, Paris: Gallimard, 1956, pp. 15–23.

38 P. Feyerabend, *Against Method*, London: New Left Books, 1975, end of chapter 15.

9

Too short for a book? *The Thousand and One Nights:* the short story and the book

'Longtemps je me suis couché de bonne heure.' 'For a long time I have gone to bed early ' – eight words only in the first sentence of a book several thousand pages long, Proust's *A la recherche du temps perdu, Remembrance of Things Past.* How we know, reading that sentence, that we are beginning to read a very long book, and how Proust chose it as the opening of his great work, are among those many mysteries of literature that, thank God, no one is able to elucidate. It is part of the same mysteriousness that each text of fiction that we write should come with a first sentence, or a sentence or rhythm somewhere, that dictates the length the thing is going to be. We know at once whether it will be 5, 20 or 150 pages, and if someone asks, 'Can you write a text of such and such a length', something in us knows what kind of a prose to look for. Often the initial or initiating sentence is a spontaneous birth, something that comes and demands to be, alas, not just born but painfully gestated, fed, laboured at. Perhaps this is also true of verse. Valéry used to say that one line may be given: never two.

What concerns me here is length. The length of the story, as a genre, if it is a genre; and its relation to the book, the thing that is got together, printed and sold as a book. I am concerned with the question for reasons of my own. I am in the process of writing two 'long' stories which have nothing to do with each other, come from different parts of me, are in a different prose, and I realize that I may not be able to publish them because each will be thought too short for a book, which each ought to be, and it would be nonsense to publish them together, which would amount to the right number of pages.

182

I have also recently had a volume refused by several publishers in France on the grounds largely that it was odd. The attempt was for a book that would be neither a collection of short stories nor a novel proper. It was made up of three stories totally separated by time, place and style, but connected by theme and an undercurrent of imagery to do with water, all kinds of waters and liquidities. It also had the same name for the central character in the three stories, but it was not necessarily the same person. Some of the readers had very enthusiastic reactions, others evinced puzzlement and a sense of alienation. Of course, I may have missed my target, not got the thing right. But it is a form that holds a fascination for me, that combination of distinct identity (the story and its difference from other stories) and flowing in and out, interpenetration, and some day I shall return to it. So the question of the story and its relation to the book has urgency for me.

I connect the western development of the short story as an independent genre with that of magazines and reviews in the nineteenth century, as Poe did, and as Doris Lessing has done recently in a French interview. The short story perfectly fits the space given to fiction written by a number of contributors inside the format of a magazine. Poe argued that it did so better than the serial, which meant cutting up a novel, producing formally artificial units. I am not sure I agree (for reasons I shall develop later, and that are evident today in the vogue of soap operas). Still, Gide had a point when he said that 'the short story is made to be read at once, in one sitting' (a phrase which is being used as the epigraph to a new magazine, *Nouvelles*, made up entirely of short stories in France). Gide may be right as far as the magazine in concerned. But what about a book?

A story, unlike a novel, may be read at one sitting, but is it made with that intention, so that it, alone, will be read at that sitting? (Which is what does happen to the tale in Balzac's 'La Grande Bretèche', or in James's *The Turn of the Screw*.) Or is it intended that other stories by the same author (in a collection) or other stories by other authors (in a magazine, or collection such as *Fathers by Daughters*, edited by Ursula Owen for Virago) be read at the same time? And – is it written at one sitting?

From the writer's point of view, the short story has the

advantage that it will be done more quickly – though there are some quintessential, particularly intense or poetic stories that take as long to be written as novels: one of my friends, Anne Roche, has just spent two years over a hundred pages that have been shrunk and cut to ten pages, a text called 'Saïs'. But generally speaking, the time of the writing of the short story is easier to adjust to the time of living. If you are a busy woman (man, sometimes), continuously interrupted by household or career duties, then the shorter span of the story will accommodate that fragmentation better. I personally find it so, but I also remember that extremely busy and interrupted women like Mrs Gaskell and Harriet Beecher-Stowe and George Sand wrote very long novels rather than stories . . . More importantly, if you do not have much time to write, and if you write relatively fast, the story will be easier because you will have less occasion to change and move beyond it by the time you have finished it. I speak from experience, since in the last six years or so I have started at least eight volumes, some, collections of stories, some, long stories, others, novels – and have completed none. But I now find that the long stories are those which I still have a chance to finish. For there is a time to write a thing, and you change, and since good writing is that which creates a correspondence between what is happening to you now and form-giving, since it is a way of finding out that you knew things you did not know you knew, then if you make yourself go back to things conceived and begun too long ago, you are resurrecting something no longer appropriate, and destroying some of the potential you have for finding out through writing. The great problem, when you want to write a novel, is to find a form that will have it in itself to accommodate large things, that will be able to take in the future that is not yet but that will be part of the time of the writing, as well as the past, 'Longtemps je me suis couché de bonne heure.' The sentence treads water, it is about habit, repetition, what persists, it plays in years and years which will become the time of the writing. Stretching before and after (but *not* a waste sad time; a meditative, child-like – for children are those normally who go to bed early – familiar and even good one: 'de *bonne* heure'). In this respect, the short story demands less, and if it turns out to have the power of habit or recurrence in it, to embody something that occurs again and again (as I tried to do with one of the stories in *Shades of Grey*, 'The Immaculate Conception', which is about compulsive house-cleaning), then it achieves that through intensity, a truth that hits, that will be remembered for its impact: as does Katherine Mansfield's 'Miss Brill' in its evocativeness of the veil of illusion the old and lonely may weave for themselves and of the cruelty with which the young will tear that veil.

But the problem of the short story today at any rate is that its length does not fit the format of the book. Short stories do not sell, publishers tell you. A young friend who has translated stories by a magnificent French writer who died three years ago, Geneviève Serreau, has had them repeatedly rejected: 'We can only sell stories if they're by people who are already famous'.

Why don't people buy short stories? Or do they? (Grace Paley, for example, recently has been a great success). Is it that when people buy a book, they want a whole? A *thing*. Because the pleasure of having your attention held over time by the same thing, of having to begin and to end once, and once only, is a powerful element in what you expect from a book? Is there a fetishism of the Book as One?

I began *The Thousand and One Nights* this summer. One of the delights they give is that they are too bulky to make a single volume, unless it be printed like the Bible, so you have to say 'them'. They play with multiplicity and refuse to totalize anyway. If you regard the Bible as *The Book*, you would have to say that *The Thousand and One Nights* are *The Stories*, plural, earlier and better than *The Decameron* or *The Canterbury Tales* or Perrault's or Grimm's fairy tales or any other western collection of stories. (I imagine the Chinese must have their stories, too, but have not read them yet.) Their plurality expresses for me what is one of the prime pleasures of the story, that it plays or should play with abundance, with the contrasts and contradictions of life, with high and low, not trying to make a *whole* out of them but letting each exist at its own pace and its own tone, letting each man and woman tell their story in their own words and with their own degree of wit, flamboyance, eloquence or rumbustiousness. They are a *vivier*, a trout-farm, of stories. But also (since what concerns me here is the story and the book, how they hold attention), *The Thousand*

and One Nights not only show how multiple stories can co-
exist, interrelate and spawn others inside a vast and infinitely
mobile form, one that demands as much or more time in
the reading than *A la recherche du temps perdu, but* the stories
ceaselessly rupture the unit. And so, there is no risk of totaliz-
ation, by which I mean the drive to homogenize experience
by making what is diverse and specific into a unified whole,
which is the overwhelming temptation of the Book. No formal
tyranny or terrorism can work though Scheherazade nightly
survives the death-threat of an all-powerful monarch.

Remember. King Shahriar, made furious by his wife's multiple infidelities, takes a new, virgin bride every night and
has her put to death at dawn. The vizir's elder daughter,
Scheherazade, says she can end the devastation. She gets married to the king, but asks that her little sister Donaziade be in
the bridal room and as soon as the king has finished with her,
should say, 'Tell me one of those wonderful stories that you
know'. Scheherazade asks the king's permission, and this
being granted, embarks on the first of her many nights.
Nightly, in order to gain her reprieve, she has to stop a story
midway, or just after the beginning or before the end: 'She
saw the dawn and, discreet, grew silent'. Her discretion may
have to do with her knowledge that night-time is story-telling
time, that the time of the story is night (and any kind of
hollow moment, a pause in a journey, a stalemated siege),
while the time of living, of politics, is day-time. Indeed, the
king goes on to his divan where he rules his kingdom, deals
out justice, then when the night comes, returns to Scheherazade. So that a space/time, the time of living, the time of reality,
separates each night. Story-telling is an alternative to reality.
When it starts, reality stops, life is suspended. There is nothing
of the confusing western bind to realism here. Proust evidently
knew this, starting as he did his long narrative with the many
nights at Combray, and the magic lantern in his childhood
bedroom casting its variegated glow on the walls and ceilings.

But in *The Thousand and One Nights* no night can correspond
to a full story, since interruption is of the essence. A night
may hold several short stories, bits of poetry, aphorisms, or
one long story may span many nights. And Scheherazade is
also discreet in the sense of cunning. She knows that by stop-
ping under pretext of morning she is holding the king in

suspense, and that suspense gains her reprieve. Next night, she reprieves the king from his suspense, his wanting to know, 'What next? And then?' And begins a new process of suspense. She tells to save her life, and in many of the stories she tells this same thing keeps happening to other story-tellers who, of course (the overall story-teller is an interested party), always in the end gain their reprieve, for poetic or comical reasons. Sometimes the story is so beautiful it gives immense pleasure to the listener who was going to have you killed, and he is bountiful in exchange (the gift of your life for your gift to me of pleasure). Sometimes, as in the tale of the hunchback and the barber with the seven brothers, the listener is so over-whelmed by the endless supply of stories that he can not take any more, he says, yes, they do make the sum after all. Bargaining is of the essence of story-telling, it is an *exchange*, riddled with analogies. Story-telling is also playing against Death: your life or your story. Your life for a story. But it is many-coloured and fun and proliferating and gameful, not stern and northern like the Knight's game of chess with Death on the beach of Bergman's *Seventh Seal*. Not a few of the story-tellers have brushed with death, suffered mutilations. There are one-eyed men, blind men, men with one hand or fingers or toes or ears or noses missing, eunuchs, women who have lost their husbands or their dowries; but they all have robustly survived their various ordeals. The stories are oddly like the tellers, since not a single story appears whole, that is, they all have to be cut in some way by the morning. Their truncated telling *is* what ensures their reprieve: the king will want to know the end, but the end will lead to more, Scheherazade saying, 'this is nothing compared to such and such a story'.[1] But the truncated telling of the stories is also the sign that they have brushed with death. On the other hand, from the moment when you become master or mistress of suspense you are as powerful as the king.

I see in *The Thousand and One Nights* an archetypal model standing behind all stories, collections of stories, story-telling, even when people are least aware of them. It is the power of great texts that they are of relevance even to those who do not know of them. For any writing that is real puts things at play that are deeper and bigger than consciousness, and that continue to exist beneath what historical moments make visible. Of course, I must not underestimate the influence they have had over the west. Robert Hampson, who knows about them, tells me that it is believed that Cervantes had come across them while he was in North Africa. And translations of various kinds had made them widely available in the eighteenth and nineteenth centuries: traces of their impact can be found everywhere, probably from Montesquieu and Voltaire and *Rasselas* and Beckford and Southey to Dickens and Conrad and Joyce's 'Araby' in *Dubliners*. Stendhal used to say he wished he could forget so that every year he could have the pleasure of rereading both *Don Quixote* and *The Thousand and One Nights*.

I fear that we lost (or failed to hang on to) something when we in the west established a tradition of the story as *single*. Even when they belong with each other, as in *The Decameron*, each story still lasts a day, the span of a day corresponds to the time of story-telling.

Units fit time, something mechanical, eventually perhaps marketable, comes into it. Quantity begins to rule instead of potential infinity. The Sienese banks have become established, Pound would tell us. Measures fit, already as in the metric system, ten times ten; the link with the body, with organic rhythms, has been lost, and with it something of the intense and multifarious nature of suspense. Interestingly, it is the *novel* in the west that seems to have inherited something of the suppleness and multiplicity of *The Thousand and One Nights*. No wonder Stendhal mentions *Don Quixote* in the same breath with them. Also heirs to them are the picaresque tradition up to *Pickwick*, or the structures 'modernist' novelists like Conrad and Joyce or post-modernist ones like Marquez, and perhaps Doris Lessing in *Shikasta*, have been creating. In *Don Quixote* the knight keeps coming across shepherds who tell him stories, innkeepers who read to them manuscripts that have been left with them, and there is sometimes the same chinese boxes effect one finds to the hunchback's tale, the same internal relevance between the inserted stories and the overall story one finds so many examples of in *The Thousand and One Nights*. But perhaps those of us who write short stories have much to learn from the internal congruence of such structures, and from the fountain-head, the Oriental book. Certainly, the collections of short stories I most admire are those which make up an *organic* whole, establish correspondences, some secret and some visible, between the stories that make up the volume. And yet they do not totalize. I am thinking in particular of Geneviève Serreau's *Ricercare* and *Dix-huit mètres cubes de silence* as well as of Tillie Olsen's *Tell Me a Riddle* (and, to a lesser extent, Grace Paley). In *Dix-huit mètres cubes de silence*, 18 stories, 18 cubic metres of silence, Geneviève Serreau sets up space, volume, perspective (something like the way in which Dutch genre paintings play with perspective and infinity), speech and silence, the way people try to, and often, not always, fail to communicate with each other, are immured in their lives, language, preoccupation with themselves, relations to objects. There is in those stories a dialogue of speech with silence, of the sayable with the unsayable, that is not unlike the way night-time dialogues with day-time in *The Thousand and One Nights*.

I wonder though: does the dialectic of life and death, day and night, function in the same way for men and for women writers? Is it gendered? Is has struck me very much in *The Thousand and One Nights* that in the stories told by mutilated tellers, the – what in our contemporary preoccupation with Freud and Lacan we would call 'symbolical castration' – is different for men and for women: the men are lame, one-eyed or eunuchs; the women have lost a husband, or a dowry. Lack strikes directly at the bodies of the men, it hits women through the money or men that give them access to marriage, that is, to social existence. It would be interesting to find out whether that entails further differences, to the kinds of stories they tell, for instance. It is true, however, that Scheherazade, whose life (not social position) is directly under threat, is the overall narrator. The overall overall narrator or gatherer of the stories and inventor of Scheherazade is unknown: the stories were written between the tenth and the sixteenth century so 'he' (one imagines that narrator somehow as male) is multiple, or compound. But one could then say that the stories are both male and female, since at any rate the overall overall narrator *needs* Scheherazade and her position in relation to the king for the stories to be told. But I ask the question because reading Colette I have been struck by the way she subverts patterns.

She wrote a number of longish short stories, or very short novels, which she calls her 'whites'. Her 'blacks', she said, were the novels, novels about love (from *Chéri* onwards, novels written in the third person). But the 'whites' are supposedly autobiographical, narrated in the first person by somebody called Colette or Madame Colette. They are in effect a complex mixture of fiction and autobiography corresponding to periods in which, the narrator says, she was not in love so nothing was happening to her. Often they are about what you can as reader only guess at, about being mistaken, and wavering, in your interpretation of people, in the kind of identification you seek with others, about gender, evil and good. The stories also subvert night and day (as well as subvert normative notions of fiction and autobiography, black and white, male and female).

'Rainy Moon' in the story of that name is a day-time pheno-menon, a little rainbow globe of light diffracted by a defect in the window-pane on to the wallpaper of a flat which the narrator visits, where she brings copy to a typist, and which turns out to be the very flat where she waited and suffered a number of years before after the break-up of her marriage: in her old bedroom, the typist's young sister waits and seems to suffer, also longing for a lost husband . . . The story turns out to be about magic, beneficent white magic like rainy moon, but also black magic since in effect the young sister is weaving a spell to kill her husband, and succeeds by the end of the story. It ends with a seventh full moon, and the narrator throwing away the text she had been bringing to the typist: what kind of magic is writing, black or white?

There is, in 'Rainy Moon', a redistribution and a spreading of the parts to be found in *The Thousand and One Nights*. Madame Colette is the Author, in a position of power, visiting the sisters, making a story out of their lives, trying to get at Délia's, the younger sister's, secret: she is the Sultan. She is also a teller, in that she is trying to interpret; and Délia is her alter ego, an image of her younger self, who holds her in suspense, for not only is she attracted to her, but Délia makes it clear that what she is weaving, the thing she is making inside her head (which turns out to be the spell that kills her husband), is as hard to make as a book, and very like it. Délia is a rival teller, a possible mirror image. But there is also ambiguity as to whose life is at stake. Maybe it is Délia who

190

is the Sultan? For Madame Colette is in the position of the threatened husband: she is attracted to Délia, sexually, and as to a child: she penetrates the recesses of her bedroom as Prince Charming might enter into Sleeping Beauty's chamber. And at least once, a spell that had been prepared for the husband almost gets her. Does she destroy the text she'd been writing because there has been no reprieve? But though suspense and power, like night and day, black and white, the parts of listener and of narrator, are redistributed in that story, it yet captures something of the multiplicity that is in the Oriental tales. For white is magical, white is seven colours, the spectrum of the rainbow, interpretation shifts endlessly as you read and reread . . .

Quite appropriately I hope, I have been using *The Thousand and One Nights* for a multiplicity of purposes. To suggest how storywriters could learn from their ways of making the many into a whole that is yet many, and how some have done so; to show how a woman writer can redistribute the gendered or power parts that are in their telling, and yet retain some of their multiplicity. I want to finish by celebrating the way they themselves could be used to shake some modernist assumptions.

Joy, reached in telling and listening as well as in lovemaking, and reached to its 'extreme limit', repeatedly, is central to the stories. Excess, a lack of the western taboos on sexual representation and the voyeurism that goes with the transgression of those taboos, are ingrained in them. They seem to provide that *jouissance* which Barthes was seeking from the *modernist* text – and this, despite the fact that as narrative they are the reverse of modernist, they are *stories*. They also seem to me to be the Devil's or a genie's gift to Bataille. He celebrated eroticism (in *L'Erotisme*) because it partook of the nature of the Gift which had been described by anthropologist Marcel Mauss in his famous essay. Eroticism should be excess, should be gratuitous, celebratory, the drinking of champagne at a feast. Since the exchange of women which Lévi-Strauss had shown to be a cornerstone of 'culture' in *The Elementary Structures of Kinship* had first been used by man to assert his humanity, renounce the satisfaction of the only instinct that can be deferred in order for him to enter into exchange and communication with others, just so now, a further turn of the screw, eroticism should rupture the established taboos to gain access to a new form of humanity, or freedom. Implicit in Bataille as well as explicit in effect if not theory in Lévi-Strauss is the position of women as objects of exchange: for Bataille, an excessive gift, champagne to be drunk at a feast. And that position seems to me to remain that even when, as in the *Histoire de l'Oeil*, the girl (one of the girls) initiates some of the erotic ventures. By contrast, I find it fascinating (and it goes against my stereotypical notions of Arab culture) that so many of those who *do* the exchanging in *The Thousand and One Nights*, from Scheherazade onwards, should be women. That joy, freedom, excess, should also be the portion of the listener, the listener to poetry as to a funny story: that it should not be hooked on death, sacrifice, transgression, sulphur. Pity nobody took that one up with Bataille.

Pity nobody said, 'It's not *the* Story or the *History* of *the* eye we want, Monsieur Bataille. It is stories. And most people tend to have two eyes, Monsieur Bataille. And if you've lost one, as the three one-eyed men have in *The Thousand and One Nights*, at least they don't mind that much, and they have wonderful stories to tell. In exchange. The stories of themselves. Not an exchanging of their women. Let us have some more such stories. Let us not make *the* story tend to the dangerous Oneness of the Book.'

NOTE

1 Comparatives, unlike superlatives, open up on infinity. When you say, 'the greatest', you are introducing closure. But when you say, as Scheherazade does, 'Ah, but what is hearing the language of men to hearing the language of animals?', you are opening a door on to a multiplicity of new stories.

10

A rook called Joseph:
Virginia Woolf

'Tell all the truth, but tell it slant'
Emily Dickinson

As far back as I can remember, rooks have always nested in
the oak trees of our neighbour, a Mr – let's call him Dawson
– , an octogenarian cantankerous misanthropist aggressive and
miserly farmer. He was an English version of Balzac's Père
Grandet and Zola's Père Fouan rolled into one: the black wings
of the rooks were well-suited to his lowering roof. Alas! Who
could have guessed I would ever say alas? When he died, his
land was sold to an affluent, friendly, nice and modern estate-
owner. He was modern, he modernized. The hawthorn hedges
all vibrant with nests, the mushroom-growing canal-slopes,
the covers and the great trees that barred the waterlogged
fields, everything has been ploughed up, drained by machines
that clogged the roads with mud. A naked plain, potatoes,
rape-seed or winter wheat, now borders the river. The farm-
house is left abandoned. The rooks have swarmed away. Black
flights now weightily hover over our own roof. Lustrous
wings, of a sinister size and colour, with a great clatter come
to rest upon the ash tree in our yard. In the space of five
years we have jumped over two centuries, lived through the
death of an equilibrium which we now nostalgically call
'natural'. A death which likewise affects the village and the
manor house, the family and the feudal community, a death
which English literature has never ceased to bemoan since
Wordsworth and Scott and Clare. We have moved from the

relatively thriving community of the opening part of *To the Lighthouse* to the general débâcle of the manor-house in *Between The Acts*.

Apart from three farmhouses on the outskirts of the village, not a single household draws its living from the land any more: where there were labourers and tenant farmers or cattle-dealers, there now are a brigadier, a sea-captain, a retired headmaster, teachers, writers . . . Chaos prevails in the animal world. Mutant caterpillars, the survivors of the holocausts of the pesticides, devour our cabbages. A primary schoolteacher and a tender-hearted ex-model have so many half-savage cats that the birds are decimated. Red tigers lie in wait for the downy crops of the thrushes' nests at the foot of our laburnums. The daughters of the tender-hearted neighbour, handsome twins with strong ecological leanings, members of the RSPCA with a 'Chicken Rights' sticker on the rear window of their black-and yellow Diane Citroën, took pity on a caged puppy at a fair: he gleefully tore off the necks of our six goslings. We bought six more. Four of them died of sunstroke. In North Yorkshire, that takes some doing.

But oh, wonder of wonders, one of the two surviving geese laid eleven eggs. Began to sit on them. The other goose kept her company, mounted guard by the shed. Was it a gander, we asked? That was the question. My son enlarged the pond. We were all dewy-eyed at the prospect of butter-coloured baby goslings, clumsily paddling . . . I, who had taken little care of the geese before, was now bringing food, fresh water to the mother, heroically still on her bed of straw. The consort – girlfriend? – anxiously allowed me near, took its share of the feast outside the shed. Then it raised its neck, its head, uttered boastful screeches. As soon as they heard me open the kitchen door into the yard, fifty yards away, cackle cackle, the geese screamed their welcome.

Five, six weeks went by. If the eggs had been fertilized, a farmer said, they would have hatched by the third week. The mother continued to sit, its eye, its plumage, duller every day. 'She will continue to sit till she dies of exhaustion. Remove the eggs, they're just rotting. And whatever you do don't you break them. It would be days before you'd got rid of the stench'. A huge crow was prowling, laying siege to the pen. It stole the bread, the left-overs I threw out for the geese.

Every day it became bolder. It began to eat from the geese's bowl. The able goose, who at the start had driven it away, bewildered or discouraged by her friend's long confinement, now was letting herself be plundered. Did the crow smell the eggs? The nearing death of the sitting goose? Or did it simply take advantage of an easy feed, make hay while the sun shone, take each day as it came? I loathed its black effrontery, and the cawing that chimed in with the now plaintive cackle that welcomed my sallies into the yard.

In the end, my son and a friend, a great-hearted, bearded and bespectacled Joyce specialist, had the courage, the one to gently pull the sitter outside and keep her there, the other to delicately extract the large white eggs from their straw nest without breaking a single one, put them inside tight-lidded plastic boxes, and to shove those into the dustbin. The sitter recovered her shine, grew fat again. But at Christmas, how on earth could we have eaten the hard-tried survivors of such an ordeal? It was a fox, the following spring, that got them . . .

Now the crow, the sinister prowler who used to lie in wait for the rotting eggs, has elected our orchard for its domain. Every time I go to throw left-overs for the birds, or even, for the tiger-cats, thinking that if they're full they'll leave the birds alone, the huge black beast homes in from the sky, materializes from distances in which I thought it was lost. It even sits on my bird-table, gets away with entire loaves of bread. Then, from the elastic branches of the ash tree, it talks to me. It does. I shout insults and threats at it, I grumble that he's a thief and a murderer and that one of these days I'll go to a gallery and learn to shoot and pelt his evil hide full of lead. He answers, proudly, he caws, as friendly and talkative as a goose.

In the end I called him Joseph. In *To the Lighthouse*, there is a crow – a rook, rather – called Joseph. Mrs Ramsay protects him:

And then, while the children rummaged among her things, she looked out of the window at a sight which always amused her – the rooks trying to decide which tree to settle on. Every time they seemed to change their minds and rose up into the air again, because, she thought, the old rook, old Joseph was her name for him, was a bird of a very trying and difficult disposition. He was a disreputable old bird, with half his wing feathers missing. He was like some seedy old gentleman in a top hat she had seen playing the horn in front of a public house.

'Look!' she said laughing. They were actually fighting. Joseph and Mary were fighting. Anyhow they all went up again, and the air was shoved aside by their black wings and cut into exquisite scimitar shapes.[1]

Worthy of note that Woolf should have called him Joseph. Joseph, the patriarch, but also the father who isn't a father: a little like Mr Ramsay, kindly in his way, lost a few feathers, a bit of a 'seedy old gentleman' himself, but who bullies his children, shoves aside the air ('standing, as now, lean as a knife, narrow as the blade of one, grinning sarcastically, not only with the pleasure of disillusioning his son and casting ridicule upon his wife',[2] James thinks) and yet doesn't realize what he's doing, the effect he's having, nor what's going on in his own house. He only becomes a father when he becomes a mother – when, after Mrs Ramsay's death, he finally takes his son to the lighthouse whose access he'd once taken pleasure in denying him. Worthy of note also that Mrs Ramsay should shelter a colony of rooks, be a mother and a hostess to them – and a spectator at a rather frayed show. And that she should so acutely feel the sharp-edged grace of their flight as, a little later on, she is to respond to the harmony which for a short while prevails over the conflicts at her dinner-table. 'Of such moments, she thought, the thing is made that remains for ever after.'[3] On her eccentric island (with everything slightly faded, the furniture and paint rather the worse for wear, the greenhouse that needs to be repaired, the weather beating down on things, not just James's hope of going to the lighthouse), in the house whose light shines at nights and which the 1914 war is soon to effectively and symbolically sack, Mrs Ramsay, the mother of a large family on a straightened budget, the wife of an ageing and increasingly obsolete academic, still attempts to maintain a feudal order. The order of a very ancient England (the England Woolf so loves in Vita Sackville-West, that she will further celebrate in *Orlando*) – an order sung by Ben Jonson's 'Penshurst', and Marvell's 'Appleton-House', and Pope, and Scott (whom Mr Ramsay reads in the evenings and whose volumes will mouldily survive the war, revived by Mrs Bates's ministrations) – an order that never ceases to die, and to attempt to perpetuate itself: in which there are bonds of loyalty, hospitableness, courtly love, grace. A maternal order also, almost a matrix. If she promises James that it will be fine tomorrow, she makes his future into a luminous vista, focused by the shape of the lighthouse. The inclusion of Lily the artist within the merciful and organic whole that radiates from Mrs Ramsay, however intermittent and ephemeral her beams, enables Lily, in the end, also to have her 'vision'. To trace the line that will harmonize the painting, focus it, straight as the tower of a lighthouse. Unless the gesture, of course, also signifies her enduring separation from Mrs Ramsay, the womanhood that can never be complete, splits the mother from the artist, inexorably. But then their short-lived co-existence, the mothering of the one by the other, are also what the vision is made of.

For she knows, Mrs Ramsay knows, as of course Virginia Woolf knows, whatever Nathalie Sarraute may have said, she knows how the slightest thing, the beauty of rooks' flights, the minute in which a disagreeable young man blossoms, a child's anguish at the prospect of bad weather tomorrow – how everything is political. Rooks' fights, children's fights.

> Strife, divisions, difference of opinion, prejudices
> twisted into the very fibre of being, oh that they should
> begin so early, Mrs Ramsay deplored. They were so
> critical, her children . . . It seemed to her such
> nonsense – inventing differences, when people, heaven
> knows, were different enough without that. The real
> differences, she thought, standing by the drawing-room
> window, are enough, quite enough. She had in mind
> at the moment, rich and poor, high and low; the great
> in birth receiving from her, half grudging, some
> respect . . . but more profoundly she ruminated the
> other problem, of rich and poor, and the things she
> saw with her own eyes, weekly, daily, here or in
> London, when she visited this widow, or that
> struggling wife.[4]

Even when it is the general condition, life, that is being

reflected upon, the question of the choices made has a sexual politics edge to it. Mrs Ramsay, the great matchmaker, has doubts about her own options – her own efforts to perpetuate life; her own mothering:

> There it was before her – life . . . for the most part, oddly enough, she must admit that she felt this thing that she called life terrible, hostile, and quick to pounce on you if you gave it a chance. There were the eternal problems: suffering; death; the poor. There was always a woman dying of cancer even here. And yet she had said to these children: You shall go through with it . . . And here she was, she reflected, feeling life rather sinister again, making Minta marry Paul Rayley . . . she was driven on, too quickly she knew, almost as if it were an escape for her too, to say that people must marry; people must have children.[5]

Moments of harmony, moments of vision: a frail dam, as frail as a book. A dam which violence carries away, ceaselessly threatens to carry away. Inside 'The Window', Mrs Ramsay is confronted less directly than Clarissa Dalloway with social and political violence. She doesn't have, under her own roof, to face up to a Sir William Bradshaw, the patriachal Pharisaical psychiatrist who has just topped four years of war and caused the death of Septimus Warren Smith. But Mrs Ramsay is also more powerful than Clarissa. Her house perpetuates life, allows an artist to come into her own. Mrs Ramsay's house is still chthonian. Now that I think about it, so was our Mr Dawson's farm. Disagreeable as he was, the old miser with his grumpy dog, an order that was kind to life prevailed over his land. The ducks throve in the marshes of his unproductive fields, moths, tits and yellow-hammers in his unkempt hedges and bushy thorns. No fish in the river were poisoned by fertilizers. He drew blackness to his own roof. Rooks and crows only went to his yard. He was our lightning-conductor.

The 1914 war passes over Mrs Ramsay's house. She dies: between brackets. The 1940 war nears the manor-house in *Between the Acts*. Planes fly over it. They are not yet black, but they might be: black signs, crossed Z, will soon mark out the planes flying in from the east. There no longer is a coping-stone, a lighthouse whose intermittent beams focus and illumine the night, no longer a Mrs Ramsay. A disparate collection of hosts, several generations of them, all in disagreement with each other, none willing to be host or hostess. They barely welcome, they just allow the descendants of those who once were their vassals, their clients, to crowd into their grounds, their outside buildings. The feast has turned into a mechanical ritual. In vain does the gallant artist, the modern troubadour, Miss La Trobe, in the once ideal space of the Park, a gramophone hidden in the bushes, attempt to focus, to harmonize. 'Dispersed are we', the gramophone wails, 'Dispersed are we . . .'

> Flowing, and streaming, on the grass, on the gravel,
> still for one moment she held them together – the
> dispersing company. Hadn't she, for twenty-five
> minutes, made them see? A vision imparted was relief
> from agony . . . for one moment . . . one moment.[6]

But violence rules, in continuous bursts of anger, aggression, rage, misunderstanding, treachery. Creative gestures abort. A crow, ever bolder, is lying in wait for the rotting eggs. In the interval of Miss La Trobe's play, on the sunny path that leads to 'the Barn, the Noble Barn, the barn that had been built over seven hundred years ago and reminded some people of a Greek temple, others of the middle ages', the barn that, like the play and however modest or home-made, is like a compendium of the history of English civilization, the barn where the buffet is laid out, Giles encounters a snake curled in an olive-green ring:

> Dead? No, choked with a toad in its mouth. The snake
> was unable to swallow; the toad was unable to die. A
> spasm made the ribs contract; blood oozed. It was birth
> the wrong way round – a monstrous inversion. So,
> raising his foot, he stamped on them. The mass crushed
> and slithered. The white canvas on his tennis shoes
> was bloodstained and sticky. But it was action. Action
> relieved him. He strode to the Barn, with blood on his
> shoes.[7]

Action. Between the acts. What is there between the acts? Inverted births? And which are the acts, the moments of vision, or the awful dispersion that occurs when the music stops and real blood is spilled in what is called an act?

'You fool. It isn't a rook, or even a crow, the beast that you imagine is almost tame, and sits on our ash tree', my husband said. 'I've asked. It's a carrion crow. A scavenger. A new phenomenon. They didn't use to be about. It's since they've stopped using DDT that they've spread again. Same with the hawks.'

When Joseph was lying in wait for our goose eggs, I kept thinking about somebody I loved, whom we had just put under the sod.

Miss La Trobe's play is a flop, or so she feels:

Panic seized her. Blood seemed to pour from her shoes.
This is death, death, death, she noted in the margin
of her mind; when illusion fails.[8]

Perhaps at the moment when she finished writing *Between the Acts*, in 1939, Virginia Woolf remembered Mrs Dalloway's reaction, twenty years earlier, when told of Septimus Warren Smith's suicide?

There was one thing which counted; one thing . . .
which he had preserved. Death was a challenge. Death
was an effort to communicate, people who felt the
impossibility to reach the centre which, mystically,
eluded them.[9]

It is not only mystically that the centre is eluding Virginia Woolf and Miss La Trobe. Disorder, violence, have become too great. The world in which the tutelary figure of a Mrs Ramsay allowed one's 'vision' to occur is no more, whether it be the now too remote world of childhood, youth, or England before two world wars. There is no one left to sit over fertilized, living eggs. Nothing but inverted births. No wonder she felt that only death was left to try and reach 'the centre'.

Where does my Joseph begin, where does he end? If the snake and toad of *Between the Acts* signify the Second World War, what should I think about the eggs of our geese, the multiplication round us of carrion birds?

Precisely: do not think about it. Remember Mrs Ramsay. (And her doubts?)

I shall put a roof over my bird-table, so that only the little birds can feed there. I shall hang a netful of seeds at my kitchen window, so that only the tits and the great-tits can hang from it.

'Did you see that extraordinary beast?', another neighbour asked. 'I've never seen a crow like it. He talks to you, he lets you come near. Most unusual you know. Almost tame. After all, they've got the right to live also. You know, he's so friendly we call him Jack. Or Jim.'

NOTES

1 *To the Lighthouse*, London: Dent, 1967, p. 93.
2 ibid., p. 4.
3 ibid., p. 123.
4 ibid., pp. 9–10.
5 ibid., pp. 69–70.
6 *Between the Acts*, London: Hogarth Press, 1960, p. 117.
7 ibid., p. 119.
8 ibid., p. 210.
9 *Mrs Dalloway*, Harmondsworth: Penguin, 1964, p. 204.

Index

abstract knowledge 155, 157
adult–child relationship 22–5 *passim*
Africa 121–4, 144–9
ageing image 112–13
alienation 96
Almanach des femmes russes 75
anabas 37–9, 44–5
ananas/pineapple 37–45
Anglo-American pragmatism 92
anglophone tradition 53
Anglo-Saxon feminism 47–8, 49, 62
animal instinct 80
anonymity 26–7
anthropology 80–1
anxiety of influence 9
Auffret, S., *Des couteaux contre des femmes* 83
'August Voice' 95
Austen, Jane, *Pride and Prejudice* 162–3
author–reader relationship 162, 170–1, 177
authorial voice (Lessing) 157–77
authority 77, 174
autobiography: Cixous 91, 92, 95; criticism as 1–12; de Beauvoir 110; *see also* Lessing, Doris

Baader-Meinhof group 71, 75
badness (and sin) 22–3, 26–7, 42–3

Balzac, Honoré de 135, 141, 174, 183
Barthes, Roland 2, 191; *Writing Degree Zero* 93
Basque separatists 71, 75
Bataille, George 80, 81, 192; *L'Erotisme* 79, 191
Baudelaire, Charles 41
Beach, Sylvia 64
Beauvoir, Simone de 66; contemporary feminism and 101–15; *Force of Circumstances* 112; *L'Invitée* 112; *Memoirs of a Dutiful Daughter* 110; *The Prime of Life* 112; *The Second Sex* 78–9, 104, 106–15, 150
Beckett, Samuel 44
Beckford, William 188
Beecher-Stowe, Harriet 195
Benda, Julien 78
Benjamin, Walter 28
Bergman, Ingmar, *The Seventh Seal* 187
Between the Acts (Woolf) 144, 194, 198–200
biblical imagery 51, 52
Biedermeier model 106
Bildungsroman tradition 134, 136, 140
bilingualism (and translation): slippage 37–45; translating French feminists 46–58; writing in two languages 17–36
biologism 49

biology, culture and 114
birth throes state 28, 29
birthing 72
bisexuality 68
bodily knowledge 152–3, 155–7
body 54; language 92, 95–7;
   -that-writes 95–6; 'writing the'
   82–8
'body' passages 152–3
bonds (connections) 30–4
Borges, Jorge L. 44
Bowlby, Rachel 48
Briefing for a Descent into Hell
   (Lessing) 134, 161
Brontë, Charlotte, *Jane Eyre* 63,
   66, 151; *Villette* 151
Burns, Gordon, *Somebody's*
   Husband, Somebody's Son 61

Cahiers du Grif, Les 62, 76, 81
Cambodia, play about 97, 98, 104
Camus, Albert 163–4
capitalism 2, 3, 104, 135
Cardinal, Marie, *Les Mots pour le*
   dire 77
castration 76, 81–2, 84, 91, 189
'Castration or Decapitation' 91
'caves and woods' 95, 96
Ce Sexe qui n'en est pas un 68
censorship 25–7, 61, 83–4, 151
Cervantes, Miguel de, *Don*
   Quixote 188
change (and change of heart)
   139–42
characters: authorial voice and
   157–70, 174–7; creation of 30–2;
   detached observer 159–60, 161,
   164, 175, 176; experience of
   146–8, 175; heroine (language
   of) 157–9; -narrator gap 161–2
'chastened style' 84
Chawaf, Chantal 69, 84, 85
childhood: adult relations 22–5;
   Lessing on 137, 142–4
Children of the Violence, The
   (Lessing): language 157–77;
   logic of sequence 119–42; roots
   142–57
China 67–8

choices 10, 146–9, 174, 177
chronological sequences 172–3,
   174–5
circularity 32, 175–6
Cixous, Hélène 24, 44, 104–5;
   Angst 91; Editions des femmes
   62, 69, 76, 81–3, 85, 87;
   L'Histoire terrible et inachevée de
   Norodom Sihanoukroi du Cambodge
   94; *L'Indiade* 94, 98; inner/outer
   theatre 91–9; *Inside* 91; *Limonade*
   tout était si infini 97; *Le Livre de*
   Prométhéa 97; *Manne pour*
   Mandelstams pour Mandelas
   98–9; *Le Nom d'Oedipe* 94;
   Préparatifs de noces au-delà de
   l'abîme 94, 96, 97; translation
   into English 46–57; *La Venue à*
   l'écriture 91; *see also* individual
   titles of major works
'classic realist text' 163, 172
Clément, Catherine 41, 83; *La*
   Jeune née 84–5, 104
clitoris 82, 83, 84
Cohen, Annie 69
coherence, change and 140–1,
   142
Colette 43, 110, 111, 112, 189, 191;
   The Break of Day 11, 113; 'Rainy
   Moon' 190
collective voice (Lessing) 128–30
Collin, Françoise 62–3
communication, exchange and
   79–81, 191–2
Comparative Criticism 101–2
concentric circles 32
connections (possession) 30–4
Conrad, Joseph 188
'conscious' language 25
consciousness 1, 8, 10–11, 19, 69;
   of characters 136–7, 143, 145,
   147, 175, 177; trans-individual
   155–6, 170–1
consensus 5
Construction 7
'contemplative' state 141
contemporary feminism, de
   Beauvoir and 101–15

contemporary French women's writing 75–89
contradictions 139–40, 142, 169
Courtivron, Isabelle de 61
creation: of characters 30–2; of self 10, 11
'creative' French 22–4, 26, 39–40
creativity (of Cixous) 94–5, 96
crisis: criticism and 7, 9, 12; -like passages 160–61; private/public events 32–3
criticism as autobiography: crisis and 7, 9, 12; de Man 1–2, 7, 9; Nozick 2–5; relations (construction) 10–11; Rushdie 4–5, 6, 8; self-knowledge 2, 6–8, 10
cult of the new 8–9
cultural oppression 71
Cultural Revolution 67
culture: biology and 114; communication and 79, 81–2, 191–2; experience and 146–8; women in 41

Dante 98
de Gaulle, Charles 41
de Man, Paul 1–2, 7, 9
death 10, 82, 187
Declaration of Women's Rights proposals 68
Deconstruction 7, 11, 68, 72, 87
Delphy, Christine 61, 67, 70, 105
Derrida 52, 63, 68, 83
Des femmes en mouvement 67
'detached observer' 159–61, 164, 175–6
deus ex machina, author as 168
Dickens, Charles 188
discourses 7, 9, 67, 68, 77, 85; communication and exchange 79–81; French feminism 48, 49, 52, 53
discretion 34
displacement 34, 49, 62, 82, 83
dissidents 71
divided self 10
Divine Comedy 98
documentary (Lessing) 121

Dolto, Françoise 66
domination 71, 72; see also master–slave relationship
drama 49, 78
'drift of translation' 49
Duchen, Claire 61
Duras, Marguerite 44, 77, 144

écriture féminine 54, 82, 84, 85, 92
Editions des femmes 19, 27, 97; contemporary French writing 75–89; Psych et Po group 62–3, 69, 71, 72
education (access to) 78
ego 5–6, 64
elemental imagery 152
Eliot, George 30, 103, 152; Daniel Deronda 162; Middlemarch 162, 163; The Mill on the Floss 151, 156, 162
elites 3, 43
Elle (magazine) 18
Emecheta, Buchi 44
empiricism 47, 53
English: of bilingualist 18–28, 39–42, 44; translating French feminists into 46–58
Entremise, L' (Ward Jouve) 27, 30, 33
epithets 56
eroticism 79, 80, 191–2
erotogenic zones 82–3
essays 10, 49
essence (female identity) 47
'essential' noise 28
essentialism 49, 54
essentiality 80, 82
estrangement 23–4, 147–8
European dissidents 71
exchange of women 79–81, 83, 191–2
excision 83
exile 149, 176
exogamy 79
experience 146–8, 175
'express the voice' 37
expulsion 65

'fads' 32

Fairley, Ian 7–8
fantasy 8
fathers 149; -and-sons game 9
Fathers by Daughters 183
female body 95, 149–57
feminine: knowledge 155; male
  writers 152; process of
  translation 28
femininity 28, 114, 149–50, 152
feminism, contemporary 101–15
feminisms, French *see* French
  feminisms
feminist aesthetics: Lessing
  119–77; short stories (and
  Thousand and One Nights)
  182–92; Woolf 193–201
feminist criticism, French 50–8
feminist theory: casting women
  in moulds 114–15; position of
  Psych et Po 61–3; reception of
  47–50; trends 102–8
feminists, French (translation)
  46–58
féminité 54
feminization 83
Feyerabend, P. 174
fictions of Cixous 49
Fisher–Spassky chess
  tournament 33
Flaubert, Gustave 168; *Madame
  Bovary* 106
'flocculation' 30
fly/steal (meanings) 46–7, 49
foot-binding 83
forclos 62, 73
Forest, Eva 75
Fouque, Antoinette 94, 97; Psych
  et Po group 62–9, 72, 73
Four-Gated City, The (Lessing)
  120–1, 124, 127–34, 137–8,
  143–4, 155–6, 158–61, 164–6,
  175
Francophile feminists 53
Francophone 92
Frankfurt School 3
freedom 26, 177, 192
French (of bilingualists) 18–28,
  39–42, 44
French feminisms: Cixous 91–9;

contemporary writing 75–89;
  de Beauvoir 101–15; Psych et
  Po group 61–73
French feminists (translation
  into English): Cixous
  misrepresented 49–57; English
  response 47–9; translator (role)
  46–7, 56–8
French Restoration 106
French Revolution 75, 107
French women's writing (and
  Edition des femmes):
  development 75–8; reading list
  88–9; woman as other 78–82;
  writing the body (inventing
  difference) 82–8
Freud, Sigmund 67, 68, 70, 82,
  150, 189
futuristic modes 93

Gagnon, Madeleine 84
Gandhi, Mahatma 97–8, 99
Gang of Four 67, 75
Gaskell, Elizabeth 195
Gaullism 78
Geist 43
gendered self 114
generation gap 64
Genet, Jean 31, 85
Gide, André 183
gifts 79, 80, 98, 99, 191, 192
Giono, Jean 112
Giving Woman 52
God, Man and Mrs Thatcher
  (Raban) 6
Going Home (Lessing) 121, 124–5,
  126, 144, 155
Golden Notebook, The (Lessing)
  130, 140, 146, 148–9, 155, 171
goodness (and righteousness)
  22–3, 42–3
'grail-seekers' 121, 149
'grass' passage 121, 123–4, 131,
  145–6
Grass is Singing, The (Lessing)
  132, 145, 147, 171
Grelard, Marie 76, 82
Griffin, Susan 57
'*grosso modo*' 173, 174

growing up 22–3, 24–5
Guérillères, Les 64, 86, 114

'half-chicken' 18–28
Hall, Stuart 4
Hampson, Robert 188
Heath, Stephen, 'Difference' 103
Hegelian model 78, 80
heroine (language) 157–9
heterosexuality 68, 70
Histoire de l'Oeil 192
historical novels 175
History, female 84, 151, 156
'Holy Trinity' of French feminist
    theory 48–9
homosexuality 70, 82
'hostility' 2, 3
houses (in Lessing) 124–7, 144
humanity 31, 80, 191, 192
hysteria 67, 97, 98, 104;
    knowledge and 95–6
Hyvrard, Jeanne 69, 85; *Mère la
    mort* 77

iconic signs 96
id 54, 56
identification, acts of 96
identity 56, 94, 96; bilingualism
    and 17, 42, 44; shifts 49; stable
    47; and translation 28, 29, 40,
    46
idioms 19–20
Imaginary 52, 96, 150, 151
imitative rhetoric 24–5, 39, 173
'Immaculate Conception, The'
    (Ward Jouve) 34
impersonality 131–3, 139, 143,
    165
incest taboo 79, 80
India, play about 97–8, 104
individualism 2, 3, 26; trans-
    individuality 155, 156, 170–1
individuals 7, 136–7, 173–4
'inessential' woman 80
inferiority/superiority 109–10
'inner life' 26
inner theatre (to world theatre)
    91–9
innocence 98, 169

instinctive emotions 33–4
instincts 80
Ionesco, Eugène, *The Bald Prima
    Donna* 18
Irigaray, Luce 48, 53, 70, 84–5,
    103–4, 150; *Speculum* 68, 105

Jalousie, La 159
James, Henry, *The Turn of the
    Screw* 183
Jameson, Frederic 104
Jeune née, La (Cixous/Clément)
    84–5, 104
Jones, Ann R., 'Writing the Body'
    53
Jonson, Ben 197
jouissance 54, 68, 72, 92, 96, 191
Joyce, James 44, 57; *Dubliners* 188
Jussieu group 70

Kafka, Franz 93
Kennedy, Margaret 111
Khmer 97
Kierkegaard, Soren 108
knowledge: abstract 155, 157;
    authorial 162–3, 165–6, 169,
    171, 173, 177; bodily 152–3,
    155–7; hysteria and 95–6;
    through self-knowledge 2, 6–8,
    10, 94, 96, 97; world 128–32,
    137, 139
Kristeva, Julia 32, 38, 48, 52, 53,
    85, 103, 150

La (Cixous) 95, 114
Lacan, Jacques 10, 52, 81, 95, 103,
    113, 189; Psych et Po group 68,
    70, 73
Landlocked (Lessing) 120, 123,
    126–7, 138, 153–8, 163–8
language 1, 5, 7; authorial voice
    157–77; development of
    tongues 84–5; differences 85–8;
    exchange of 81; as law 38;
    masculine 150; maternal 23–5,
    28, 38, 40; 'meta' 162–3;
    'naked' 169, 176; 'natural' 24,
    25, 28; patriarchal 23, 25;
    sounds and 37–9, 40;

speech–sex links 82–4; translator's role 46–7, 57–8; women's alienation from 67

'Laughter of the Medusa, The' 49, 91

Leclerc, Annie 77

Le Dantec, Denise, *Les Joueurs de go* 77

left-wing feminist theory 48

Lehmann, Rosamond 111

Leiris, *L'Age d'homme* 110

Lejeune, Philippe 2, 6

L'Entremise (Ward Jouve) 27, 30, 33

lesbianism 70, 82

Lessing, Doris 32, 44, 105, 183; *A Hundred Years of Solitude* 174–5; *In Pursuit of the English* 121, 149; language 157–77; logic of the sequence 119–42; *La Nausée* 139; *The Pig* 150, 155; *Resurrection* 135; roots 142–57; *The Trinket* 150, 155; *see also individual titles of major works*

'Leur unique prénom' 64

Levinas, E. 78

Lévi-Strauss, Claude 80, 174; *The Elementary Structures of Kinship* 79, 104, 191–2

lies and lying 28, 34

lighthouse image 9

Lispector, Clarice 44, 77, 97; *The Apple in the Dark* 93

Littré 37, 38

livres-cassettes 69

logic of the sequence (Lessing) 119–42

'logos' 114, 151

Lomas, Peter 95

Luccioni, Eugénie 104, *Marches* 77

Lukács, George 7–8

McCabe, Colin 104, 162

Magli, Ida 81

male writers/artists 57

Mallarmé, Stéphane 103

Mandela, Nelson and Winnie 99

Mandelstam, N. 98–9

Mansfield, Katherine, 'Miss Brill' 185

Mao Tse Tung 67

Marquez, Gabriel 188

marriage 79–80

Martha Quest (Lessing) 119, 121–2, 125–6, 131–2, 139, 144, 157, 159, 162, 169

Marvell, Andrew 197

Marx, Karl 67

Marxism 8, 48, 71

masculine: female writers 151; history 53; knowledge 155; language 150; law 83, 151; Order 76; style 150; thought 63

masculinity 42–3, 81

'mass' forces 136

master–slave relationship 71, 78–9, 86

'maternal' language 23, 24, 25, 28, 38, 40

matriarchy 66, 80

Mauss, Marcel 41, 79, 191

May, George 6

meaning, binary system of 53

meaning-language 28

meanings (in translation) 46–7, 53

Memoirs of a Survivor (Lessing) 121, 132, 133, 142–3, 148

menstruation 80, 87

'meta-language' 162–3

metaphor 83; private expression of public events 32–3; as relation 11; of weather 136

Michel, Louise 106

midwife role (of translator) 46–7, 57

Millet, Kate 75

misogyny 51, 62, 79

Mitchell, Juliet 61

Mnouchkine, Ariane 97

mobility, bilingualism and 17

model construction 173, 174, 177

modernism 150, 191

Moi, Toril 48, 62, 96; *Sexual/Textual Politics* 50–2

'Moitié-de-poulet' 18–28, 29, 34

'moles' in Psych et Po 61, 63, 65

Molière, *Le Bourgeois gentilhomme* 37
Monde, Le 68, 85
Mondo Cane (film) 39
Montaigne, Michel de 10
Montesquieu 188
Montrelay, Michèle 104
mother: –daughter relationship 82, 111, 143–4; role (of translator) 46–7, 57
motherhood 9, 71, 83, 109, 111, 113, 149
mothering 69, 197, 198
Mouillaud, Geneviève 77
moulds, casting women into 114–15
mouth–sex link 82–4
Mouvement de libération des femmes 69–70
movement, communication and 80, 81
Mrs Dalloway (Woolf) 31, 200
'mud' passage 121–4, 127, 133–4, 136–7, 145–7, 152, 154–5, 177
multilingualism 43, 44
mysticism 130–32, 141
'mystification' 53, 111
mythological imagery 51, 52
mythologies (Cixous) 94, 97

Nabokov, Vladimir 44
naked language 169, 176
'Name-of-the-Father' 28, 63, 64, 65
narrator 189–90
'nationality' 32
'natural' language 24, 25, 28
natural rules 41
nature 57
Nawal-el-Sarawi 75
Nehru, J. 98
Nerval, Gérard de, 'El Desdichado' 56–7
neurosis (in *Martha Quest*) 144, 149
New Continental Criticism 1
New Rights 105
Newly Born Woman, The (Cixous) 46–7, 49, 91, 93, 95

Nin, Anaïs 9
nomadism/nomads 176
nouns, epithets and 56
Nouveau Roman 93
Nouvelles 183
Nouvelles questions féministes 70
Nozick 3–5; *Anarchy, State and Utopia* 2

objectivity (in criticism) 5
observing subject (in criticism) 1–12
Olsen, Tillie, *Tell Me a Riddle* 189
openness 5, 57
Order 63, 76
Oriental tales 188, 191
Other 95; of Anglo-Saxon pragmatism 48, 62, 77; and otherness 68, 72, 78, 81; in *The Second Sex* 110–11; women as 78–82

painting image 57
Paley, Grace 185, 189
pamphlet 6
paradoxes 12, 35, 48, 61, 94
parents of writers 143
Paris Commune 106
Parole de femme 77
particularity 134–6, 137
partitioning of material 145–6
'patriarchal' language 23, 25
patriarchy 78
patrilinear law 83, 151
patronymic 64
Paul, Jeffrey, *Reading Nozick* 2–3
'people-ness' 128
Perse, Saint-John 38
Phaedo 92
phallocentric delusion 54
phallocracy 65, 72, 87
phallogocentrism 63–4, 65–6, 67–8, 71
phallus 81
philosophy 10
placenta 66–7, 69
Plath, Sylvia 77
Plato 92, 105
Poe, Edgar Allan 183

poetry 57, 88
political: equality 78; lesbianism 70, 71; position of bilingualist 20–1
politics 11; in Lessing 153, 154, 157; psychoanalysis and 67; sex and 157
Pope, Alexander 197
Portrait de Dora (Cixous) 91, 94, 95, 104
possession 30–34
post-feminism 103
post-modernist fiction 93
Pound, Ezra 103
pragmatism of British tradition 47, 48
pre-Minoan civilization 72
pre-Oedipal state 24, 52, 57, 96
prephallocentric discourse 53
present, writing in 93–4, 96
preterite 93
primary sounds 38–9, 40
private events 32–3
process approach 10–11
professions 78
'progress' 174–5
Proper Marriage, A (Lessing) 119, 123, 139, 146, 147, 152–3, 157, 166, 169
Proust, Marcel, *Remembrance of Things Past* 182, 186
Psych et Po group: members 64–6; position (misrepresented) 61–3; positions (and goals) 71–3; presentation of 66–71
psychoanalysis 10, 48, 52, 67, 71, 79, 82, 94, 95–6
psychological realism 141
psychology 163–4, 165
psychotherapy 95
public events 32–3
publishers (Editions des femmes) 19, 27, 62–3, 69, 71, 72, 75–89, 97
puns and punning 56–7, 96

Quang Jin 67–8, 75
Questions féministes 66, 70

Raban, Jonathan 6
radical feminism 53
Rasselas 188
reader–author relationship 162, 170–1, 177
readiness 57
reading-in-the-present 93
realism 168–9
realist texts, classic 163, 172
reality 8, 186; in Lessing 170, 172, 174, 175, 177; principle 72; world 128–32, 137, 139
reglées, women as 41
relations, construction of 10–11
relativity principle 2, 175
religious, transference of the (to art) 27
representative experience 49, 134, 135
repressions 63, 67, 82–4, 96
reproduction 83
retrospective knowledge 169
re-writing (translation solution) 30
Rhys, Jean, *Wide Sargasso Sea* 63, 66
Rich, Adrienne 25
right-wing theory 48
Ripple from the Storm, A (Lessing) 119, 121, 123–4, 138–9, 145, 152–3, 155, 157, 164
risks 5, 6, 35
Risset, Jacqueline 28, 31, 46, 47, 49
Robbe-Grillet, Alain 159
Rocard, Michel 41
Roche, Anne 184; *La Cause des oies* 77; 'Sais' 184
role-playing 131, 141, 143, 144
Romanticism 114, 131
Room of One's Own, A (Woolf) 4, 88, 105–6
roots (Lessing) 124–5; Africa 144–9; body 149–57; childhood 142–4
Rousseau, Jean-Jacques, *Sophie* 106
rue de la Roquette 69, 75
rue des Saints-Pères 69, 75

Rule 41, 42
Rushdie, Salman 6; *The Satanic Verses* 4–5, 8
Ruthven, K. 49–51, 52–3

Sackville-West, Vita 196
safecracking, truth and 35–6
sainthood 171
salvation, writing as 27
Sand, George 184
Santos, Emma 77
Sarde, Michèle 61
Sarraute, Nathalie 44, 77, 163–4, 197
Sartre, Jean-Paul 78, 79, 93, 108, 113; *L'Age de raison* 110
satire 6
scarcity model 79
Scheherazade 101, 186–7, 189, 192
schizophrenia, translation and 28–30
Schreiner, Olive 148
science fiction 93
sciences 47, 173–4
Scott, Walter 64, 103, 197; *Robert Count of Paris* 106; *The Waverley Novels* 156–7
Screen 103
second, woman as 110–11
Second Sex, The (de Beauvoir) 78–9, 104, 106–15, 150
secrecy: connections and 32; need for 22–3, 25–6, 27, 39; truth and 34–6
self: criticism as autobiography 1–12; demystification 2; -denial 80; -discovery 96, 98; -knowledge 2, 6–8, 10, 94, 96, 97; -love 69, 96; reflectiveness 97
selfhood 11, 94
Sellers, Susan, *Writing Differences* 91
semiotics 6, 62, 85
sensations 152–3, 154, 156
'sense' 147–8, 171
sequence: logic of (Lessing) 119–42; progress and 93–4

Serreau, Coline 76
Serreau, Geneviève 185; *Dix-huit mètres cubes de silence* 189; *Ricercare* 189
sex: politics and 157; –speech link 82–4
sexual difference 72; inventing (in French women's writing) 85–8
sexuality 53, 67–8, 70–1, 82, 95, 154, 156
Shades of Grey (Ward Jouve) 23–4, 26, 29, 33
Shakespeare, Judith 88
Shikasta (Lessing) 132, 143, 157, 170, 171
short stories 182–4; *The Thousand and One Nights* 185–92
Showalter, E. 53
Signoret, Simone 66
'silence' 2, 3
silencing 65
sin (and badness) 22–3, 26–7, 42–3
Sleeping Beauty metaphor 67–8, 76
'snakethinking', truth and 34–6
Sollers, Philippe 30, 32, 40, 41
sounds 37–40
Southey, Robert 188
space, de Beauvoir's 111–13
spaces, women-only 69
specificity 136
speech 47; –sex link 82–4
spider's dance 85
Spivak, Gayatri 63, 65, 72, 83
stability of identity 47
Staël, Mme de 106
Stalin, Joseph 99
Steiner, George 43–4
Stendhal 141, 188
story length 182–5
Streetcleaner, The (Ward Jouve) 42
structuralism 21, 48, 53, 79, 80, 104, 150
'struggle discord' 52
subjecthood 7, 10–11, 95
Sun Tse 76
supression of women 114–15